AFC BOURNEMOUTH

The fall & rise

AFC BOURNEMOUTH

The fall & rise

THE ASTONISHING RAGS-TO-RICHES
TALE OF THE PREMIER LEAGUE'S
SMALLEST CLUB

NEIL MELDRUM

First published by Pitch Publishing, 2018
Reprinted 2019

Pitch Publishing
A2 Yeoman Gate
Yeoman Way
Worthing
Sussex
BN13 3QZ
www.pitchpublishing.co.uk
info@pitchpublishing.co.uk

A CIP catalogue record is available for this book
from the British Library.

ISBN 978-1-78531-442-1

Typesetting and origination by Pitch Publishing
Printed and bound in India by Replika Press Pvt. Ltd.

Contents

For Neve and Caleb...
My two constants from
League Two to the
Premier League xx

ACKNOWLEDGEMENTS

I ALWAYS thought I had a book in me. But having worked in the relentless, cut-to-the-quick newspaper industry since my early twenties, I can only admire the likes of Mike Calvin, Ian Ridley, Matt Dickinson and Ian Herbert for simply finding the time to craft and polish their extended prose to such an awe-inspiring standard. They are the benchmark and the inspiration.

Leaving the *Daily Echo* after 15 years in 2017 was not as much of a wrench as I had feared. My time had come, as it does for most senior newspaper executives in a media age where making both print and digital pay becomes harder with every passing week. I departed with handshakes, embraces and fond memories – none more ingrained in my psyche than my time as sports editor, covering AFC Bournemouth between 2006 and 2015.

I must pay tribute to the people who got me to this point, who believed in me when a career underwriting mortgages beckoned.

The late Neal Butterworth, a giant of regional journalism and a loss to it still felt today, gave me my first freelance job at the *Echo* – sub-editing sports pages on Sunday afternoons – before offering me a permanent position in 2002 as I was about to book myself in for CMAP revision. I miss his wisdom, his wit and his love of the Beautiful Game.

Andy Goodall, my first sports editor, recommended I take the reins despite me being just 26 and with a mere four years of press experience. I am forever grateful for that opportunity.

A man I had first met as a student in 1999, Neil Perrett is a well-known and much admired reporter on the AFC Bournemouth beat. From the old school, he taught me too much to mention here, then embraced my role as his boss despite the gap in years. More importantly than that, he is a friend and I thank him for so many laughs, for red wine and Wensleydale, ill-advised bets and so many near misses on the M6. His name features heavily in this book, such is the influence he carries around the corridors of Dean Court.

My other colleagues on the *Echo* sports desk over the years, Ian Wadley, whose help proofreading this book was much appreciated, Ned Payne and Paul McNamara in particular, also provided professionalism and good humour often in the face of impossible workloads. They are some of the most dedicated people I have ever met and ever will.

My thanks, also, to Andy Martin, who made me his deputy editor in 2015 but allowed me to continue covering AFC Bournemouth and who permitted me to raid the *Echo*'s picture archive and print the astonishingly good images you see in this book.

I met a wonderful bunch of journalists over the years covering the Cherries. Graham Nickless of *The Sun*, Alex Crook of M&Y News Agency and Kris Temple, Johnny Cantor, Paul Scott and Andrew Hawes of the BBC must all be thanked for their banter and expertise in their fields. I was also lucky enough to bend the ears of the likes of Kevin Kilbane, the former Republic of Ireland midfielder, and other high-profile pundits.

Thanks, also, to Jacqui Oatley, who offered her support in promoting this book. I first met her covering the Cherries' match at Brighton's Withdean Stadium in 2010 and I can confirm she does have lovely eyes (*she'll get the joke...*)

During my time covering the club, I met some seriously talented footballers and some wonderfully honest, down-to-earth and humble sportsmen. The likes of Warren Cummings, Danny Hollands, Neil Young, Mark Molesley, Stephen Purches, Marvin Bartley, Alan Connell, Brett Pitman, Matt Tubbs, Shwan Jalal, Shaun Cooper, Anton Robinson, Ryan Garry, Josh McQuoid, Steve Fletcher, Steve Lovell, Danny Ings, Marc Pugh, Harry Arter, Simon Francis, Shaun MacDonald, Steve Cook and Tommy Elphick were and are a pleasure to deal with. Most, if not all, fronted up during the tough times and faced difficult questions. I thank them for that.

I must also mention the managers. Kevin Bond faced an impossible task but did so with grace and a smile. He was still smiling when I met him late in 2017 for this book and I thank him for his honesty and for his time.

Also Lee Bradbury, a loyal and sincere man who wiped the slate clean to meet me and discuss one of the club's most tumultuous periods. We fell out, had our differences as most journalists and managers do at one point or another, and wasted far too much time on phone calls where neither of us would budge. But Lee doesn't do grudges and welcomed both myself and this project into his life with open arms.

Jimmy Quinn's spell at the club was brief. He was on a hiding to nothing if truth be told, but again he dealt with the media in a professional and engaging manner even if his threat to 'get the boys over from Belfast' does still send a shiver down my spinal cord.

The club's media team has grown along with its presence in the English game. I must thank the late Mick Cunningham, a red and black supporter through and through and a truly gifted sports photographer. He is much missed on both a personal and professional level.

Thanks go to Max Fitzgerald, the club's first proper head of media, who has gone on to achieve great things with both West Ham United and now Wolverhampton Wanderers. He banned the *Daily Echo* in 2012 only to find out the next day that the newspaper had banned the club in return. A learning experience for both of us, yet we remain friends.

Anthony Marshall is the club's current head of media and a former newspaper man who sees things from the other side of the fence. Thank you, Anthony, for your assistance and support alongside Becky Stimson and Rob Mitchell in the commercial department as I toiled through penning this book.

Keely Stamou, Eddie Howe's PA, was instrumental in pinning down both her boss and myself during busy schedules and thanks go to her for her patience!

As I reach a close, I must thank both Jeff Mostyn and Steve Sly for their wit, commitment and unprintable humour during the most difficult of periods for the club. It's a well-known fact that had Jeff's pockets not run as deep as they do, this football club would not exist. They deserve the utmost respect. I will never forget the look on Jeff's face in the tunnel at Dean Court after the *Echo* boys informed him the players had just been paid in readies from a Marks & Spencer carrier bag.

On a personal level, my love, admiration and heartfelt thanks go to my wife Stephanie and children Neve and Caleb simply for being there and loving me back. I could not have completed this book without their support and patience. My love for you all cannot be put into words.

I send thanks to my parents, Les and Kay, for allowing me to pursue a career in newspapers when, if they're honest, they would have preferred me to become a plumber or an electrician. I hope my successes have repaid your faith.

Finally, my respect and admiration for Eddie Howe and Jason Tindall, two of the most hard-working and inspirational people I have ever met. This story is their creation and would have been very different had Eddie not said 'yes, Adam' on that monumental New Year's Eve of 2008.

ACKNOWLEDGEMENTS

To steal a quote from Tommy Elphick, this is their 'masterpiece' and I thank them both. We all do.

Neil Meldrum
Poole, January 2018

FOREWORD
BY EDDIE HOWE

WHO'D get into football management? Me, as it happens, although I'm still to this day not completely sure how it *did* happen.

It's a funny old game, as they say, and the night Adam Murry phoned to ask me to take the team changed my life forever.

The story of what followed has been well covered in newspaper articles and TV documentaries but those only tell part of the tale. This is the first comprehensive piece of writing to document everything that happened to this wonderful football club from the summer of 2006 to that glorious, memorable night in April 2015 when we sealed Premier League promotion.

I have tried and failed on many occasions to put it all into words, but one thing I can say is that it has been a journey inspired and underpinned by dedication, hard work and a lot of very talented and loyal people in the playing squad, management team and behind the scenes.

This is the story of what can be achieved when those things come together. Our club motto is 'Together, Anything is Possible' and it really is. I feel both humble and proud to have played a part in the football club's rise to the Premier League.

This is also a story written by someone who, alongside his colleagues at the *Daily Echo* in Bournemouth, witnessed first-hand the ups, the downs, the successes and the failures. Neil even reminded me of moments I had allowed to slip away from my mind when we met – but I used the pressures of Premier League management as an excuse for forgetting a few things!

Football has given me so much and I am forever grateful for that. It is a sport that transcends all races, colours and creeds and has the ability to spark huge emotion and depth of feeling.

I hope you enjoy this story as much as I have enjoyed being a part of it.

Eddie Howe
Bournemouth, February 2018

INTRODUCTION

'FOOTBALL, bloody hell.' He was the doyen of winning, Sir Alex Ferguson. But he had all the tools to succeed – would you describe any of Manchester United's 13 Premier League titles under the great man's leadership as a sporting miracle? Probably not.

For all of the certainties in sport, though, like Phil Taylor winning world darts titles, the driver with the fastest car claiming Formula One's world championship year after year, or Celtic lifting the Scottish Premiership crown by February, there are the moments of breathtaking wonder, where you're not quite sure how something you have just witnessed happened. You just know it *did* happen. Stories of taking inconceivable odds, throwing them in the air and knocking them out of the park, into the stratosphere. Emotion, heightened by success and failure. Sport that makes us 'feel' and the triumph of the underdog that takes us even further into the wonder of the bright lights.

Ferguson might have used more colourful language alongside that most famous of soundbites when attempting to comprehend Leicester City's 5,000-1 Premier League title win in 2016, Jamie Vardy, Wes Morgan, Robert Huth, Claudio Ranieri et al the Rocky Balboas of a season that will surely never be repeated.

Further down the table that year were AFC Bournemouth.

'Bournemouth? What, skint Bournemouth by the beach, with the little ground in the middle of a park?' Yes, that Bournemouth.

'How did they manage that?' Good question, which brings us appropriately on to a sporting miracle that surely rivals the achievements of Ranieri's men. Maybe even Boris Becker's 1985 Wimbledon victory at the age of 17? How about John Daly's 1991 USPGA title win, or Buster Douglas flooring Mike Tyson in 1990? Surely Liverpool's Champions League comeback of 2005 on that sweltering night in Istanbul?

Like Leicester, the Cherries were forced to battle back from the precipice, but the achievement of Ranieri's side in 2016 emerged from the ashes of a Premier League relegation near miss rather than falling through the trapdoor itself. Their success on the back of failure also spanned only two seasons, while Bournemouth's saw them recover from what looked a certain drop into non-league, even extinction, before an assault on three divisions in seven years led them to the Premier League's promised land.

Yes, Ranieri's squad was formed on a shoestring by Premier League standards, but the likes of Morgan, Huth, Danny Drinkwater, Marc Albrighton and Ranieri himself all had good, solid experience. The mental strength and capacity to go again after disappointment. They also had genuine talent in Kasper Schmeichel, Vardy, Riyad Mahrez and N'Golo Kante.

Yes, Cherries owner Maxim Demin's millions enabled Eddie Howe to take the club beyond the shattered imaginations of its loyal supporters by purchasing talent in the same vein.

But consider the years before Demin's arrival in 2011. Howe was 31 and had never managed before when he took the reins in 2009, while his squad comprised the likes of Anton Robinson, Liam Feeney and Mark Molesley – hard-working, reliable, talented professionals but all rising from the lower reaches of non-league with only one Football League appearance between them.

Ranieri's side received their wages each month, without fail, while they plotted the club's pathway towards the Premier League title. Howe's side in the manager's early years often went several months without their salaries, while also being forced to watch as the club publicly lurched from one crisis to another off the field. At one point during the administration of 2008, the Cherries were five minutes from being liquidated. Five minutes.

Does all that make little AFC Bournemouth's fall and rise more miraculous than Leicester's achievement or anything else that has gone before it? I believe it does. You may feel the same by the time you reach the end of this book. You may not.

But one thing is for sure, when it comes to sporting stories, the ones that make you 'feel', AFC Bournemouth's takes some beating.

DREAM THE IMPOSSIBLE DREAM

T OMMY Elphick moved his food from one side of the plate to the other with his fork, as if playing an imaginary match. His girlfriend Hannah looked on, a smile through gritted teeth masking her simmering displeasure at yet another meal spoiled by football distractions.

The Chewton Glen Hotel just outside Highcliffe, a small Hampshire–Dorset border town, is the kind of five-star luxury reserved for wealthy, successful businessmen and their families. Or Premier League footballers. But Elphick was trying not to think about that prospect.

Championship front-runners AFC Bournemouth were two games from the promised land. Its riches, its glamour and its glory. Sky Sports, though, had moved the club's penultimate match against Bolton Wanderers at Dean Court to a Monday night. The broadcaster had the same feeling Elphick was trying to keep penned in, a surge of emotion just waiting to break free.

Elphick is sitting, but leaning forward intently and speaking directly into my iPhone recorder, as if to be certain no memory is overcome by the din of a Friday lunchtime crowd in The Belfry's Brabazon Bar just outside Birmingham. Donning jeans, trainers and a fitted jacket, the Aston Villa defender is tall and broad, yet unassuming, without the 'he's a footballer' look perfected by so many of his colleagues in the Beautiful Game.

He sips his cappuccino and takes up the story of Monday, 27 April 2015, AFC Bournemouth's day of destiny.

To Elphick, though, its build-up was more like a painful 72-hour boot camp for the mind.

'We'd trained on the Saturday and the gaffer got the lads together after the session and told us not to waste our energy watching the scores come in,' he reflects, his eyes locked on mine. 'We knew if results went our way we could get promoted against Bolton on the Monday, but he didn't want us to get involved so I made a point of booking the Chewton Glen restaurant at 3pm on the Saturday with Hannah so I could get away from it.

'Of course my intentions were good, but I couldn't help myself and wanted to have a look at the scores. I couldn't get a signal on my phone, though. It was agony. I spent most of the meal dithering with my food as I couldn't shake off the feeling of not knowing what was happening.

'My missus wasn't happy so I did my best to try to forget what was happening in the other games. By 5pm when we left the restaurant and I got a signal, my phone started going wild as all the messages and missed calls started flashing up. The lads had obviously totally ignored the manager but could you blame them?

'Our group message was going crazy. If we beat Bolton on Monday night, we were going up. The Premier League! Everyone was just so excited.

'On Sunday morning we trained again and everyone was flying. I promise you now, I would have bet my life on us winning that game. I was that confident. It was meant to be and we were giving it everything in that session.

'I woke up on the Monday morning and tried to be as normal as possible. I took a few phone calls from the family but I was trying to be normal. Of course you can't though, can you? I read the papers and I was double-checking the league table every two minutes in case we'd got it all wrong.

'The *Daily Echo* had done a front page that day which was black and red stripes with the words "DREAM THE IMPOSSIBLE DREAM" on it. It sent shivers down my spine – how could I be normal after that? I still have it today.'

For Howe, his role was keeping his men grounded. As it had been throughout a breathtaking season that had propelled little AFC Bournemouth into the mainstream media's hearts.

'The gaffer is a genius,' grins Elphick. 'He was great at producing key team talks at big moments in the season. We came in as normal on the Monday morning of the game and walked through a few set pieces, then he told us all to get to bed and do what we normally did. He was dampening it down as much as he could, but you can imagine what we were like.

'We got to the warm-up before the game and then he called us in as he normally did. He was his usual self, but once we had sat down in the dressing room, the lights went off.

'A big screen came up and he had produced a montage of footage on the club's history. This was five minutes before we were due to go out so he'd normally be doing his team talk.

'The footage was incredible. I swear if you could bottle the feeling it produced, nobody would ever lose a game again. It was a stunning bit of management. We got up and my heart was racing, the hairs on my arms standing up.

'We got into a team huddle in the dressing room and he calmed everyone down just enough, as we were revved up to the eyeballs.

'It was a magical atmosphere inside the ground, a Monday night under the lights and in front of the Sky cameras, and we got off to a great start. Marc Pugh scored so early, I just knew it was going to be our night. Pughie had been at the club for a long time and it was just so fitting that he scored. Matt Ritchie made it 2-0 and then Callum Wilson got the third. By that stage everything was just a blur. We'd done it – we were going into the Premier League. The crowd poured on to the pitch and I was carried aloft towards the tunnel. It was just monumental.

'It was probably one of our best performances of the season and some of the football we played that night was just stunning.

'Every player in that dressing room had a story and it was just pure emotion after the game. I'd come back from a double Achilles rupture with people saying I'd never play again, Yann Kermorgant had battled leukaemia, Matt Ritchie had dropped down the leagues to rebuild his career, Harry Arter the same when he went to Woking, Simon Francis had got brutal stick at Charlton as apparently he couldn't cope, Steve Cook had gone out on loan in non-league and Charlie Daniels was released from Tottenham. It was band of brothers stuff as we were a complete bunch of misfits thrown together, but we just clicked.

'We did it our way and when you actually look at the results like Leeds, Watford, Derby and Huddersfield and what these huge clubs were spending, we battered the lot of them. There can never be any doubt how much we deserved to reach the Premier League. We'd done it and proved everybody wrong.'

Mighty oaks from little acorns grow...

CHAPTER ONE

SETTING THE SCENE
2003–06

INTERVIEWS with Warren Cummings were, at times, unnerving experiences for those of us in the media.

Daily Echo photographers past were squirted with water or forced to witness more than they bargained for when Cummings would yank down the shorts of his fellow players during the annual pre-season photo call.

A match merit mark of less than 6/10 in Monday's paper, meanwhile, would be followed by Cummings's unique brand of training ground banter come Tuesday morning. On one occasion, the defender requested my mobile phone to speak directly to *Echo* sports writer Ian Wadley, whose 4/10 in that Monday's paper had not gone down at all well. With Cummings, though, things were never truly serious, yet inside the joker lay a character of fearsome determination.

Those kind of characters gravitated towards the club between 2002 and 2015. The difference in that 13-year period? Four divisions, administration, two relegations, a Greatest Escape and four promotions. Hard to believe isn't it? But this is not a story of far-fetched fiction. Cummings is seated and ready to talk when I walk into a coffee shop in the popular Bournemouth suburb of Westbourne, close to his home.

He is a picture of calm, dressed in a fitted jumper, jeans and brogues. Nonetheless, given the Scot's decorated history with practical jokes, I drink my latte, generously purchased by Cummings before my arrival, with one eye on the contents and one eye on the subject...

In many ways, Cummings's spirit and humour, not to mention his talent in the left full-back position, tell the tale of AFC Bournemouth's fall and rise on their own.

A leader committed to the cause and a marauding full-back ahead of his time, the Scot would have become an international regular had injury not struck at the worst possible moment. Nevertheless, he did play for his country once or, as he prefers to put it, 'Me and Kenny Dalglish won 103 Scotland caps between us.'

Raised in the dressing room of Chelsea, alongside the likes of 1998 World Cup winners Marcel Desailly, Frank Leboeuf and Didier Deschamps, as well as close friend John Terry, Cummings could have been forgiven for thinking Bournemouth was somewhat beneath him when he arrived at the club on loan at the dawn of the new millennium.

'Far from it,' he laughs, sipping his coffee from a disposable cup. 'I went away after that initial loan spell in 2000 and did a year at West Brom then a year at Dundee United in 2002/03.

'Very quickly that turned out to be an awful move for me because the manager at the time was sacked and I couldn't wait to get back to Chelsea, even just to be in the reserves. I wasn't in the first-team picture at Dundee United and wasn't being treated particularly well, but I wasn't in the first team at Chelsea either.

'In January 2003, Peter Grant gave me a call. He was still at Bournemouth coaching under Sean O'Driscoll and asked me if I fancied coming back on loan again.

'I said I was up for it if they could get the paperwork done. Because I'd signed on loan at Dundee United for that whole season it was slightly difficult but they got it done and I arrived at the end of January.

'My first game was away at Kidderminster Harriers and we lost 1-0 but I was just glad to be there. I'd loved my first spell at Bournemouth and it was great to be back.'

Inexplicably relegated from Division Two under O'Driscoll in 2002, the squad Cummings returned to in 2003 was brimming with talent and, with Dean Court having been spun around 90 degrees and rebuilt, albeit partially, in 2001, the infrastructure and belief was firmly in place for a return to the third tier.

'Things had changed a lot while I'd been at West Brom and in Scotland,' Cummings admits. 'They had a new stadium which was fantastic and the squad was highly talented.

'But they'd had their difficulties in 2001/02 and been relegated to Division Three. They'd started pretty well in 2002/03 but had tailed off a bit in December and January and I think Sean had received an ultimatum from the chairman Peter Phillips that he had two or three games to get the team up the league as they'd had a poor couple of months.

'The squad was talented without a doubt. We had big Steve Fletcher up front, Carl Fletcher in midfield who was outstanding, Garreth O'Connor, Brian Stock and Wade Elliott, plus James Hayter up front.

'But when I arrived at the end of January we were fifth in the table and should have been higher. We knew we should have been in the top three with the squad we had.

'My first home game after the Kidderminster defeat was against Wrexham who were right up there with us but we beat them 2-0 and it was comfortable. Warren Feeney got both goals and we knew then we had a chance of going up.

'I signed permanently in April, but for whatever reason we didn't get into the top three and ended up in the play-offs. I couldn't tell you whether Sean was happy or angry about it because he was the same every day! You never got a huge amount out of him either way, but he was highly knowledgeable and we were supremely organised.'

For what O'Driscoll lacked in an extroverted personality, he more than made up for in coaching that was beyond its years in the lower reaches of the English league. Having endured criticism for taking the Cherries into the bottom tier in 2002, the Midlander was hell-bent on a return to Division Two to silence doubting supporters who had been scarred by the club almost going out of existence in 1997, owing the Inland Revenue £350,000 and Lloyds Bank £2.1m.

'I felt Sean was ahead of his time,' reflects Cummings with a smile. 'We watched DVDs and videos on the opposition in 2000 and that was unheard of for a Division Two side at that time. He also used to give us all a booklet, 16 pages long, every week detailing everything about that weekend's opposition. It had detail on set pieces, every individual on the team. It was amazing and he expected us to digest it all.

'His training methods were revolutionary, although I didn't always enjoy it as it sometimes lacked a competitive edge.

'But he was excellent and streets ahead of everyone else in the lower leagues at that time.'

But even O'Driscoll couldn't pilot his talented squad into the Division Three automatic promotion places come April 2003, despite six wins from their final nine league games.

'We were disappointed with missing out on automatic promotion but everyone always says if you can win them, the play-offs are the best way to get promoted,' says Cummings.

'We had Bury in the semi-final, who were difficult to play against, very physical and just not very nice.

'They had Colin Cramb up front and he was a real playground bully. He was horrible. We went up there for the first leg and the pitch at Gigg Lane was awful and they were getting right in our faces, which was their way. Nothing suited us but we scraped a 0-0 and took them back to Dean Court where it was comfortable for us. We won 3-1 and there was a bit of afters with Peter Grant and Cramb on the touchline, but it was straightforward other than that!'

With a final against Lincoln City at Cardiff's Millennium Stadium to come, Cummings decamped north of the border while O'Driscoll toiled on the best way to overcome another side famed for their physical presence and single-mindedness.

'The final wasn't until ten days after the second leg against Bury so I went back up to Scotland to see some friends on the free weekend and it definitely helped remove some of the pressure,' Cummings recalls.

'We did training as usual in the week leading up to the game and from then on the build-up was all based around Lincoln.

'They'd beaten us 1-0 from a set piece in the last few weeks of the regulation season so we were aware of their presence and knew it would be difficult. But we were so organised and Sean went into overdrive the week before to make sure we were all over what we needed to do.

'Nothing bothered Sean. It didn't matter whether we were playing five-a-side or a play-off final at the Millennium Stadium – he was always the same. He knew if we were right, we would have a chance of winning every game and the final was just another game to him.

'But after we went to Cardiff on the Thursday before the game, we trained up there on Friday morning and I went over on my ankle.

'It blew up like a balloon straight away so they took me back to Southampton Nuffield Hospital and they confirmed I'd torn some ligaments. They said I could strap it up, have an injection and have a go on it in the game but said I'd probably do more damage to it and probably not even get to the end of the 90 minutes.

'We drove back to Wales and I arrived on crutches with the ankle in an ice pack. We were staying at Celtic Manor just off the M4 so we decided I'd have a fitness test on the Saturday morning before the game.

'Peter Grant took me out and really put me through my paces. I was running with my ankle strapped right up and I got through it so they said I could play. I didn't have an injection as I knew I'd do damage and wouldn't know about it. At least without the injection I'd be able to feel the pain and know if I had to stop.'

With only a 1984 Associate Members' Cup win and 1998 Auto Windscreens Shield Final defeat to count as 'success' in the modern era, supporters flooded over the Severn Bridge in their thousands, a chance to say 'I was there' after many had thrown their contribution of £35,000 into buckets at the Winter Gardens concert hall in 1997, money which gave the club an immediate future when the threat of liquidation was a very real prospect.

'The day was just magical as we drove into Cardiff and saw all the fans lining the streets and that was when the enormity of the game really hit us as players,' reflects Cummings fondly. 'It was a beautiful day and there was a real air of expectation and we got the perfect start through big Steve Fletcher.

'The ball went forward and was flicked on and he volleyed it in but then they scored from a set piece again, through Ben Futcher.

'Luckily we got a goal right before half-time through Carl Fletcher, but it was Stephen Purches's goal just before the hour that really I remember more than anything.

'Neil Moss punched it clear in our penalty area and James Hayter broke away and fed Wade Elliott down the line.

'Purchey had run all the way from full-back and slotted it home. At 3-1 we really started to enjoy it and then Garreth O'Connor made it 4-1. The game got really stretched though and they scored to make it 4-2, but then Carl Fletcher got a fifth about ten minutes from time and we knew it was done.

'The celebrations were epic and we went out that night. The most surreal moment for me was standing in the nightclub's VIP room with Sean having a glass of Champagne. He was the same even then though and didn't really celebrate – he was more interested in talking about the game!'

O'Driscoll left his players to the rest of the night, distracted by more pressing matters.

Back in Division Two, how would he keep them there, let alone make progress?

Summer signings were non-existent, while the club was far from out of the woods off the pitch. With Phillips having replaced Tony Swaisland as chairman in 2002, the latter walking away after his proposal to sell and lease back Dean Court was met with despair by supporters, the new man at the helm was preoccupied with a partially completed new stadium, not to mention sums of money owed to builders Barr, Swaisland, Lloyds Bank, Bournemouth council and club president Stanley Cohen – a black hole to the tune of £5m just six years after the Winter Gardens buckets were put away.

Phillips would eventually seek board approval for Swaisland's sale and leaseback proposal himself in 2005, handing over Dean Court to London landlords Structadene for £3.5m in favour of paying around £30,000 a month in rent.

'We always had a feel for the fact the club wasn't too stable off the pitch,' admits Cummings. 'Our wages were late pretty much every month so we knew things weren't good.

'That didn't change for the next two seasons back in Division Two after the play-off win and when the club sold the stadium and leased it back in 2005 we knew it was getting worse.

'We also lost a lot of players between 2004 and 2005. Garreth O'Connor and Wade Elliott went to Burnley and Warren Feeney went to Stockport, but the biggest loss was Carl Fletcher to West Ham. He was outstanding and sold for a pittance, but we knew the club would have their leg lifted quite easily because the financial situation was so bad.'

With Structadene talks well under way in the spring of 2005, Cummings was to suffer injury agony that would stall both his international ambitions and a play-off push sparked by defender Eddie Howe's signing from Portsmouth. In peak AFC Bournemouth fashion, supporters started an 'EddieShare' scheme that raised £13,000 in 48 hours to secure the centre-half's return to Dean Court from Fratton Park.

'We almost got to the play-offs in 2004/05 and should have done really,' Cummings recalls solemnly. 'But I broke my leg at Swindon in March and I was never the same after that.

'I'd won my only Scotland cap in 2003 but was doing well in 2004/05 and I was looking at a recall. It was a very tough thing to go through for myself and the team. We had a very small squad and we didn't win any of our remaining six home games after I broke the leg so it killed our season really.

'We needed a win against Hartlepool on the last day of the season to make the play-offs and we could only draw 2-2. There was a fire sale of players like John Spicer, Brian Stock and James O'Connor and we knew it was going to be difficult after that.

'We had a very poor second half to the season in 2005/06 and finished 17th and I think Sean knew he was done after that. He wouldn't have *wanted* to leave but I think he knew he had to in 2006. There was no money and the squad was not as talented as in previous years. He was constantly trying to pull rabbits out of hats and I think it took its toll on him.

'We'd lost Peter Grant and Richard O'Kelly had come in as a coach but Sean only really had Richard. Everything else he was doing himself and I think that also got to him.

'I'd signed a new contract while I was laid up with the broken leg, but I think I would have left that summer in 2005 if I'd been fit. Sean knew that, too, but with the situation I was in with the injury I was grateful that he wanted to offer me a new deal.'

Phillips, too, had endured enough and decided to 'step off the rollercoaster' at the start of September 2006. Just over a week later, O'Driscoll left to become the new manager of Doncaster Rovers.

'Peter Phillips stepped down and his vice-chairman Abdul Jaffer took over,' Cummings says, before breaking out in a wry smile. 'Days later, Darren Anderton signed and Sean left the same day!

'It was an odd situation and even though Darren is now one of my best friends, his signing at the time just didn't feel like a Sean O'Driscoll signing, so it was not a huge surprise when Sean left for Doncaster. I think Darren's signing was instigated higher up in the board room for PR rather than playing reasons and that was probably the last straw for Sean.

'You could see from that point, with other people getting involved in transfers, he knew he had to go.

'He was the only manager I really knew and so I went and got some bottles of Champagne for the end of his last game against Crewe. A couple of us stood up and said a few words and it was an emotional moment.

'But it was typical Sean when he told us to halt the Champagne because we had another game on Tuesday!'

With Jaffer in place and perhaps enjoying the limelight that comes with a managerial search a little too much, a host of other big names were rumoured to be following midfield signing Anderton south – but into the Dean Court dressing room as manager.

'The speculation on Sean's replacement started straight away,' laughs Cummings. 'Les Ferdinand and Robert Lee looked like the early favourites and then Kevin Bond, Andy Hessenthaler and Phil Brown came into the running. I know they were all interviewed. I didn't enjoy that period, to be honest. People like Les and Rob Lee were massive names and it just seemed like a little bit too much for Bournemouth.

'It was too much of a change and I wondered how people like them would have reacted had they come in and then suddenly seen everything that they *didn't* have. If they had known what a state the club was in when they were interviewed they wouldn't have touched the job with a barge pole.

'It was all done very publicly too and people were getting photographed going into the ground. It was like the club was running a competition to win the job – it just wasn't done professionally.

'It went on for about six games at the start of the 2006/07 season and during that period Joe Roach, the youth team boss, and the goalkeeping coach Stuart Murdoch steadied the ship pretty well as caretaker managers.'

Jaffer's planned 'Bond is Back' moment in the press conference unveiling had been spoiled by the *Daily Echo* revealing the former Dean Court defender was the board's choice the day before. Nonetheless, the miffed chairman sat alongside the new man and chief executive Laurence Jones as the gathered handful of scribes and broadcasters fired questions.

'Kevin Bond was a good appointment on paper,' says Cummings. 'He had a connection with the club and a good relationship with his dad John and Harry Redknapp. It wasn't as left-field as Ferdinand and Lee and seemed like a good option at the time.

'But Kevin did too much too soon. In 2006/07 he didn't really bring in too many new faces and we ended up finishing 19th, which was poor but at least we had stayed up in tough circumstances after Sean had left.

'But the following year he brought in too many bodies. He took Jo Kuffour, the striker, who turned out to be a good signing for us but he also brought in a lot of loan players during the summer of 2007/08.

'He took Paul Telfer from Celtic and we were thinking, "He's got to be a good signing. He's only just finished playing in the Champions League!" Jason Pearce also came in from Portsmouth. He didn't play much in 2007/08 until the end of the season, but I could talk about that boy all day. What a player. He was just outstanding and his attitude was as good as I have ever seen.

'Darren Anderton was fantastic too. He was at the end of his career and it had initially seemed a bizarre signing the previous season, but he was superb in 2007/08.

'I'd never rated him as highly as I should have when he was playing at Tottenham and for England, but he was just outstanding on the ball and was a great lad to have around. He really bought into the club even though it was very different to what he was used to.

'Kevin used to give him time off during the week because his legs weren't what they were and he was picking up a few injuries, but he was a real globetrotter and would text us on a Wednesday after a Saturday game and he'd be somewhere like New York or Miami with a tight hamstring!

'He trained like a demon when he was back here though and was a huge influence on that team and is still close to a lot of the boys from that era now. His ability was outstanding.

'In his first game for us against Scunthorpe in 2006 we had a free kick from 35 yards and we were both stood over it. He said, "I'm having this one. I'm going to fade it."

'I said, "What do you mean, fade it? Like a golf shot?"

'He said "Yeah", struck it and it bent like a banana and went into the top corner. I just thought "wow".

'Several of Kevin's signings just didn't work though. The worst decision he made was to bring in four lads from Reading, Jem

Karacan, Scott Golbourne, Alex Pearce and James Henry. It really upset the apple cart.

'They were decent players but they just didn't fit in and we were struggling as a group anyway. The four of them arrived in October and November of 2007 and I understand why Kevin did it as he really didn't have much choice. We'd played Northampton at home in September and I broke my arm, Ryan Garry broke his leg and Russ Perrett tore his hamstring, all in the same game!

'Three defenders were gone in a flash so Kevin had to do something, but it was the wrong option to take four from one club.

'Individually they were good players and all of them have gone on to have good careers above the level we were at at that stage, but it created a huge divide in our dressing room. It was a "them and us" scenario and they were divisive in my eyes.

'When young players come in on loan from bigger clubs, they have to be selfish because they are trying to make a career for themselves. I get that.

'But in that situation you don't have an affinity for a loan club and the divide it created couldn't be overcome, although there was worse to come.'

Indeed there was. Off the pitch a further divide had been created when Jaffer, part of a three-man consortium bidding to take overall control of the club from fans' group the Community Mutual, resigned as chairman in February 2007. The two men remaining pressed on with their takeover as Bond's men toiled for the rest of the year, but choppy waters were on the horizon.

CHAPTER TWO

HEAD EXAMINATION
2006–08

J EFF Mostyn stood at the back of the room, surveying the
scene as Gerald Krasner held court in front of the media. The
cameras continued to point towards the brash Yorkshireman
at the head of the table.

It was 29 April 2008, just after lunchtime, when Mostyn
nodded his head, a moment witnessed by only those who had
chosen to take their eyes off Krasner for a moment. Had Mostyn
shaken it, this paragraph would be the end of the story.

Mostyn loves a 'cuddle' and welcomes me with one as I enter
his office in Dean Court's main hub ten years on (almost to the
day) from the moment that handed AFC Bournemouth a lifeline.

Manchester-born and a lifelong football fan from the blue half
of the city, Mostyn had become firm friends with former City
defender Bond and his father, the former manager John.

Running a successful financial business had provided Mostyn
with a comfortable life in affluent Chilworth, near Southampton
and close to the home of Bond Jnr.

He harboured utopian ambitions of owning a football club,
although he admits it was a dream rather than a genuine quest.

Around 30 miles down the M27 and A31, AFC Bournemouth
were welcoming Bond into the Dean Court hotseat as a

replacement for O'Driscoll. Behind the scenes, chairman Jaffer was in talks with a consortium featuring Bond's long-term friend and colleague Harry Redknapp but with the club's perilous financial state laid bare, Jaffer soon found himself back at the drawing board.

Bond picked up the phone.

'I got a phone call from Kevin and he invited me to meet with Abdul Jaffer to look at a potential investment,' recalls Mostyn. 'Kevin had made me fully aware that the football club was on its knees financially and that consortium after consortium had fallen away, including one with Harry Redknapp.

'I'm not sure what discussions took place between Harry and Abdul but you'd think that Kevin getting the manager's job when he did was part of that.

'He invited me to have lunch with Abdul in October 2006 and during the course of the meeting Abdul gave me a bit of a tour and introduced me to some of the directors and associate directors.

'I committed myself to a few quid, around £20,000, to help the club but the truth was they needed to raise somewhere in the region of £1m, predominantly for HMRC who were working up to a winding-up petition for unpaid PAYE.'

Despite the chasm swallowing up money at Dean Court, Mostyn was hooked. He was walking into a hailstorm yet something engulfed him as he strolled out into the main stand to watch Bond's men slump to a 3-1 League One defeat against Rotherham.

'As soon as I walked through the door, I loved it,' he says, gesticulating with his hands. 'I'd never been to a lower league club before apart from when Manchester City were going through a blip. Kevin was the catalyst – he has been my best friend for 30 years and my wife Rose and Kevin's other half Trina are joined at the hip. Rose talks to Trina more than she talks to me.'

As Mostyn took the club to his heart, Jaffer's focus was on money and the chairman-by-default following Phillips's resignation had managed to bring together a further group of like-minded individuals looking to invest.

'There were around a dozen people looking to contribute as part of Abdul's consortium,' says Mostyn with a smile, 'but I think Abdul had his Fantasy Football head on because to get 12 people to throw in £100,000 each and be loyal, committed people but lacking in sense, was a big ask. Essentially, he was asking people to throw £100,000 into a dark hole.'

'I came in on the crest of a wave thinking "Christ, I've got the chance to buy a football club here and I can save Kevin's job." I hadn't engaged my brain. It was left at home and my heart was pumping thinking I could make a go of it.'

By November 2006, though, 12 had become three. Mostyn and associate director Steve Sly, a giant of a man, tattooed and imposing, yet decorous when it came to the club he had followed as a boy, looked on as Jaffer's consortium crumbled away.

'The issue we had was that the football club was controlled by the Supporters' Trust and they were effectively ministers without portfolio,' says Mostyn. 'They weren't about to simply relinquish the reins of the football club and I realised very quickly why all the other potential investors had moved away.'

Mostyn was undeterred and alongside Sly and Jaffer, pushed on with plans to take control of the club from the Community Mutual, set up as the UK's first football supporter-backed boardroom in the wake of the Cherries' Winter Gardens bucket collection of 1997.

But just a month after Jaffer announced a shareholders' Extraordinary General Meeting to vote on his consortium's plans, the chairman walked away following a leaked board meeting in February 2007. For Mostyn, realisation was biting hard as the 12 that became three were now down to just two.

'Very quickly I realised we were in the shit and my sole focus from then on was, "Where do we get the money?"

'I had already gone in way beyond what I had budgeted for so the relationship with Abdul deteriorated quite quickly in early 2007 when we realised he wasn't going to be putting in any more money himself. He did have a great desire to take money out, though, and he believed he was owed.

'Like many people at the time, he had loan notes. He also had shares, but as far as I was concerned as soon as Steve and I took control in March and changed the articles, those shares were worthless.

'I'd already contributed around £850,000 even before I had taken over the club. What an idiot. Steve said at the time that, as someone with intellect and who worked in the financial services industry, I should be ashamed of myself. But I had helped to stabilise his football club so he still loved me.'

Mostyn and Sly's takeover was ratified on 16 March 2007 inside the 'Inn Off The Bar' watering hole attached to Dean Court's main stand, a space that now houses the Premier League club's press and media lounge. Installed as chairman, Mostyn could have probably done with a drink when the true picture of the club's finances emerged following his takeover due diligence.

'Football had been my passion since I was five and now here I was realising a dream of becoming chairman and owner of a football club, but the dream was becoming a nightmare simultaneously,' he says.

'I remember the lawyers saying, "Jeff, listen. Don't say a word. We're sending over the full due diligence report by courier, but these are the headlines. You get into your car and drive as fast as you can back to Manchester and never think about Bournemouth again for the rest of your life, let alone visit."

'Of course I ignored them. It made no sense and I was an idiot. I sat down with the chief executive at the time, Laurence

Jones, and we did the sums. The average attendance at the time was 2,500–2,750 and the wage bill was £1.2m, or £100,000 a month. So you take the income from ticket sales and three burgers and an orange juice and it doesn't go into £1.2m. I did that basic maths but still thought somehow I could make the club different. I was mad.'

While Bond guided his new team to League One safety in the face of off-field upheaval, by the summer of 2007 Mostyn was left carrying the burden of an insolvent football club, unable to overcome its mountain of debt.

As Bond's side embarked on a poor run of five defeats in six during September and October of the new season, Mostyn went to business and accountancy advisers BDO Stoy Hayward for advice.

'I wasn't an expert on administration at the time, although you could say now that it's my specialist subject,' laughs Mostyn. 'I bought the club with my heart rather than my brain and by October 2007 I needed to know whether administration was the right way to go. What were the pros and cons and where would it leave me and my family?

'At the same time I was wearing an incredible weight of being the custodian of a football club. It weighed heavily on me and still does even today. I felt responsible for the club.

'The stress was unbelievable and I was just throwing money into a pit.'

Having watched from afar as Leeds United had entered administration 12 months earlier, Mostyn had at first been intrigued by the 'pre-pack' deal that saw the Yorkshire club purchased by a new company set up by chairman Ken Bates, essentially wiping out the club's debt with a 1p in the pound dividend deal for creditors and starting on an even footing. Having got wind of Mostyn's interest in the controversial pre-pack scenario, the *Daily Echo* took a flyer when, as expected, Mostyn placed the Cherries in administration on 8 February 2008.

'The plan was never to do a pre-pack deal, the *Echo* was wrong on that,' Mostyn says sternly with a pointed finger for added value. 'The principle was correct in that I was hoping to get some money back, but my intention was always to find a buyer or at least someone who could join me to share the burden. I didn't make one rational decision during that first 12 months at the club, so I just wanted to hang in there long enough to see some of my money again.

'What Leeds had done was create a ghost company which essentially bought back the business the day after entering administration, wiping out the debt and then carrying on as normal. I didn't like that because it left the creditors with next to nothing. Why should the person who delivers the milk lose out because of ten years of mismanagement? But unless I wanted to destroy myself financially, administration was the only route we could go down. It gave me the chance to continue to support the club while we searched for a buyer who could either take it on from me or become a partner. By the time we went into administration in February, I'd put £1.5m into the club.'

The debt was marginal by the lofty standards set by Leeds, a mere £4m compared with the £35m Bates claimed had been racked up during Peter Ridsdale's reign at Elland Road.

But everything is relative. While Leeds continued to boast crowds upwards of 30,000, even the Cherries' core support of 2,500 was waning as the reality of administration dawned and Bond's side looked doomed to drop into League Two following a ten-point Football League penalty.

Mostyn is clearly still hurt by those supporters who questioned his motives, even after he had written yet another cheque for £100,000, against wife Rose's wishes, following the now infamous 'head nodding' press conference of 29 April 2008.

'I had a choice of administrators and we had BDO Stoy Hayward come down and do a presentation for the directors,'

Mostyn recalls. 'I wanted to make sure that everyone knew what we were doing. I have always tried to do business with honesty and integrity yet during that period all people did was question my honesty and integrity!

'If I had put both feet in central Bournemouth at that time then I could have joined the Lord for Easter. I'd put £1.5m into the club and people still wanted to lynch me.

'BDO were the chosen administrators but I felt I owed it to the board to look at other options and at that stage the most high-profile insolvency expert in the country was Gerald Krasner.'

Mostyn can clearly see where the *Echo*'s Leeds pre-pack link came from. As soon as Krasner was confirmed as the club's administrator, the journalists began to salivate.

A bold, quotable and thick-set Yorkshireman, Krasner had led a consortium of local businessmen in purchasing Leeds United in 2004 before selling to Bates in 2005.

'Gerald seemed to have an ability to find buyers as well as run an administration in a sporting manner, whereas BDO were very businesslike,' recalls Mostyn.

'Gerald understood football clubs, so I met his lawyer David Hinchliffe in London to talk about him. He said he could set up a meeting with Gerald and act as the lawyer for the administration.

'That meeting was at the five-star Chewton Glen Hotel near Highcliffe and I should have known what was coming because every time Gerald came down from Leeds with his team, they stayed at the Chewton Glen. I was paying for that.

'I had to commit to the administration when we met with Gerald and also commit a minimum of £500,000 to fund it or Gerald wouldn't take it on. He said it would take a minimum of three months and we were looking at more than £100,000 a month to pay the players and fund the administrator. I got out of jail for a couple of months because he sold Sam Vokes to Wolves for £400,000. That was the first stroke of luck I'd had although I'm sure Kevin didn't see it that way.

'Those were the first steps of the marriage between Gerald and I. Whether it was made in heaven or hell I don't know.'

As part of the administration process, Krasner, who had placed a value of £3m on the club, was duty bound to hold monthly press conferences to update the club's creditors, of which there were many, ranging from the might of HMRC to small local businesses, whose money the football club had swallowed up, putting their livelihoods at risk.

Yet, in true AFC Bournemouth fashion, Krasner's briefings became infamous for their farcical nature more than their detail, none more so than on 29 April as Mostyn stood stony-faced at the back of the room.

'Gerald loved the press conferences,' recalls Mostyn with a smile. 'He always said the club's plight was in the national interest but it wasn't really. It was of interest locally first and foremost and mainly to the creditors who were going to lose all their money.

'But Gerald liked it and his chest swelled by a few more centimetres as he pontificated in front of the "world's media" as he liked to describe it.

'Gerald pulled me before the press conference in April and said to me before we went in, "Jeff, you'll stand at the back of the room and I will ask for the monthly cheque for £100,000. You'll nod your head if the answer is yes and shake your head if it's no." I said I had had enough and my wife Rose and I had agreed I wasn't going to put any more money in.

'He said if I shook my head then he would liquidate the club in the press conference.

'When he said to the journalists it was the end of 125 years of history at the football club, I nodded my head.

'I got home and Rose said, "Don't say anything. I know what you've done."

'How could I just let it die after everything? It would have meant all the grief was a waste of time and I would have been throwing away all that money I'd already put in. I couldn't do it.'

But before Mostyn and Krasner had even reached the end of April, what was already a farce had started to become a circus.

In March, just a month after the club had formally entered administration, Mostyn and Sly had seen talks with Dorset property magnate Alan Pither, of Christchurch firm Priory Homes, collapse. The pair then linked up with mysterious Dorset businessman Marc Jackson and the trio's first bid to Krasner was accepted. But by 3 April, relations with Jackson had also turned sour, with Mostyn and the man dubbed a "photocopier salesman" by supporters launching counter bids against one another.

Five days later, and just 24 hours after a creditors' meeting failed to pass a company voluntary arrangement (CVA), Mostyn's new offer alongside the ever-present Sly was given preferred bidder status in a press release issued by Krasner's company Begbies Traynor, only for the release to be retracted less than an hour later following a frantic phone call to the *Daily Echo* sports desk from one of Krasner's team.

Vaguely, the caller would only confirm Mostyn's bid had "lapsed" and that Jackson's rival bid was now in the driving seat. Jackson emerged as the frontman for EU UK, a company made up of businessman and former football agent Ian Mathison and fellow directors John Frost, Gary Oates and Simon Jordan, yet bizarrely, even by the Cherries' standards, Jackson was then jettisoned from the deal and asked to stay away from the top table when the group was unveiled as the club's new owner on 10 April.

Despite the photo call, rumours persisted that the group had yet to supply Krasner with the required funding, although Mathison told the *Echo* on 13 April that he expected the deal to be rubber-stamped before the administrator's deadline of 14 April.

'EU UK were unveiled with the scarf in the stands photo call and everything,' says Mostyn with a far from inconspicuous eye roll. 'Even though I had lost out in the bidding, for me it was pure relief that someone had come along and taken away the ball and chain that was dragging me down.

'I went to Marbella with Rose for the weekend after they had been unveiled and we were sitting in the hotel in Puerto Banus at around 1pm, the bells in the church nearby chiming. It was lovely.

'We'd just sat down with a drink and I hadn't even got the glass to my lips when the phone rang and it was Gerald. "Jeff, the EU UK cheque has bounced."

'He told me I was back in and he needed me to cover funding of £80,000. Within five minutes of Gerald's call I had another from Andy Williamson at the Football League saying the fixture list was due to come out at the end of the season and they needed an update or they would withdraw the Golden Share allowing us to play in the League.

'He said if we were going to come out of administration with a CVA in place, it needed to be for 10p in the pound. Where the hell was that money going to come from when we had no assets? From me, that's where.'

The club's CVA proposal at the 7 April creditors' meeting had been doomed to fail. With HMRC holding 17 per cent of the vote due to the mountain of PAYE owed, their policy on voting "no" when it came to football club CVAs seemed almost certain to land the Cherries with a further points deduction to add to the ten they had lost in February. Krasner needed 75 per cent of creditors to vote in favour of the 10p in the pound dividend proposal and fell well short.

With a second points deduction a certainty, Mostyn and Sly, complete once again with preferred bidder status in the wake of the collapsed EU UK deal, set about renewing their efforts to attract investors to the table.

'Steve Sly and I were travelling the country trying to find a buyer,' says Mostyn. 'David Hinchliffe said he had had some dealings with a guy called Paul Baker at Chester City, who was looking to invest at another football club as he was only a minority shareholder at Chester.

'We flew up to Manchester and met at the Radisson Blu at Manchester Airport and Paul had brought along his business partner Alastair Saverimutto. Very quickly it became clear that Savi could sell sand to the Arabs but it later transpired he couldn't afford a matchday programme let alone a football club.

'Savi had sold Paul the idea of buying shares in his marketing company, Sport-6, and Paul was a bit like me – too trusting. He put a substantial amount of money in and the idea was that Sport-6 would buy AFC Bournemouth.

'This is awful, but at that point I didn't really care whether I trusted them or not because Paul had written a cheque for David Hinchliffe while we were there, for £50,000.

'His courier business UK Sameday was thriving at the time so we agreed a deal pretty much there and then.

'We'd met so many people by then and witnessed so many false dawns that we were simply doing a mirror test – we shook hands with Paul and put a mirror in front of his face. It steamed up showing he was breathing so that was good enough for us. We were desperate.'

Baker and Saverimutto were unveiled to the media on 17 July, two months after Bond's braves had succumbed to the club's ten-point deduction and dropped into League Two on the final day of the campaign at Carlisle United.

With Sport-6 having purchased 100 per cent of the club from administrator Krasner, Saverimutto and Baker agreed a deal with Mostyn for his shares.

But this was a club fanbase now shrouded in suspicion and the Sport-6 PR machine did little to ease the scepticism.

'You can talk all day about what you hope to achieve but, ultimately, you will be judged on what you deliver. Delivery is my gospel,' Saverimutto told the gathered media at the press conference confirming his role as the club's new chief executive.

Baker, meanwhile, was equally into the soundbites, proclaiming: 'The football club has been on a life support machine for the past five months and it is in a period of intensive care.

'Jeff Mostyn, along with Steve Sly, has held the intravenous drip throughout that period, but we're now getting very close to the period where the club will come out of intensive care and into a period of aftercare.'

Mostyn and Sly remained in non-executive roles, to ease in the club's new owners if nothing else. Mostyn was also keen to support the under-pressure Bond, whose start to the 2008/09 campaign had been less than impressive against the backdrop of administration and a 17-point deduction for failing to pass the CVA proposal.

'Sport-6 came up with the money and everything appeared to be in order,' says Mostyn, 'although I had to beg the Football League to give us the Golden Share to actually play in League Two. I won hearts and minds with what I had done through funding the administration and I think they appreciated that I kept them up to speed with what was happening, so they eventually gave us the share alongside the 17-point deduction.'

Bond, though, knew his days were numbered. Just five games into the new League Two campaign, the points column remaining in negative numbers and without a win, Saverimutto sacked the manager in front of his friend Mostyn and brought in former Cherries striker Jimmy Quinn as his replacement.

Mostyn and Bond would not exchange a word for two years following that day, although Mostyn will only describe the fall-out as 'private'.

'Steve and I stepped aside about three months after Savi and Paul arrived and after Kevin had been sacked because we oversaw the transition from the old company to the new one,' he adds. 'Paul became the new chairman in November and we went to a few games after that to show our support but that was all.'

But no sooner had Sport-6 arrived, the circus was about to start up all over again – and the club's recently sacked manager would play an unexpected part.

CHAPTER THREE

WE'VE GOT NO CHANCE
2007/08

KEVIN Bond was used to unexpected phone calls, often in the hours of darkness. After he and decision-maker-in-chief Harry Redknapp had made the move from Portsmouth to Southampton in 2004, Bond was subjected to sustained and prolonged abuse from disgruntled Pompey fans, apoplectic that the south coast club's management team had hauled anchor and sailed along the Solent to St Mary's.

Bitterness and rage, even the historical rivalry and hatred between the two clubs, doesn't tell the sorry tale. Bond was threatened over the phone almost nightly, the perpetrators promising all manner of horrible, disgusting scenarios for both the coach and his family.

But when the phone rang at Bond's home just outside Southampton in the latter months of 2008, it wasn't abuse on the mind of the caller but a yearning for advice.

Two years earlier, Bond was embarking on his maiden job in league football management with the Cherries. Cash-strapped and hanging by a thread in financial terms at least, he was a glutton for punishment.

A combative and hard-working central defender, Bond had learned the arts of both pragmatism and idealism from father John, the former West Ham full-back who racked up 381 appearances for the east Londoners. Bond Snr was as colourful as they came, in an era when the Upton Park boys ruled the roost, strutting along Green Street, mop-tops bouncing in the East End breeze. As a manager with Bournemouth, Norwich and Manchester City he was bold and fearless yet tactically aware and intelligent. His son got the best of both worlds.

We meet in a quiet corner of the Chilworth Arms public house, just outside Southampton and close to Bond's family home. It's busy for a Thursday lunchtime so seeking space out of the earshot of business people and parties of families is tricky.

Bond, dressed in a puffa-style jacket and a trousers and trainers combo, stirs his cappuccino slowly, pondering, reflecting, remembering his late father, who died in 2012 at the age of 79. A batch of *Daily Echo* cuttings is sifted through with a genteel approach by the man whose soft centre is encased by the hard exterior left on many a Division One striker back in the 1970s and 1980s.

The passing of his father undoubtedly changed his perspective and it is a very different Kevin Bond today to the one that sent in a speculative CV to Cherries chairman Abdul Jaffer in 2006.

Having finished his playing career in Devon with Exeter City, Bond moved into the world of real work by opening a transport cafe, serving bacon rolls to long-haul truckers.

'It was bloody hard work,' he laughs. 'I had to go to London once a week at the crack of dawn to buy my bacon and chicken but I had to earn a living.'

If anything, Bond's desire for a route back into football was intensified by the early mornings and grumpy truckers. Then came a chance meeting with Alan Ball and he was back in the game.

'I bumped into Bally at the races one day and he had just started as manager at Manchester City. He asked me if I fancied coming to work with him as one of his coaches and I said I'd love to. He said he'd give me a call, but he certainly made me wait.

'I said to my dad, "Do you reckon I should ring him?" He told me not to and said I should wait and sure enough a couple of weeks later Bally rang and I ended up going up to Maine Road as reserve team coach. But less than a month in I was wondering if I was about to get the bullet.

'It was bizarre really,' smiles Bond. 'Alan lasted three games after I started. He was gone and it was an unbelievable shame. The chairman was Franny Lee and I knew him from when I played at City, I knew him well. But business is business.

'I survived Alan leaving and then they took on Steve Coppell who I didn't know. He was a very quiet man and never really spoke to me so I thought, "OK, I'll just crack on and keep my head down."

'But I'll never forget, Steve came up to me one day when I was training and said, "Kevin, I just want to let you know you are going to be completely autonomous." He patted me on the shoulder and walked off.'

Bond arches back and chuckles. 'I wasn't too sure what "autonomous" meant, so I ran off the training ground and into the office and told one of the secretaries to get her dictionary out and look it up. I was convinced I'd lost my job, but she looked it up and said "self-ruling". I'd gone from thinking I was about to get binned to being the happiest bloke on the planet.

'But then just as I was rejoicing, Steve only lasted six weeks. He was gone and I was back at square one – and we were only six weeks into the season. Eventually they brought Frank Clark in and I stayed until March of that season. I was only on a year's contract and I asked Frank if he had any thoughts.

'He said he needed to think about things. We were doing well and won the reserve league so I thought I'd done okay. But I needed clarification so I went to see him. He was going to leave it until the summer but I jumped the gun and he came out and said he was going to change everything. I left that day after just nine months but three managers!

'It was certainly a grounding in the rollercoaster of football coaching and management and becoming a victim of circumstance.'

Bond's voice drops an octave. 'I spoke to Bernard Halford, a wonderful man who is still involved at City now and he said, "Kevin, to survive in this game you have to have the heart of a lion and the skin of a rhino." Never a truer word was spoken and here I was out of work again.'

A stint at non-league Stafford Rangers followed where Bond took on his first management role, before Ball again came calling, impressed by Bond's relentless work ethic with City's fringe players. Bond's time in the North West was over and Portsmouth was his destination, this time as assistant manager.

But again it wasn't to last and in late 1999, Bond linked up with Redknapp as West Ham United's European scout. When Redknapp took the Pompey job in 2002, Bond followed as first-team coach.

Redknapp was already gaining a reputation as a man-manager who made things happen. Pompey won the Division One title in 2002/03 and the Premier League door was open. But drama was around the next corner and Redknapp's relationship with owner Milan Mandaric was unravelling.

'Harry felt that Milan had undermined him,' says Bond. 'They had a great relationship in many ways and Milan did an amazing job for Portsmouth. Him and Harry loved each other but Harry is his own man and Milan ended up bringing in Velimir Zajec as director of football and Harry didn't like it.

'Their relationship was fairly fractious at that time and he decided to leave. Everyone put two and two together and made five when they said he knew he was going to Southampton.

If that was the case then I certainly didn't know about it,' he laughs.

Redknapp's home on the banks of Poole Harbour on the upmarket Sandbanks peninsula was an idyllic escape for the manager. Win, lose or draw, he'd return home, often in the early hours, to long-suffering wife Sandra for comfort in defeat or celebratory relaxation. The halcyon location, however, left Redknapp open to the abuse Bond was also receiving by telephone following their move from Fratton Park to St Mary's Stadium.

'I had no future at Portsmouth when Harry went,' insists Bond, sternly, 'but I used to get telephone calls at all hours of the night from guys who had been up the pub. It was scary, the things they said.

'One day I had a call from this guy who was hurling abuse at me and threatening my family but the bloke hadn't withheld his number so I rang him up after training one day. He said, "Who's this?" I said, "Kevin Bond. You've been ringing me."

'I asked him what he'd do if he lost his job in Portsmouth and couldn't get another job there. Would he take a job in Southampton? He said, "Yeah, of course." So I had a conversation with him and after about ten minutes he was good as gold.

'After that he'd ring me up every week to ask how I was doing and he called me one day and told me about this terrific young player at Aldershot. He said me and Harry had to take him because he should be a Premier League player. He was saying this boy would do for us at Southampton – who he hated! It was unbelievable.

'Harry had it worse though. He used to get Portsmouth fans on boats sailing past his house in Poole abusing him when he was out in his garden. It was wicked, but you know that it's part and parcel if you're in football.

'He was available and Rupert Lowe contacted him. I was in the same boat again after Harry left Pompey. I played at

Southampton so I was made up when Harry asked me to go there with him.'

Bond smiles. 'Rupert was an interesting character and brought the old England rugby coach Sir Clive Woodward to the club while we were there. He had some unconventional ways of looking at things. He used to talk about eye coaches and peripheral vision and it was all a foreign language to us, really.'

The last bits of froth remaining, Bond takes a final slurp of his Italian coffee and leans in close. The disappointment etched on his face is the same expression I saw post-match at Carlisle's Brunton Park on 3 May 2008, save for the ravages of time.

'We should have kept that Saints team up,' he says with more than a hint of regret. 'That's pretty obvious – it was a good squad but certain games cost us. We were at home to Everton and 2-1 up in stoppage time. We had to win the game. Peter Crouch got the ball and instead of running into the corner and running down the clock, he had a shot and it went over the bar.

'The goalkeeper took a quick goal kick, somebody flicked it on and Marcus Bent volleyed it into the back of the net. The last kick of the game and it was 2-2 – an absolute nightmare. We'd just take one step forward and two back all the time.

'We'd beaten Middlesbrough away in March and I thought we'd done it, then we didn't win in five games and had Manchester United on the last day. We went 1-0 up but got beat and went down. It was horrible.

'Midway through the following season Harry was asked if he wanted to go back to Pompey as they were in the mire again and he did. There was no way I could stay at Southampton so I went with him.

'We stayed up at Portsmouth in 2006 by a miracle, but there was talk about Tony Adams coming in to coach. Harry didn't fancy another row with Milan so left it well alone, but I wondered where that would leave me and I didn't feel comfortable.

'Glenn Roeder offered me the chance to go to Newcastle as his assistant as I'd worked with him at West Ham, but it was short lived.'

We briefly discuss the BBC's *Panorama* programme *Undercover: Football's Dirty Secrets* with eyes widening as another round of coffees arrives. The programme, broadcast on 19 September 2006, cost Bond his job in the North East and tested the resolve of that thickening rhino skin.

'Unfortunately our relationship didn't work out how we had hoped and, ultimately, it was the *Panorama* programme that cost me at Newcastle. It was disgusting, but I've said all I want to say on it and I had to move on.'

Rather than recoil into the confines of home in a bid to escape the circus, Bond opted to throw his hat into the ring at another club close to his heart.

O'Driscoll's sudden departure from Dean Court was the story of a coach seeking solace with a club on a sounder footing. Bond, meanwhile, was seeking a different kind of refuge.

'Sean had left to go to Doncaster so I applied for the job,' Bond reflects. 'I didn't know the chairman Abdul Jaffer but he took advice from people and I had a couple of interviews. I was known at Bournemouth because I played there and my dad was the manager, so it was a club very close to my heart.

'They had to ask me about the *Panorama* stuff and I don't blame them for that. They had to do their due diligence but Abdul offered me the job.'

Jaffer, the flamboyant Kenyan-born businessman who owned a series of care homes and a recruitment business in Bournemouth, was not a football man in the truest sense of the word but had learned quickly as vice-chairman under Phillips until he stood down just a week before O'Driscoll headed north.

Short and stocky with a bullish nature to match, Jaffer's 'I'm an honest man' catchphrase formed a distinct yet dubious impression with the local press pack, but Bond was simply glad to be the boss again after a stop-start coaching career held back by circumstance and reliance on the fate of others.

Arms folded and sitting back, Bond smiles. 'It was a good time for me to get back into management. It was in League One, near where I lived and at a club I loved, so it was a massive opportunity for me. I knew the club didn't have money as such but I didn't care. Nobody had any money at that level! It was all on a shoestring so I didn't feel like I was taking on a club in the mire.

'When I took over in October 2006 the team wasn't doing very well so I tried to go in and paint an optimistic picture, but the reality was harder than that. I made numerous mistakes in my time as manager there and one of them was in recruitment. Abdul knew I could get players in on loan for a pittance and he encouraged me to bring people in – he said the club would find a way to pay for them.

'If I had my time again, I probably would have taken more time to assess my squad. Eddie Howe was forced to work under a transfer embargo when he took over in 2009 and I think that helped him bring the squad together. The mistake I made was going straight in for loan players. I was leaning on Harry a lot in a bid to bring in some quality when actually I probably didn't need to. I needed to try to get the best out of what I had and I didn't do that. It was inexperience as a manager.

'I should have taken my time a bit more and then fed a couple in as and when. Abdul was very good but it was all a bit rushed and I think it hurt us in the end.'

Bond's start was as bad as it gets. Five defeats from five, including heavy beatings at home to Rotherham and away at Swansea, turned supporters scarred by years of uncertainty against the new manager. Bond had played 126 games for the Cherries between 1988 and 1992, but the new breed cared not a jot about that. In the minds of the terrace regulars, he was taking them down.

'Abdul was probably wondering what the hell he'd done,' laughs Bond, his hands clasped as if to extenuate his defences. 'We were beaten 1-0 at Millwall and then shipped three at home to Rotherham. We didn't win again in the league until December when we beat Forest 2-0.

'In January we started to string a few results together and then won three on the spin in March before finishing the season with three wins, three draws and three defeats. It was enough to keep us up, but we were fortunate. There was no issue with togetherness in the squad,' insists Bond. 'They'd had Sean for a long time and like everything, they needed to adapt to a change. The training changed and sometimes it's a good thing, sometimes not. The lads were great with me, but it was hard.'

Bond had brought along close friend Mostyn to some of those early home encounters, in part to watch his new side, but mainly for him to enjoy some boardroom hospitality laid on by the effervescent Jaffer. Born in north Manchester, Mostyn was a spit and sawdust football man and had followed the ups and downs of life at Maine Road from the north of the city.

Bond smiles as he continues to flick through cuttings, edging nearer to the focus of our next subject. The *Daily Echo*'s back page headline confirming Mostyn's takeover is hard to miss. What had started as a nice day out quickly became a costly obsession.

'I was very close with Jeff at that stage and I took him to my first and second games in charge,' recalls Bond, with a fondness. 'He came into the boardroom with his wife and sat next to Abdul. He was my pal and I thought he'd love the hospitality, which he did, but by the end of the game Abdul had persuaded him to part with 20 grand and that was it. He was basically on board.

'He realised very quickly that the only way he was going to get his 20 grand back was to loan him another 20 grand. Before he knew where he was, he was half a million pounds deep in the club.'

With Jaffer having resigned in February 2007, the odd man out in that three-pronged consortium, Bond continued to settle in the Dean Court dugout, while Mostyn and Sly drew up their mandate to gain control of the club from the Community Mutual.

Bond was boosted further after Mostyn was installed as chairman a month later following the much-publicised extraordinary general meeting.

With League One safety confirmed, Bond added some youth and experience to his squad during the warmer months of 2007. Paul Telfer, the Scottish full-back, was signed on a free transfer from Celtic and young goalkeeper Asmir Begovic drafted in on loan from Redknapp's Portsmouth.

Ryan Garry, a central defensive prospect, but one blighted by injury, was picked up on a free from Arsenal. The additions made little difference, though, as déjà vu struck and Bond's side were left with just two wins from their opening eight games.

'I was encouraged by others to bring in Asmir,' Bond reflects with an eye-roll he'd rather have stayed hidden, 'but it was my decision ultimately. I knew him and thought he'd improve us so I took him. It was so difficult to tell Neil Moss, who was a legend at Bournemouth, he wasn't playing before that first game against Nottingham Forest in 2007/08.

'Nobody knew that Asmir was going to be such a good keeper at that stage and Mossy was really loved by the fans so it didn't go down too well.

'But Asmir did okay those first few games. Then we played Carlisle at home at the end of September and a ball came flying into the box at height from the halfway line.

'Asmir didn't know whether to catch it or not but ended up doing so and falling backwards. He was so tall his hands hit the crossbar and the ball popped out. Joe Garner tapped it in and we lost the game. The fans were chanting Mossy's name after that and I really felt for Asmir as he was only a young lad.

'His days were numbered after that unfortunately and it was partly my fault because I didn't need to put him in the team. I knew he would be a superb keeper and he has gone on to great things. He was a big lad and I was doing it for all the right reasons but it wasn't something I needed to do.'

Off the pitch, the vultures were circling and the unrest growing. Speaking up in the din of the Arms' lunchtime crowd, Bond knows what is coming.

Mostyn and Sly's initial investment had not even touched the sides of the club's mounting debt, which was now closer to £4m. Stadium rent following the controversial stadium sale and leaseback and poor crowds, meanwhile, were crippling the bank balance.

'We started the 2007/08 season poorly,' reflects Bond. 'We lost six games before October and we were struggling. There were stories starting to do the rounds that the club was going to go into administration because things had become so bad. It was very hard and I found it tough. We somehow managed to keep our heads above water but then in February we went into administration and were docked ten points. That left us 11 adrift of safety, so we knew it was going to take a miracle to stay up.

'Jeff gave it to me slowly, bit by bit. The negative effect administration had around the club was horrendous. People were losing their jobs but we had to try to go out and win a football match. We had no hope really.

'At that stage I thought we had no chance of avoiding relegation so we talked to the players and we knew we couldn't do anything about the points deduction. It wasn't our doing so we said if we could get relegated by nine points or less, at least that meant we would have stayed up without the points deduction. That was all we could aim for.

'The club was in a downward spiral. We had no money and a points deduction and it would have been an almighty feat if we had stayed up. I thought we had no chance. Our results still weren't coming together and we were just about hanging on to the coattails of the teams above.'

But all was not lost. A frantic March saw six points yielded from five games, before a 2-1 win against Tranmere at Dean Court saw a change in mentality. Bond's voice quickens, his glasses folded away.

'We got the bit between our teeth and found some belief from somewhere,' he says, enthused by a run of games that so nearly yielded a miracle. 'Finding that is hard – you have to build it and it takes time. You can't just switch it on but when you have it, look out.

'Things went our way a little bit too. We got an amazing result away at Swansea when we were 1-0 down and they were flying. Joe Partington scored a late header and I still have a photograph at home of Max Gradel, Sam Vokes, Brett Pitman and all the rest of them on top of Joe celebrating. It was fantastic and the confidence came back.

'We were a different outfit all of a sudden. Jason Pearce was different class and really stood up for me. He was a Terry Butcher-type centre-half and you could have seen him in a bandage with blood running down his face, still putting his head in. Brett Pitman was just coming into form. He is a good player and a nice boy and he did the business for Bournemouth after Steve Fletcher had gone the previous summer.

'Fletch had been tremendous for me the season before, but I let him go in the summer of 2007 and I shouldn't have done,' Bond admits. 'I should never have done that. We spoke about it as a group, all the coaches. We were so dependent on Fletch and his style and we didn't want to be "just get it up to Fletch". We wanted to evolve, but it was a mistake and Eddie Howe, who was on my coaching staff then, knew that which is why he brought him back when he took over in 2009.

'It was nothing personal. I loved Fletch – he is a great guy and was a terrific pro. But I wanted to move the team on. It was the wrong thing to do though. It really hurt him.

'We had taken Max Gradel on loan from Leicester and he was great for me. He was terrific in the dressing room, a real livewire. I took David Forde, the goalkeeper from Cardiff, and he was superb. He did fantastically well for us and saved a penalty against Millwall in March in a game we needed to win. We'd have gone 1-0 down and I think that would have been curtains for us. We got a penalty and Max scored and we ended up winning 2-0.

'It was clear by then that we weren't going to get relegated by ten points or more. We were buoyed by that and we had some momentum. We went into the final game at Carlisle on the back of six straight wins and they needed to win to go up automatically. We needed a draw and if Doncaster, who were also going for promotion, had beaten Cheltenham, we'd have stayed up.

'Cheltenham were right in the mire and needed a win. It was all set up for a thriller, but I wasn't looking at it quite like that! I knew Cheltenham were fighting for their lives.'

Bond recalls inviting the *Daily Echo*'s two sports writers to the team hotel, funded by supporter donations, at lunchtime on Saturday, 3 May. In a sprawling conference room, sat watching rolling footage of the Cumbrians, were Bond, assistant Rob Newman and young coach Howe, whose playing career had been ended at 29 by a crippling knee injury.

Bond had seen something in Howe, even in those early days with him yet to mark his 30th birthday, and invited him to join the ranks. Newman made the tea and the footage was restarted. Bond laughs at a suggestion that he was calmness personified in those hours leading up to the game at Brunton Park. 'I was like a duck on water, I promise you that.'

It was a typical May afternoon, with the kind of warming sun that makes supporters despise the summer recess after such motorway toil during the ravages of winter. A Cumbrian youngster called Andrew Johnson, who had warmed the nation's hearts both with his voice and story of being bullied at school while a contestant on TV show *Britain's Got Talent*, sung beautifully as 1,500 travelling supporters from Dorset crammed into the Petteril End. For Bond, though, it was agony.

'The last half an hour of that game was a blur,' he says, his eyes deepening. 'I was a spectator really. We were drawing 1-1 after Scott Dobie had given them the lead and Brett Pitman equalised with about 20 minutes to go. But I'm there in the dugout hearing Cheltenham were beating Doncaster. I couldn't believe it. Forest ended up getting promoted and Donny went up via the play-offs. It was a mad, mad day.

'It was without doubt, and always will be, the biggest disappointment in my football life. It always will be, no matter what I go on to do in the future. It was so tough to take. The lads had a real go and couldn't have done any more, but it remains my biggest disappointment.

'Jo Kuffour did well for us that season. Darren Anderton was terrific, but thinking about it now, I should have found a better role for him – I played him off one side and it was wrong. He was top drawer. An unbelievable player. I should have played him as a number 10 – he was so good.

'It just wasn't quite enough and it still hurts me to this day. It always will.'

Dusting himself down, Bond knew he was on a hiding to nothing during a summer of discontent. The Cherries were hit with the 17-point deduction for exiting administration without a CVA, the only positive ahead of the inevitable battle for league survival being Rotherham and Luton suffering the same fate, the Hatters to the tune of 30 points for further misdemeanours.

With Mostyn keen to step away after an administration period that had tested not only his business resolve but threatened to tear apart his family, Bond's concern turned to the arrival of Sport-6's Saverimutto and Baker. With the comfort of friend Mostyn's boardroom influence slipping away, Bond could have been forgiven for packing up his things and walking away. But he stood firm. That rhino skin was coming in handy.

'I knew the next season was going to be difficult, even without the 17-point deduction,' he admits. 'The administrator Gerald Krasner had sold Sam Vokes, our young striker who was hitting form, to Wolves for about £400,000 and I couldn't do anything about it. I didn't have a choice.

'It had to happen for the club to survive. Anything that was worth any money was sold and Sam was worth a few quid, no doubt. Sam would have been happy to stay. He was a local boy and happy, learning his trade. But it had to happen and he was pushed into it.

'I had heard all kinds of rumours that the club was going to go to new people once the administration had finished. That was the case when Savi and Paul Baker arrived and Jeff took more of a back seat. I'd heard even then that Jimmy Quinn was waiting in the wings to take over as manager, as he had a relationship with Savi and Paul, and I felt really unstable.

'My days were numbered really and it was very difficult for me at the start of that season. We lost to Port Vale and Exeter after draws against Gillingham and Aldershot and I went in and Jeff, Steve and Savi were inside. Savi told me I had to go. It was tough for Jeff as we were friends, first and foremost, and I gave him a hard time. I shouldn't have done that, but I'd lost my job and I was so disappointed.

'It was no longer his decision so he had to support Savi. I understand that now, but it was hard. As expected, Jimmy came in and I was gone.'

With results failing to improve under Quinn, Saverimutto's PR abilities were tested further when bailiffs arrived on 19 November to seize goods from the club shop. But he and Baker were preoccupied by an increasing tension within the supporters, unhappy with both Sport-6's running of the club and Quinn's tenure.

Bond smiles. 'The funny thing was, a couple of months after giving me the sack, Savi phoned me at home one night in December. It was the last thing I was expecting. Things hadn't improved once Jimmy had taken over and the fans were raging at Savi, calling for his head and all sorts.

'He knew he had to make a change, even though Jimmy was his man and had only been in the job for a couple of months, so he phoned me to ask what I thought he should do. I couldn't believe his front, but I said he should give the job to someone who knew the club and had that connection with the supporters. At the time, did I think he was the right man for the job? I don't know – it was a massive task keeping an ailing club in the Football League. But I knew he had something, so I told Savi to appoint Eddie Howe.'

CHAPTER FOUR

THE ROOKIE
2009

ABOVE the manager's desk in AFC Bournemouth's 'Pavilion', the heartbeat of the club's on-pitch operation and away from the glare of the main stadium and nearby dog walking haven King's Park, is a laminate banner proclaiming '12 Lessons in Leadership'.

Pinned to the cork board behind the manager's chair are points targets for different stages of the Premier League season. It is a sprawling office space overlooking the club's training pitches behind Vitality Stadium's East Stand, flanked by a security gate, guard and pass-card door entry system.

Despite having the smallest top-flight stadium in England, everything about AFC Bournemouth is Premier League. A far cry, without doubt, from Eddie Howe's 2009 baptism of fire.

The manager is decked out in his usual training attire. Tall and with the broad frame of a former centre-half, he has retained the look of youth despite combining the cauldron of English football's top flight with turning 40 in 2017.

'So, how did it go with the Big 'Un?' Howe probes, in between thanking his PA for a peppermint tea and with a grin that suggests he knows what is coming.

'It was emotional,' I laugh, referring to the hour with the Cherries' record appearance-maker Steve Fletcher prior to sitting down with Howe.

Howe is what you might call a reluctant manager, or at least he used to be. His appointment on New Year's Day 2009 was as mysterious as it was laughable. He had no management experience, had been sacked along with Bond and Newman only months earlier and was just 31 years old, his playing career with the Cherries and Portsmouth ending at the age of 29 after a knee injury suffered on his Fratton Park debut could not be overcome. The club he was taking on? Facing almost certain relegation into the Conference after starting the season with that 17-point deduction due to administration misdemeanours.

Dorset businessman and philanthropist Adam Murry had joined the club's board of directors alongside Sport-6 owners Saverimutto and Baker late in 2008, following Bond's sacking and the appointment of Quinn.

It was Murry, tall, imposing and with a handshake that could distort steel, who telephoned Howe to change his life at the most inconvenient of times.

'I was at Richard Hughes's New Year's Eve party and the phone rang,' the Cherries manager reflects, sitting back in his seat, concealed slightly by the huge screen of an Apple iMac. 'I didn't even know Jimmy Quinn had been sacked at that point as it was New Year's Eve. I was out having a good time, the same as most people, but clearly things had been happening at the club regardless of the fact it was 31 December.

'There was hardly any signal on my mobile so I went into a room and managed to get a couple of bars. When I answered, Adam was on the other end and he said they wanted me to be caretaker manager.

'His words actually were, "I want to make you permanent manager now but I haven't got the support of everybody."

'I just said, "What the hell are you doing? Adam, no. This isn't right. I'm not the man to do this."

'Loads of things were going through my head at that point,' he laughs. 'I thought if I was lucky enough to get one shot at being a manager, is this the right time? It clearly wasn't. I wasn't experienced enough, the club was in the mire. I didn't want to be the man who took us into the Conference.

'Loads of things were filling my head, but Adam was insistent. He told me I had to take the team and he wouldn't be swayed.'

He pauses briefly, before the broad grin I see frequently during our interview emerges for the first time. 'I tried to put up a fight for a brief time but soon learned that you don't fight for too long with Adam Murry! And I also realised quite quickly that this was likely to be an opportunity I would never get again and if I turned it down I would regret it.

'I had no right to be a manager, but when I asked for advice, from people like Kevin Bond, they all said "do it".

'I felt loyalty to Kevin so I wanted to see if he was okay with me taking it given it had been his job only a few months before, but he told me to do it and was so supportive.'

Howe speaks fondly of Bond, a mentor and friend. 'I always had a brilliant relationship with Kevin and wanted to help him be a success as part of the team at AFC Bournemouth but the fact that he went through that experience and then still supported me for the job speaks volumes about him.

'He held no negative emotions and was happy for me. He is a wonderful guy. I was met with massive support from everyone.'

For Howe, it completed a whirlwind few months where he had found himself out of work following Bond's sacking, before being brought back to the club just weeks later to run the academy.

'When I was let go I felt I hadn't actually coached properly,' he says, 'although I was starting to get to grips with it when it felt like it was all going to come to an end.'

The reality of the situation was stark. 'I had a conversation with Wimborne Town, playing in the Wessex League in front of about 50 people every week, about going there as manager, although I hadn't given it another second's thought until this interview,' Howe reveals. 'I was thinking "right, what am I going to do" and the call from Wimborne came. But on the day I got the sack at Bournemouth I was in a room with the people who were making the decision and I said my bit. That was my saving grace.

'I certainly didn't take it lying down and was quite passionate in what I said. I think that might have stirred some emotion with Alastair Saverimutto because he called me quite quickly after that day and said he hadn't been aware of many of the things I had said.

'He didn't know me as an individual but told me to come back in for a chat about what he could do to keep me involved at the club.

'That wasn't my intention – I just wanted to sound off in protection of Rob and Kevin who I thought were being treated unfairly as much as anything else. In the next few days I had a chat with Savi and ended up coming back into the club to work with the youngsters.

'It had been a difficult few months after Savi and Paul Baker arrived. The difficulty for all of us as a coaching team was there were lots of rumours flying around that Kevin was under pressure and the club could look to make a change. We'd heard that Jimmy Quinn was being lined up.

'The players got wind of it and that made it very difficult. That uncertainty made it very hard for Kevin but I believed in him and the players we had and it was desperately disappointing it came to an end for so many different reasons.

'In terms of a manager's job, Kevin couldn't have had it tougher when you look at what he had to deal with behind the scenes. Usually a manager just wants to concentrate on what he does on the training field, but that was the least of Kevin's worries. It was unfair and I felt desperately sorry for him.

'We were aware of how bad things were off the field and the main link was Jeff Mostyn to Kevin as they were friends. Myself and Rob would hear what Kevin fed down via his link with Jeff, but we learned a lot from what we were reading in the *Daily Echo* and the players had that too.

'It was a really difficult time. We didn't know what to believe, whether it was what we were being told or what we were reading in the paper.

'I was really happy to be back in the club though and was happy doing my job in the centre of excellence because I had gone back to learning about coaching. I was learning how to teach ten-year-olds to control the ball and I was happy to do that.

'I had absolutely no desire to get involved with the first team again at that point.'

Thrown in to the storm by Murry, in the depths of winter and with a squad lacking desire thanks in part to never knowing if their wages would turn up from month to month, Howe's first two fixtures as caretaker boss at the start of January were away trips to Darlington and Rotherham. A northern nightmare.

The sprawling setting of the Darlington Arena's 25,000-capacity bowl was built by big characters with even bigger, and ultimately crazed, ambitions that the little club in the North East, surrounded by the giants of Middlesbrough, Sunderland and Newcastle United, could climb the ladder to the riches of English football's top flight.

If Howe felt alone on the A1M, the empty stadium, with just short of 1,000 inside, would have felt like solitary confinement. Danny Hollands's 29th-minute strike handed Howe the perfect start to life in the dugout, but the prospect of exorcising the ghost of Quinn's dire fare eluded him. Pawel Abbott, a 46th-minute substitute, equalised seven minutes from time before

Rob Purdie's last-minute penalty told the story of what Howe was up against.

Having crashed out of the FA Cup to non-league minnows Blyth Spartans, the final nail in the coffin of Quinn, the trip to Rotherham's Don Valley Stadium, another wind-swept and half-empty bowl with a running track around the pitch, was probably seven days later than Howe would have liked thanks to a third-round empty weekend.

Mark Hudson gifted the Millers an early lead and once Hollands had seen red just after the hour, the task for Howe was suddenly impossible, let alone monumental. Late chances for both Mark Molesley and Jason Pearce went begging, leaving the Cherries ten points adrift of safety and Howe assuming his days were numbered before they'd even begun.

'I didn't think I was the right person for the job when Adam phoned on New Year's Eve,' Howe reminisces with a hint of sadness, 'but after I had taken it I had to believe I was the right person. You have to or you have no chance.

'I set about preparing the team to go to Darlington but I had no idea what I was doing really. I can say that now looking back, but at the time I probably thought I knew exactly what I was doing! I tried to bring organisation to the team and a bit of confidence because that was lacking.

'I knew I would be able to unite the players straight away. The club had become very disjointed, the fans weren't happy, the players were unhappy because they were in the dark and weren't getting paid. I knew I needed to bring it all together and thought I could do that.

'I knew that was the only chance we would have to stay up.

'I wanted it to be us against the world and I felt it was, genuinely. It wasn't made up, but I had to harness it and make the players believe that everyone wanted us to fail: the league, the media, sometimes even our own board of directors.

'I told them if we could achieve it, it would be an incredible story and they would go down in history. It was chest pumping stuff.

'Darlington were flying at the time and we went 1-0 up but couldn't hang on and lost 2-1. I felt sick. It was a long journey home and looking at the league table after that game we were right in the mire.

'Rotherham two weeks later was a tough game and even though we played well, we couldn't force anything and lost 1-0. I remember clapping the fans at the end and getting some hostility from them.

'Maybe it was for the situation rather than me, but I understood it. They probably thought we were going to go down without a fight as we'd lost two on the spin with a young, inexperienced manager in charge.

'It was a real low point and I found myself in the middle of a storm thinking, "Shit, what are we going to do?"'

Howe's phone rang again.

'This time we were on the way back home from Rotherham,' he says, 'and Adam told me he was going to appoint me permanently until the end of the season. I told him he was having a laugh the first time and this time he was off his rocker.

'We'd just lost two in a row, but he was adamant he had seen an improvement and wouldn't take no for an answer.'

Howe knew he needed January reinforcements but, like Bond, the club's perilous financial position was likely to impact on the personnel. With Jason Tindall, Quinn's assistant manager, installed as his number two, Howe sought out the former Weymouth manager's non-league contacts book.

He knew it was a risk, bringing untried players from the Conference into the Dean Court storm, but what choice did he have? Anton Robinson, a combative midfielder, arrived from Weymouth alongside winger Liam Feeney from Salisbury. Howe had decisions to make on Molesley, whom Quinn had signed on loan from Grays Athletic, and striker Matt Tubbs, a goal machine who had gleaned national attention following his FA Cup exploits for Salisbury against Nottingham Forest.

'When I first took over, I knew we had the potential for a superb midfield,' Howe enthuses. 'We brought in Anton from Weymouth and had Danny Hollands who I knew was going to be a massive player for us.

'Marvin Bartley's energy was key as well, but signing Liam Feeney with his pace and Anton for his drive were game changers for me that season.

'Without Liam's pace, the front two weren't going to get chances. We needed someone to stretch things and Liam did that.

'Mark Molesley was a decision I had to make really early as he was on loan from Grays and set to go back at the end of January. I was hit with so many things so early. Having given up on fighting Adam over taking the manager's job, I was then asked, "Right, Mark Molesley, do you want to keep him or not?"

'I just put my head in my hands. I didn't even know Mark as he came in late under Jimmy and I hadn't worked with him. It was another "welcome to management" moment. Do you want to keep a player you haven't seen or send him back?

'I had sorted out Jason as my number two. Keeping him was the only bit of bargaining I did when I took the job. They asked who I wanted as my number two and I really didn't know. I looked around the club and there wasn't anyone already in situ. All my good relationships were with players who were still playing so I said I would keep JT.

'The board weren't having it and wanted to clear out Jimmy's backroom team completely. They didn't want anyone left over from the legacy of Jimmy's reign.

'I was insistent though. I said I would take the job but I had to keep JT. It was a sticking point but eventually they agreed.

'So I rang Jason and asked him about Mark Molesley and he told me to keep him. I sent Matt Tubbs back to Salisbury for no other reason than my relationship and belief in Brett Pitman, who I knew would get goals for us.'

One more signing was up Howe's sleeve. Not that he knew it at the time, but it was to be his masterstroke. Steve Fletcher was Mr AFC Bournemouth. A veteran target man of 500-odd appearances, but with rapidly disintegrating knees, Fletcher had sought refuge at Chesterfield after being released by Bond during the summer of 2007.

A home from home under Lee Richardson, Fletcher's tears dried during the long drive up the M1 while his family remained in the Bournemouth suburb of Bearwood. It was a drive he could and would only make for one season, being away from home even for three days a week taking its toll on a man whose heart was firmly in BH7.

In demand for his physical presence and canny experience, Fletcher dropped into non-league at the start of the 2008/09 campaign with ambitious Crawley Town, managed by the flamboyant Steve Evans and with their sights set on the Football League. Sipping his peppermint tea with a smile forming around the paper cup, Howe asks how Fletcher told the story of what happened next during our interview that morning, before recoiling with laughter.

'This is a true story although he obviously denied it and told you I was ringing him begging him to come back! He rang me up just after I had been appointed and said, "Come on, Ed, am I coming back?" I was like "No, no, no, that's not where we want to go, Big 'Un."

'I wanted to go a different way with young players but it was almost like a light bulb moment with me when I was driving with Jason on the way to watch a game and I said to him, "What do you think about bringing the big man back?"

'I was serious. I thought the fans would be really pleased and it would help unite everyone. It would give us a focal point from a playing point of view because clearly we weren't going to get the points we needed by playing nice attractive football. We were going to need to dig in, get nasty and try to pile into teams.

'We needed quick results and I knew he would help me in the dressing room. I was a young manager and needed that experience around me.

'I rang Kevin and asked him what he thought. He wanted to know my reasons so I told him and he said "don't hesitate, do it".

'Again it was amazing from Kevin because he had let Fletch go 18 months before. I rang a few other people and the reaction was mixed, but I knew I had to do it.

'I phoned Fletch and said what I wanted to do and Steve Evans was fantastic and didn't stand in his way.'

Howe sits back once again in his seat and gazes out across the training pitches that, in 2009, were a dust bowl used by yobbos in cars stuck together by gaffer tape and brainlessness.

'I've learned over the years that there is always doubt with a transfer,' he says, making eye contact once more. 'Every transfer I have done I've felt that. It doesn't matter who you sign, you always ask the same questions. Is he going to be popular? Can he still play and make a difference? How will he take *not* playing?

'There were so many doubts with Fletch but he just wanted to come back and when I look back, he has to be my greatest signing for so many reasons.

'I looked at the squad and felt we had enough quality to stay up, but we needed that leader.

'I was lucky to have seen a lot of the games leading up to my appointment so I knew what we had.

'I had an idea who was on the fringes in the reserve team as well as I had taken them under Kevin so one of my first thoughts was "Brett Pitman has to play." It was amazing because under

Jimmy, Brett looked as if he was going to leave the club and go into non-league. He was really unhappy and hadn't got on or been playing under Jimmy but I knew I could revive him.

'We needed goals and I thought Brett would link well with Fletch. The big man would nod them down and Brett would finish them. He is one of the best finishers I have ever seen, even to this day, and still is now for Portsmouth.

'Once I had Fletch in and Brett smiling again, I felt better, but the players were low on confidence so I had to bring that siege mentality, try to get a couple of wins from somewhere and then we'd have a chance.'

As well as his permanent recruits, Howe drafted in loan goalkeeper David Button from Tottenham and midfielder Jake Thomson from neighbouring Southampton. With high-fliers Wycombe Wanderers next in Howe's first home game in charge, Fletcher went straight into the starting line-up.

It was to be a huge turning point for the young manager, but not before that sinking feeling when Matt Harrold put the visitors in front after just nine minutes. Howe, though, felt calm, rather than the surge of fear that flowed through his body during the trips to Darlington and Rotherham. That siege mentality was emerging.

Pitman equalised before Jason Pearce gave Howe's side the lead after 32 minutes. Thomson's strike just after the hour put the gloss on the finish and Howe was up and running.

'Wycombe was a huge turning point,' he says, leaning in. 'We went 1-0 down after a mistake from David Button, the goalkeeper I had brought in, so I was already thinking "oh God". But Brett Pitman scored a free kick with an unbelievable strike and we went on to completely outplay them and won 3-1.

'Fletch was the catalyst, no question. He came back and suddenly everything was different.'

A 1-1 draw at home to fellow strugglers, the doomed Luton Town, the following Tuesday provided more stability before a topsy-turvy visit to Lincoln that ended 3-3, a game during which Howe's men were 3-1 in front, ensured the manager's feet would remain firmly rooted in the sticky mud of Sincil Bank.

But Howe's tub-thumping had made an impact. His side became experts in nicking results. One-nil wins against Shrewsbury and Accrington saw the Cherries keep pace as winter thawed into spring, but still knockbacks were only around the next corner.

With both Thomson and Button back at their parent clubs, their stays brief and differing in success, a visit to Fletcher's old club Chesterfield yielded nothing, the potent Jack Lester scoring the only goal of the game. Two steps forward and one back was better than the traditional saying, however.

The Saturday–Tuesday relentlessness continued. Howe's side travelled to Dagenham on Tuesday, 24 February, with Pitman fit again following a short lay-off. Howe, though, saw his resources stretched and was forced to name Tindall, long retired, among his substitutes.

'Dagenham was another massive game, but we were short of players and Jason had to be named as a sub,' the Cherries boss recalls with a wry smile.

'We were under the cosh for pretty much the whole game and Matt Ritchie was killing us for them. He was on loan from Portsmouth and only a youngster, but his pace and trickery even back then were way better than the level. He was a nightmare for us.

'Jason was giving it the big one at the back of the dugout for the whole game, saying, "Ed, get me on, get me on."

'Then Ryan Garry went down injured and I said "Jase, are you ready?" He turned to me and said "Nah, he's all right, he's fine." I couldn't believe it. I said "Jase, he's not all right, he's getting stretchered off." He carried on, "Nah, nah, nah, he's all right, you don't want to put me on."

'He'd spent all game badgering me to get him on and then suddenly the moment had come and he didn't fancy it! I said "Jase, you're going on. Get ready." He went on and he was unbelievable and set up Mark Molesley's goal right at the death. It was a massive high.'

Molesley's strike, deep into stoppage time, remains a YouTube hit among the Dean Court faithful. The midfielder advanced and skipped past two defenders before beating goalkeeper Tony Roberts with a low, angled drive. *Daily Echo* reporter Neil Perrett spilled the Haribo sweets handed out to the press as a 'meal' such was the unexpected, critical nature of Molesley's strike. Intros were frantically re-written and copy filed as the visiting fans headed out on to the streets in time for last orders.

Post Dagenham, Fletcher's first goal since returning to Dorset sealed a 2-0 win at Aldershot, before Howe's side secured a hard-fought 0-0 draw at home to Port Vale. Tuesday, 10 March, with Howe still looking over his shoulder at the likes of Grimsby Town and Chester, saw the Cherries travel to Exeter, flying high under Paul Tisdale and with the prowess of Marcus Stewart up front.

Around a thousand visitors from Bournemouth packed into the open end on St James Road as Adam Stansfield put the home side 1-0 in front. But something was in the air and Howe's men got themselves on top. Hollands levelled the scores just before the hour as a head of steam built in the chilly Devon air.

Pitman, in form and relishing Howe's backing as the main striker, made it 2-1 three minutes later before adding his second three minutes from time. Fletcher started again, making a mockery of both his birth certificate and ailing knees as he continued to make life a thorough misery for League Two's lumpy centre-halves.

The St James Park result was backed up by two Fletcher goals in a 4-1 win over Bradford and a Lee Bradbury double in a 2-0 triumph at Macclesfield. Bradbury, a striker by trade, took centre stage at Moss Rose having been an unsung hero at full-back as Howe continued to battle with a lack of numbers in his squad.

Pitman bagged a hat-trick in a 4-0 home win over Rochdale which appeased defeats against both Bury and Notts County, but Barnet and Brentford both edged 1-0 wins ahead of the Cherries' clash at Chester on 18 April.

Howe knew how big that game was, both in terms of the long-term future and as a catalyst to end the toxicity seeping through the pores of a football club still pinned down by off-field uncertainty.

Chief executive Saverimutto had departed in March, finally bowing to pressure from supporters unhappy with Sport-6's tenure, but holding strong on false promises of Middle Eastern investment. In a hard-hitting comment piece in the *Daily Echo* following his resignation, Perrett wrote: 'Delivery was his gospel, failure, ultimately, was his legacy.' It was a line that spoke volumes when, that same month, director Murry was forced to pay off a creditor's winding-up petition to the tune of £33,000, while Sport-6 had also fallen into rent arrears with stadium landlord Structadene, who had instructed the bailiffs to lock the stadium and seize more goods from the club shop.

In a departure statement as bizarre as the man himself, Saverimutto neglected to mention his appointment of Quinn and the mysterious director of football Ted Sutton, a flamboyant Scouser dubbed 'Sun Bed Ted' who claimed to have secured Everton's deal with Chang Beer and who backed up Savi's Eastern Promise with Chinese investment claims of his own.

Elsewhere, a statement from Baker issued to the press just two days before the crucial visit to Chester's Deva Stadium confirmed Murry was preparing a deal to purchase his share of the club alongside two well-known fellow investors – Mostyn and Sly. The circus and back-biting between Baker and Murry continued apace, an unwanted sideshow as Howe and Tindall prepared for the game of their young management lives on Baker's old stomping ground.

'It was poor, really,' Howe reflects sternly. 'Jason was fuming and I know he had words with the *Echo* boys before the game after they had run Paul's statement. But once I had thought about it, I knew I could use it in our favour. That game was probably the most nervous I have ever been before a match. We knew how big a game it was for the future of the football club.

'There was so much riding on that game for both clubs and if you look at what's happened since, it shows how massive it was. We could have ended up where Chester did, down in the depths of non-league. If we'd gone into the Conference, we might have even gone into extinction. That's what I was told at the time and I genuinely believe that now.

'We used the situation of Paul being a Chester fan to galvanise the team further. It was all part of the siege mentality and convincing the players everyone was against them, even the owner of the club.

'I told them he probably wanted us to lose and they reacted. I felt it too. I just thought, "How can this be happening?" How can we be in a situation where we are playing the team who our owner has supported since he was a boy in such a crucial situation? It didn't feel right and made everything more intense than it already was. It felt very personal and as a squad of players and coaches, we felt very alone.

'But Brett Pitman took a free kick early on and it went straight in and then Anton Robinson got the second which was an incredible feeling. We'd given ourselves a great chance.

'Adam Murry was a constant supporter throughout but the situation off the field felt very toxic at that time and it was certainly dominating the thoughts of many supporters.

'I didn't really have any relationship with Paul Baker and my communication was mainly with Adam and a little with Savi up until the point he left in March. We were just trying to get an idea of what we could and couldn't do and, sometimes, whether we could even train or not.

'It was little things like making sure we had enough bibs, enough balls and cones, things like that. At the time trying to book the astro pitches at the local leisure centre, Littledown, to train on when the weather was bad was even difficult because of the club's historical payment record. We were met with "no" almost every day from somewhere.

'We'd been kicked out of everywhere pretty much and if we wanted to train somewhere then we had to bring cash to pay for it as nobody trusted the club.'

It wasn't just the Littledown Centre. The players were among those not being paid. Sport-6's disastrous 11 months at the helm started to unravel at the worst possible time as Howe's battlers had given themselves a chance to complete a miracle.

Much of their February and March wages still outstanding, members of the press had looked on in the tunnel after the game at home to Port Vale on 7 March as around £40,000 in a Marks & Spencer carrier bag was taken into the dressing room by a member of the club's media department. The gate receipts had enabled Howe's squad to pay their mortgages, while the colour of Mostyn's face matched the grey skies above Dean Court as the press pack informed him of the readies being dished out among the playing staff.

No matter, though. On the pitch, a home win over Grimsby on 25 April would seal the club's Football League place against the longest of odds.

In front of a sold-out crowd, Nathan Jarman silenced the din by handing the visitors the lead on 41 minutes and final-day drama at Morecambe a week later looked to be on the horizon for Howe's heroes. But the stars were aligned and Fletcher had written his own script.

CHAPTER FIVE

THE BIG MAN COMETH
2009

T HE tunnel at Dean Court is adorned with the stars of 2018. Jermain Defoe, Nathan Ake, Jordon Ibe – players worth millions both in transfer terms and personal wealth. It wasn't always like that. The corners of the stadium are filled in with huge images of successes past, yet in 2009, save for the two Football League Trophy final appearances in 1984 and 1998 and 2003's play-off final in Cardiff, the club's only joys had been in celebrating failure.

Steve Fletcher was part of both the 1998 Auto Windscreens Shield Final defeat to, of all teams, Grimsby and the 2003 play-off final victory over Lincoln, O'Driscoll's big moment in a reign dominated by intense firefighting that would become commonplace as the new century ticked on.

On the afternoon of 25 April 2009, Fletcher lined up in the dour magnolia-walled tunnel at Dean Court with destiny in mind. In July 1992, he didn't even know where Bournemouth was.

'I'd gone into pre-season with Hartlepool and the manager Alan Murray called me into his office and said Tony Pulis had been in touch and Bournemouth were interested,' recalls Fletcher, who even at the age of 45 carries a physique that would give centre-halves nightmares.

He sits in the players' lounge in the Dean Court pavilion, fully focused on memories as Tyrone Mings and Ryan Fraser, two of Howe's current Premier League crop, play *FIFA 17* on a games console as if their lives depend on it. To the right of them, some youth team players, perhaps the Fletchers of the future, enjoy a riotous game of darts.

'I didn't even know where Bournemouth was on the map,' continues Fletcher, 'which was stupid really because I'd been down for a game, although I didn't get in the team that day and watched from the stands.

'I'd played against Bournemouth in Harry Redknapp's last game in charge where they'd needed to beat Hartlepool to get in the play-offs and we won 1-0. I'd played pretty well that day and Tony had seen something in me.

'I went home and spoke to my dad and we decided to go down to have a look. Alan had said if I wasn't keen then I could go back to Hartlepool and fight for my place so I had options.

'We got in the car about midday and arrived in Bournemouth about midnight! It was so far, but it was a scorching day in July and Tony had put me up in the Royal Bath Hotel, which was the top place in Bournemouth back then with a view out over the sea. He knew what he was doing, Tony.

'It was a million miles from Hartlepool and felt more like Spain than England. I looked out over the hotels and the beach and it was glorious.

'They paid for a meal and Tony picked me up the next morning and took me around the training ground. He totally sold it to me and I signed that day.'

Quick decision-making and following his heart was engrained even then in the young Fletcher, essentially an untried prospect after just a handful of games for his home-town club. But Pulis, a pit bull of a defender with a hard man reputation during his playing days with Bristol Rovers, Newport County, Bournemouth and Gillingham, loved Fletcher's physical stature ahead of what was to be another tough Division Two campaign.

Fletcher, though, struggled in the early days of life on the south coast and missed the comforts of home.

'I moved into digs with Ken "Nimbus" Sullivan and his wife Audrey,' he reflects, turning down the offer of a cup of tea from Eddie Howe's PA. 'Most of the new lads lodged there initially, and I never really got back to Hartlepool after that until several months later.

'I found it really difficult to settle in as the only contact I had with my parents was when Audrey would let me use the phone for 50p a go.

'Tony always tried to make sure I was okay, but he was old school and didn't have a massive amount of time for people moaning about being homesick. He wanted me to get on with it and it was sink or swim for me early on. I needed to grow up quickly.

'My mum and dad were publicans and the lads in the pub back home were all saying I wouldn't be able to hack it down south as I liked my home comforts too much.

'It was tough, but it gave me a lot of independence, although as a squad we had things go against us from day one. Tony was just trying to keep the club afloat and had to sell anyone who came through, like Joe Parkinson who we got big money for back then.

'Keith Rowland went to West Ham, Joe went to Everton and Neil Masters went to Wolves and they all went for up around £400,000 which was big money then. Tony kept the club in the league but we were languishing down near the bottom of the table and he was sacked after two years in charge.'

For Fletcher, Pulis's departure placed him at an early and unwanted crossroads. Having failed to fully establish himself between 1992 and 1994, the natives were becoming restless, bewildered by the young man from the North East who had been recruited to replace Jimmy Quinn, who had left Dorset for Reading after a prolific goal-every-other-game spell under Pulis.

Fletcher's rapid North East tones drop. 'I had another year left on my contract and I didn't know where I stood after Tony went. But Mel Machin came in and I got a good vibe from him so I stayed and kicked on under him. But it could have gone either way for me in 1994.

'Mel was a disciplinarian like Tony, but Tony was all about fitness. He wanted us to be big, strong and physical but Mel brought in players like Steve Robinson, Neil Young and Steve Jones and wanted some younger, more creative lads in the squad.

'He kept Mark Morris, the captain, but wanted to go in a different direction. He had a softer side though and as much as he used to hammer me on a Saturday, by Monday morning he had his arm around me and was telling me he loved me!

'He also brought through Scotty Mean and John Bailey so we had a lot of leaders in that team, really big characters.

'We had a horrific start in 1994 and had ten points at Christmas. If we'd started the season in January though we'd have got promoted as we went on an unbelievable run which was the first Great Escape. It cemented Mel into history and I won supporters' player of the season which was my defining year. My first season was tough as I had come in and replaced Jimmy Quinn who was a machine. Goals hadn't come for me and I took a lot of stick from the fans.

'But Mel changed me and I grew up that season in 1994/95. The supporters got behind me and then I realised Bournemouth could be my home for the immediate future.'

Machin, though, moved upstairs in 2000 as director of football with O'Driscoll returning to the club where he had made more than 400 appearances between 1984 and 1995. For Fletcher, the Midlander's appointment as manager was a tonic after several seasons plagued by persistent injuries.

'People don't realise I had 16 knee operations in my career,' reveals Fletcher, clearly still pained. 'It was my weak point, my left knee mainly. I lost four seasons in total through injury in my career.

'Towards the end of Mel's reign I started to play well again and got a new contract, then Sean O'Driscoll took over and he made me captain which was a whole new level for me.

'I'd met my future wife and she was pregnant but the club was in the mire off the field so all wasn't well. I didn't know a lot of what was going on but we were hearing things on the radio and reading stuff in the *Echo*. It got to a point where we weren't getting paid so I kept putting the mortgage back every month and asking my mum and dad to help. It was tough.

'You keep going because you just keep thinking about the football, but looking back at it now it was a nightmare. The club could have easily gone under and it would have been horrendous.

'We just missed out on the play-offs under Sean in 2000/01 and we had a great team. We should have got promoted and Eddie Howe agrees when I talk to him about it now. I never played in the Championship and I should have done with that team. It was criminal that we didn't get promoted.

'By the time we got to 2005, we'd been relegated to Division Three in 2002 and then promoted in the play-offs a year later. It was a rollercoaster even then as money at the club was still tight. I had my testimonial and then, before I knew it, it was 2007 and I had been there for 15 years. It flew by so quickly.'

With O'Driscoll sensing trouble off the field, his unease got the better of his heart's desire to remain at Dean Court, his family settled in nearby Verwood. The manager closest to Fletcher opted for ambitious Doncaster Rovers, a club a far cry from the struggles he had become used to.

The arrival of new manager Bond was to commence a rapid countdown for Fletcher, whose character was fully established within the dressing room. He leans back into his seat and, for a moment, his eyes look down.

'Kevin came in and for the last seven or eight months of the season in 2007 I played quite a bit, but at the end of the season I went in to see him and he told me he wasn't going to give me a new contract. I was gutted.

'My wife phoned me and I told her I was being let go. I was 34 and had spent 15 years at one club so I had no idea what I was going to do, but I was playing okay. I thought I would get a new club but I was resigned to the fact I might have to travel. I had two kids by that point and we were settled in Bournemouth so I was never going to uproot the family at that stage.

'My wife Lynne told me one of the fans' websites had set up a tribute page for me so I went online and took a look – this was the same day I had been released.'

His eyes reignite once more, the emotion and pride still clear. 'It was amazing,' he says. 'There were over 700 messages from fans and I printed them all off and still have them in a folder today.

'It wasn't just football. Lots were about hospital visits and how I had made a real difference to someone who was sick. You don't think about that kind of thing at the time, you just do it because you feel you should give something back to the people who come to watch you and spend their money.

'But I sat reading the messages in floods of tears because the enormity of what had happened hit me. I'd been an influence on people and I didn't realise it at the time and it was a lot to take in, reading those messages.

'Football can touch people's lives and it was only then that I realised it. But I was still without a club and it was only when I read the messages that it dawned on me that I had left Bournemouth.'

Two more managerial saviours were to step in and once again Fletcher took guidance from his heart. It was a sign of his development as a man that he was able to regroup quickly in the wake of personal turmoil at the club he had fallen in love with.

'Within 24 hours I had a call from Lee Richardson at Chesterfield,' he enthuses. 'I told him as he was the first to contact me that I would go up and see him. It was so far from Bournemouth and I wanted a club less than a couple of hours' drive, but Lee was insistent and Lynne said I had to see him out of respect.

'I was heading up to Hartlepool to see the family so I decided to stop off at Chesterfield and see Lee. Three hours after I got there I signed a contract.

'It felt right. I had five or six other clubs keen and was planning on seeing them but Chesterfield just felt right and I had to phone the other clubs and tell them I was committed to Lee.

'Lee was great with me. I had told him I couldn't move the family and he said as long as I kept myself fit and we didn't have a midweek game I could come up on a Thursday. I said I could use Bournemouth's facilities to train and he was happy with that.

'After a game on a Saturday I would go home to Bournemouth and go up to Chesterfield late on a Wednesday for Thursday and Friday training and press and then a game on Saturday.

'I was very fortunate and signed a two-year contract which was a year with a further 12-month option, but I had some family issues and I couldn't take the option. Lee was gutted but I had to turn it down.

'Chesterfield is a fantastic club with amazing supporters and we only just missed out on promotion that year. I went back with Bournemouth on the last day a couple of years later and I was mobbed by their fans. It was the last game at Saltergate and it was hugely emotional. I was 36 when I left Chesterfield in 2008 and had only just got home when I got a phone call from Steve Evans at Crawley. I wanted to stay within a couple of hours so I went to see Steve and again within a few hours I'd signed.'

The Red Devils were ambitious, but Evans knew he needed some canny experience and a dose of muscle to out-gun and out-think the wily campaigners of the Conference. He got both in Fletcher, but agony was around the corner.

'Steve said if I kept myself right then I could have similar time off in the week to what I'd had at Chesterfield,' remembers Fletcher, speaking fondly of both Evans and the Broadfield Stadium side. 'I signed a contract for two years on the same money as Chesterfield so it was amazing for me.

'Halfway through pre-season, though, I went up for a header in a practice match and landed on a lad's ankle. My own ankle ligaments snapped and I was out for nine weeks.

'I got myself back in but I wasn't firing. I'd had no pre-season and I needed one at 36. I started about eight games but was on the bench more often than not.'

This is where the story differs from Howe's version of events, but Fletcher is insistent. His life was about to go full circle but not before a healthy dose of soul-searching.

Fletcher laughs as he recoils in his seat. 'On New Year's Day 2009 I was doing the ironing at home and I was listening to the radio when they said Jimmy Quinn had gone and Eddie had been appointed caretaker manager.

'I ran into the other room and told Lynne that Ed had been given the job and she said, "I bet he gives you a call."

'I said, "Don't be stupid. I'm 36, what's he going to call me for?"

'But she laughed and said, "I bet he does."

'Sure enough, on 2 January the phone rang and it was Eddie.

'He said, "Big 'Un, I want you back." He was straight to the point. I couldn't believe it and the hairs on the back of my neck stood up more than they ever had before. It was almost like a sense of fear, though. I almost wanted him to say he was joking, but I knew he was serious.

'I told him I had 18 months left at Crawley and Ed, as he still does to this day, just said, "Well sort it out then. Do something about it."

'He said he needed to know and said my wages would be less than I was on at Crawley, but it wasn't about that.

'They'd gone to Darlington and Rotherham and lost and they were cut adrift. I was thinking I was about to give up an 18-month contract to go to a club that had no guarantee of survival, for less money, and for what remained of the season.'

Fletcher's voice softens and slows once again. 'In the end Ed gave me an ultimatum and said he needed to know so I woke my missus up at 2am one morning and told her I was going to sign. I knew if I didn't it would be the biggest regret of my life.

'Lynne was up front. She knew as well as I did there was a big chance Bournemouth could go down and go out of existence or at best start again from non-league. Loads of people told me not to go back because it would never be the same but I knew I had to do it. It was eating me up inside. My head was telling me to think realistically but my heart was saying I had to go back.

'I couldn't think "what if" in years to come. What if we could survive? I felt like it was unfinished business as I hadn't achieved anything other than the play-off final win in 2003. This could be off the scale if we could stay up. I went to see Steve Evans and he was fantastic. He knew how much it meant to me and said had it been any other club he wouldn't have even had me in the office.

'He was quite ruthless as a manager but he released me from my contract and if it weren't for him I wouldn't be doing this interview now. The day after I signed I started for Bournemouth against Wycombe, we won 3-1 and went on this crazy journey.'

Fletcher and his team-mates sat in their usual spots inside the home dressing room on 25 April. Howe's tactic of turning off the heating and ensuring the seating was as spoiled as possible were put into place across the other side of the tunnel, in the tiny away changing room, before the visitors arrived.

Howe was big on normality. Nothing needed to change despite the magnitude of the match.

The game carried fear for both sides. Grimsby were hovering precariously above Chester and Luton who occupied the relegation places. Above them, Howe's side knew a win would be enough to complete the miracle: seventeen points adrift before a ball had been kicked and now with a chance to stay in the Football League.

'I just wanted to get out there and get on with it that day,' recalls Fletcher. 'Eddie told us before the game that we could become part of history and I echoed that in the team huddle before kick-off. I said, "Boys, let's make sure we go down in history. Let's do it for ourselves first and foremost but also for the fans and for our families."

'We went 1-0 down when Nathan Jarman scored so what I had said obviously didn't have the effect I had intended, but we were great after that. The siege mentality had served us well and we didn't panic. We took the game to them and Liam Feeney equalised just before half-time.

'I played 836 games in my career and didn't go into a single one apart from that one knowing I was going to score. I always hoped I would score in every game but never really believed I would and that was probably a bit of a mental downfall in my career because I didn't believe enough.

'But I knew I was going to score that day. I just knew. For the whole of the second half I was thinking, "I am going to score the winner."

'I never said it at the time or for years after, but I'm telling you now I genuinely believed it. It was set up for me. It was my moment.

'Mark Molesley lost a header when the ball came into the box, which he still says to this day he did on purpose, but their lad headed it into my chest and it fell perfectly. I just smashed it through a crowd of players and wheeled away, shirt off, swinging it around as I ran.

'The last eight minutes before the ref blew for full time felt like an eternity and I just wanted it to be over. When he blew up I ran past the dugout as the crowd spilled on to the pitch and climbed the steps up to block two of the main stand and grabbed my daughters and just cried.

'Everything I had risked had paid off. We survived against all odds and it is my single greatest achievement.'

Howe had felt the same as Fletcher, kindred spirits and with a telepathy that exists to this day.

The Cherries manager smiles, picturing the moment. 'We went 1-0 down and it was another case of us never making things easy for ourselves. But the stars were aligned that day.

'We got the equaliser and when Fletch buried the winner it was right there and then that I thought "Yes, that's how it was supposed to end."

'It was an emotional moment and I remember feeling really choked up. I realised we were going to do it and all the hard work had paid off.

'Fletch had played superbly since he had come back but hadn't scored a huge number of goals and it was just meant to be.

'He surprised me in so many ways when he came back and he became indispensable really. I couldn't play without him in the side. He was magnificent. I found myself leaning on him and saying, "Big man, I'm sorry, but I need you. You're going to have to go again." He played so much football that season.

'Anything I asked of him, he did. We managed his workload but he was more professional that season than he had been at any stage of his career. He was so pleased to be back and so proud to represent the club again that really we got a brand new player when he came back.

'He played the best football of his career that season but, if anything, the next season he was even better. It was a travesty he didn't play higher than he did because I believe he had everything. Okay, he didn't have the goal record, and we joke about that now, but he had everything else to play at a higher level.

'He became the player that other teams focused on and feared playing against.'

'You could never write the script,' Fletcher smiles. 'Everyone I meet always says how they can't believe what I have been through in 25 years at this club. It really is a fairy tale.

'I wanted to play in the Premier League and the Championship and never achieved those dreams but I would never swap those for the things I achieved here. I walked out at Wembley in 1998 and scored in the play-off final in Cardiff then scored the goal that kept the club in the Football League. I would never change it for anything – not even one season in the Premier League.

'Everything that happened made me the man I am today. I played the best football of my career that season in 2009. I was 36, my legs had gone and I wasn't as mobile as I had been but I was smarter and played every game like it was my last.

'I did it for Eddie as he revitalised my career and I wanted to pay him back. If he hadn't shown faith in me in 2009 I wouldn't have what I have now, still being involved with this club in the Premier League. It changed my life, 2 January 2009. It resurrected my career but more importantly it resurrected my life.'

The Houdini act complete, Howe set his sights on greater ambitions.

CHAPTER SIX

ON THE UP
2009/10

MARVIN Bartley is running late. It's early March 2018 at Hibernian's Easter Road home and most of Edinburgh is still ankle deep in spring snow with the small matter of the visit of bitter rivals Hearts just days away.

The midfielder breezes into the stadium's main reception, where historic images of the likes of Jackie McNamara, Gordon Smith and Hugh Shaw adorn the walls, with a handshake, wide grin and an apology.

If ever one player epitomised the siege mentality fuelled by Howe during the dark days of administration and points deductions, Bartley is it. Tall and athletic, he was a unique rough diamond lining up for Kevin Bond, Jimmy Quinn and Howe in the lower reaches of the Football League. An N'Golo Kante or Claude Makélélé in red and black. A spoiler in divisions where spoilers are required yet often considered too much of a luxury. The irony of such a description is not lost on him.

'I was released by Reading at 14 because I wasn't tall enough,' he laughs. 'I was playing centre-half there and they didn't think I was going to reach 6ft so they moved me on.

'But I wasn't enjoying it anyway to be honest. I'd only started playing aged 11 so I was only really interested in having a kick around with my mates. Once you end up in an academy, it gets more serious and it just wasn't for me at that stage of my life.

'Getting released was bitter- sweet because it meant I could go back to playing Sunday league again with my mates!'

Bartley, far from disappointed at a potential professional career slipping away, did a jig all the way back to Caversham Boys, before switching to Henley in the Allied Counties League and then Hayes.

'That was when I realised I wanted to play professionally again,' he says, smiling. 'I was at Hayes in their youth team and at that point I was only setting my target to play for the first team. They were in the Conference South at that point and training twice a week so I really wanted a piece of that.

'Hampton & Richmond came in for me while I was at Hayes and were offering more money so I went there, but then ended up coming back to Hayes before going back to Hampton & Richmond again! It was all just to get an extra £10 a week at that stage!'

Combining playing part-time with fitting windows for a living, Bartley's second spell at the Beveree Stadium was to be decisive under Alan Devonshire, the wide midfielder who played almost 400 games for West Ham United between 1976 and 1990.

Devonshire loved Bartley's on-pitch aggression. An engine that shows no signs of running low on fuel is quite a commodity in the Ryman Premier League, yet Devonshire knew Bartley's quality would lead to greater achievements and did not stand in his way when a former Hammers team-mate asked the question.

'Things went well during my second spell at Hampton & Richmond and I went to MK Dons for a trial under Martin Allen,' recalls Bartley. 'Everything was in place and I was due to sign but then Martin went to manage Leicester a couple of days later! That destroyed my chance because even though Leicester were in League One as well, they were a massive club and I didn't think for a minute that Martin would want to take me there.

'I didn't really know where I was going to go from there, but I managed to get in at Bournemouth under Kevin Bond in 2007 as he was looking at a lot of triallists at that point. There was a lot of upheaval and Kevin was trying to build a squad.

'He put me in for a pre-season game against Weymouth and I got cramp after 25 minutes because I'd been at work fitting windows that day. I was heartbroken because I'd never had cramp before but I had to come off and I thought that was another chance gone. I'd only played 25 minutes so the manager wasn't going to have that – he'd assume I just wasn't fit enough.

'Kevin asked me if I had been at work so I told him that I had been up and down ladders all day carrying windows. He was impressed that I had managed to come down to Bournemouth from Reading after a full day at work and promised me another go. I was blown away.

'I started to come in for training, travelling down from Reading, and the company I worked for was fantastic. They wanted to see me do well and progress so let me leave early and take days off to train with Bournemouth.'

Bond saw in Bartley exactly the kind of ingredients he knew he would need for a proper League One tear-up. Murmurings of administration already piercing the air, too, perhaps Bond was thinking even further ahead when he took the plunge on Bartley in July 2007.

But his new signing, fresh from penning his first professional deal and eager to get back to Berkshire for some celebrations, was due an unexpected phone call.

'We played Southampton that pre-season and I signed my first contract after the game,' says Bartley. 'I didn't even look at the contract or the money – I just signed. I called my mum and brothers back home and they were made up – my brother had been released by Crystal Palace so he knew what that kind of disappointment felt like.

'I had to drive back from Bournemouth to Reading after the Southampton game and I was just delighted. But my phone rang and I didn't recognise the number. When I answered it, the voice said, "Marv, it's Martin Allen."

'I thought, "What's going on here?" Martin had been trying to get hold of me for days, as it turned out. He ended up phoning Alan Devonshire, as they had played together at West Ham, and Alan gave him my number.

'He asked where I was and I told him I was in the car on the M3. He said, "Can you get up to Leicester?"

'He said he had wanted to sign me at MK Dons and still did even though he was now at Leicester. He knew I wasn't contracted at Hampton & Richmond so wanted me to come up to get the deal done. I couldn't believe it.

'I told him I'd just signed for Bournemouth and suddenly I felt like I'd missed a massive opportunity. But I'd signed the contract and I wasn't going to try to get out of it.

'As it happened, Martin only lasted four games at Leicester so I dodged a bullet!

'By the time I got home, I was back to being delighted. It didn't take much time to shake off the Leicester thing because I soon realised that I was going to play at Bournemouth. At Leicester, I would have been a squad player, which was no good for me at that stage.'

Bond had already added one window fitter to his squad in centre-half Russell Perrett, but for Bartley, the smell of mastic and the weight of UPVC frames were a thing of the past – although the monthly wage from The Splash Group in Reading was perhaps more reliable than the salary of an ailing League One football club.

'One of the boys had said the club was going to go into administration and we'd had a few problems with our wages from time to time. It was just normal really,' confesses Bartley.

'But I used to travel down from Reading with Jason Pearce and us not getting paid meant we had no petrol money to get to training!

'I was enjoying my football and loving being at the club – I'd almost turned into a fan – so I really didn't want to face a points deduction in my first season. Kevin got us together upstairs in the stadium and said the club was going into administration and all we could do was aim to go down by less than ten points. But there was still a fight left in us and I think that showed with the run we went on at the end of that season.'

Bartley was possibly the only man in Carlisle on 3 May 2008 who felt worse than Bond, the midfielder missing a gilt-edged chance late on at Brunton Park to make the score 2-1 and save his new club from the drop.

'I felt like it was my fault that we went down,' says Bartley, the emotion of the moment still clear almost a decade later. 'It was instant. After I missed that chance in stoppage time it just kept replaying in my mind. I couldn't get over it. When the final whistle went it was just like the air had been kicked out of me. We went back into the dressing room and so many of the boys broke down in tears, myself included.

'Looking at professional footballers from the outside, as I had done for years, I had never attached emotion to the game. I never attached disappointment or administration or relegation to it either. As a young lad watching, it's all glory and you don't see the reality of it sometimes, but it really hit me at Carlisle that day.

'Mentally I wasn't prepared for losing that game and it was very emotionally draining.'

With a 17-point mountain to climb the following season in League Two, Bond sacked in favour of Quinn in September 2008 and Sport-6's ill-fated reign beginning to take effect at boardroom level, Bartley could have been forgiven for dialling Martin Allen's number. But Reading born and bred, Quinn was his hero and as

Saverimutto turned on the sales charm in a bid to convince the rest of the dressing room, Bartley's eyes sparkled.

'I remember the first meeting we had with Alastair Saverimutto and the way he spoke and the things he said the club was going to do,' says Bartley with the kind of smile that usually leads to laughter. 'I just thought, "wow". The way he spoke about Sport-6's plans, Bournemouth was going to be a Premier League club. I was love-struck and just thought, "This man is the saviour. He can walk on water."

'Very quickly, though, it went completely the other way. If Savi gave us a date of the 15th of the month for getting paid, he'd still come to us on the 25th when it hadn't happened to say it was still going to happen! And we still believed him. He certainly talked the talk!'

On the training field, meanwhile, the aura of Quinn failed to materialise in substance for the Berkshire boy.

'For me, Jimmy was a legend as he had done such amazing things at Reading,' admits Bartley. 'I had a vision of how he was going to be based on the fact he was a bit of a hero of mine and, without meaning to be disrespectful, I'm not sure Jimmy wanted to put the work in to be a successful manager.

'I know he wanted the job, but I don't think he was prepared for the graft. There was a definite dip in standards and work ethic when he came in and I noticed it because of how things had been under Kevin.

'I'd been around the club and the professional game for a year by then and I was learning about how the game operated from people like Darren Anderton. It was an eye-opener into how good people do things and how everyone else does them. For me, Jimmy didn't want to do it. He didn't give me the feeling that he wanted to be at training or coach us. He didn't come across as if he wanted to put the time and effort in. It was disappointing for me personally because Jimmy was a god to me. I still respect him hugely as a player and for what he achieved at Reading, but it just didn't work for him at Bournemouth.'

Anderton was to prove a useful ally for many of Bond's, and then Quinn's, younger players, supporting and backing them to push on as he reached the end of a sparkling career.

'Darren was in the twilight of his career so I think his legs had gone a bit,' laughs Bartley, 'but with the ball at his feet I couldn't see how even the boys in the Premier League at that time could do things any better.

'Watching him was like playing *FIFA* on a Playstation – you'd watch the things he did and just think, "That's not real life." He could do things the rest of us couldn't.

'He would just ping balls in training and find the top corner from all kinds of crazy distances and angles. He'd hit the shot and then shout at the keeper, "Just leave it, you're not going to get to it." He just knew, as soon as the ball left his foot, it was going where he wanted it to.

'He was like a wizard and when I first began to train with him I was nervous being on his team in the small-sided games because I didn't want to mess up.

'Me and Pearcey didn't think he liked us when we first arrived, but we realised in the end that wasn't the case at all – he just wanted us to better ourselves. He wasn't being horrible, he just gave us a bit of a hard time because he wanted us to do well for ourselves. I can see that now I am older.

'On and off the pitch he was fantastic. He used to do cash boosters in training, things like the first player to win a tackle would get £50. He was great to have around and if you asked me to write down my best 11 now, he would be in it because with the ball at his feet, he is the best player I have ever played with.'

Just 18 months into his Dean Court career, Bartley saw Howe become his third manager. It was a statistic that told the story of the club at that time, but unbeknown to Bartley, history and success were just around the corner, spearheaded by their 31-year-old manager.

'My main memory of Eddie from that time was him bringing in the academy kit to be washed,' chortles Bartley. 'I knew Jimmy wasn't going to last, probably even from his first week in charge, but I didn't know Eddie would be next in line.

'He had coached a bit under Kevin but was really young and only really worked with the younger lads like me, Brett Pitman and Shaun Cooper. We used to do some sessions with him and learned a lot, but it was still a surprise when he was given the manager's job as he was so young.

'But he changed everything, not just on the pitch but off it as well. The feeling around the club was toxic under Jimmy and Sport-6 and once Eddie came in it just lifted everyone.

'He was young and energetic and it was like chalk and cheese compared with Jimmy. Maybe Jimmy felt Bournemouth was a bit beneath him and that he should be managing higher up but Eddie came in and it was like Bournemouth was his baby.

'We just gelled under him and dug deep to give ourselves a chance at the end of the season in 2009.

'The Grimsby game is still a bit of a blur really – it was just crazy. But I do remember Fletch's goal and thinking at the time, "If he had got that chance in training he'd miss it 100 times out of 100!"

'One would go over the bar, another wide of the post! But it was a special moment – the shirt came off and off he went like Ryan Giggs in the 1999 cup semi-final against Arsenal, just a little more shaved!

'It was an incredible feeling and the buzz from that game just ignited everything after that.'

Howe's summer plans, though, were hamstrung by a rolling Football League transfer embargo, put in place due to the manager's January 2009 recruitment.

Off the field, with Saverimutto having retreated under a cloud in March but with League Two safety secured, Baker sought out Murry, Mostyn and Sly to compete their deal, enabling him to follow his business partner back up the M6 to Merseyside.

Finally, after months of protracted talks and newspaper statement back-biting, the Murry Group took control in June 2009, but as well as Mostyn, Murry and Sly, the group's surprise fourth member attracted the attention of both press and supporters alike.

Eddie Mitchell was a property developer most famous for his company's £4m block and render 'Thunderbird' house at Sandbanks and for his appearance on the *Piers Morgan On... Sandbanks* programme where he was oddly dubbed the 'George Clooney' of Dorset.

Mitchell, who was quickly installed as the Cherries' new chairman, had also dabbled in football as chief of non-league Dorchester Town, while son Tom had played in midfield for the Magpies.

'The club had come out of administration with a blank piece of paper, completely debt free when Sport-6 took over in 2008,' recalls Mostyn.

'But they never got around to paying me fully for my shares so the shares came back to me through default in the spring of 2009. I felt cheated, although I felt sorry for Paul Baker because two of his biggest clients at UK Sameday had gone into administration. That represented 90 per cent of his business. He was wiped out.

'But Sport-6 didn't pay a bill while they were here. The Royal Bath Hotel in Bournemouth and the local Chinese restaurant were owed vast sums of money, as well as a dry cleaning business. Everything had been expensed on the football club and nothing had been paid for.

'They had racked up around £1m in debt in the short time they were at the club.

'Adam Murry came to me and Steve Sly that spring in 2009 and said he wanted to form a consortium to get the club back fully from Sport-6. I couldn't believe it was happening but it was the only chance we had to get back some of our money from the first time around.

'Adam had spoken to Eddie Mitchell, as had I previously, and the deal was Eddie would take half of the club and I would have half while still looking after Steve Sly to the tune of 17 per cent of my half.

'My position was clear: I was happy to write off what Sport-6 owed me to get the deal done.

'At that point in time I technically owned 100 per cent of nothing, but Adam's proposal meant I could own 50 per cent of something which might give me a chance to get at least some of my money back from when I owned the club the first time.

'But I wasn't prepared to put any more money into the club at that stage.

'The money had to come from the other shareholders.'

Buoyed by the previous season's Greatest Escape and what by the Cherries' standards was classed as off-field security, the manager ploughed on as the Murry Group completed its takeover.

A 3-0 win at home to Bury on the opening day of the 2009/10 League Two season, the club's first campaign on an even points keel for two years, set the tone for an opening few weeks that would shape the campaign.

Only a 4-0 reverse at Millwall in the League Cup three days later and a 2-0 loss at Northampton on 22 August soured Howe's mood as wins over Rotherham, Aldershot, Crewe, Yeovil, Torquay, Lincoln, Darlington and Burton secured 24 points before the end of September.

An October dip in results, though, coincided with a crippling injury crisis that saw Howe field just three substitutes in league defeats at Hereford and Port Vale and a loss at Northampton in the Football League Trophy.

Tindall was called out of retirement once more, while Howe handed debuts to youngsters Danny Ings and Jayden Stockley against the Cobblers. Stockley was just 15 years old when he came on as a 79th-minute substitute for Warren Cummings.

'Jason Tindall was unbelievable that night against Northampton,' remembers Bartley fondly. 'He played 70 minutes because we only had three subs and all three of them were youth team boys – George Webb, Jayden Stockley and Danny Ings. Shwan Jalal was injured so Dan Thomas, who was only 17, played in goal.

'Lee Bradbury missed a penalty then gave one away at the other end in the 90th minute and they beat us 2-1. How on earth we kept it to that, I don't know. At one point during that game we had Ingsy and Jayden leading the line whose combined age was less than what I am now!'

A late Danny Hollands goal against Chesterfield on 10 October was in vain as Drew Talbot's double dented the Cherries' progress yet further, but with injury worries subsiding, Howe's men slowly began to regroup and maintain their place among the division's elite.

Hollands was on target again in a gritty 1-0 triumph at Accrington, while a 3-1 win over Grimsby saw strikes from Alan Connell and Brett Pitman sandwich a Paul Linwood own goal. However, the following week's visit of Rochdale saw a 4-0 humbling for Howe, whose activity in the transfer market nine months earlier had riled Spotland boss Keith Hill.

'We got a real pumping against Rochdale that day,' says Bartley glumly. 'Chris Dagnall and Chris O'Grady tore us to pieces. I remember watching O'Grady and thinking, "What is he doing in this division?" He was a world-beater and Dags was like a wasp feeding off everything. I later played with Dags at Leyton Orient and he was still just as good then.

'But O'Grady was like a mobile Steve Fletcher. I remember the ball going down the channel and he just put his head down and he was gone. We had no idea how to stop him.

'Nathan Stanton got sent off that day for cutting me clean in half late in the game but we were well beaten by that point.

'There was a lot said by their manager Keith Hill that season and that was why Stanton had smashed me. Our paths crossed late on and he said, "You think you're a bit of a hard man, don't you?" because I'd been doing my usual thing of kicking people for 80 minutes. He said he was going to teach me a lesson and he went right through me, high up. How he didn't break my leg, I really don't know.

'After the game Eddie really opened up on how much their manager had to say about us and told us never to forget what Stanton had done to me. After the game we were going round shaking hands and Eddie had told us all not to shake Stanton's hand while he waited in the tunnel.

'I think they were jealous of us. We were clubs of a similar size but they saw us bring players in that January and February when the club had not long come out of administration and they were trying to be sensible with their budget. But I also think Hill was probably jealous of Eddie because he was so young and getting so much attention for what he was doing.

'Managers like Hill have been plying their trade in the lower leagues forever and some of them didn't like that Eddie was young and having success. There was an element of jealousy, I'm sure of that, because a lot of things were said that season by people like Keith Hill and Keith Alexander at Macclesfield.'

Pitman was on target twice in a 2-1 win at Moss Rose that sparked yet more veiled vitriol from Alexander in November, while a mixed bag of results up until Christmas yielded just enough points to keep Howe in the hunt for a first career promotion. But Bartley was to experience the wrath of his young manager for the first time when the Cherries made the long trip north to Morecambe on 12 December.

With Jalal injured and youngster Thomas doubtful, Howe was forced to beg the League to relax its transfer ban so he could bring in an emergency keeper on loan for seven days. Granted his wish, Howe plumped for Marek Stech, who at just 19, was highly rated by West Ham United and a Czech Republic youth international.

He had also performed well during a loan spell at Wycombe Wanderers and, to Bartley at least, certainly looked the part. Three-nil down inside 25 minutes and 5-0 behind at full time, though, Stech was the least of Bartley's worries.

'When Marek came in before the Morecambe game I thought he was going to be like Peter Schmeichel,' Bartley laughs. 'I thought he was going to save everything because he was a real unit, but he ended up saving nothing and then we never saw him again!

'We had our Christmas party booked for the same night in Manchester but they scored three really early goals, inside 30 minutes, and I just saw red.

'They were mouthing off, on top of playing well, and I just decided to leave a bit on Stuart Drummond, who'd scored the first goal, just to get a booking and let them know they weren't going to run through us all day.

'It was like slow motion, the tackle, and straight away I thought, "Marv, you've gone in a bit hard here." I was on my knees and their players were surrounding me while the referee came charging over.

'I knew I was going off so when he pulled out the red card, the only thing I can compare it with is being drunk and in a daze and then something really bad happens to instantly sober you up.

'As I walked off I thought to myself, "Whatever you do, don't look at the gaffer." I got to the dressing room and I was just lonely. It was horrible.

'The lads had spent a load of money on the Christmas party, but obviously we'd been well and truly beaten so we were trying to decide if we should still go out. I knew I couldn't – we'd been battered and, not only that, I'd been sent off. But there were a few ringleaders in the group and they were insistent I had to come out.

'The plan was for the coach to drop us on the main drag through Manchester. When it pulled up I thought, "I'm not going. I can't." But Warren Cummings was saying, "You're f***ing coming!"

'The coach pulled over and a few of the lads started filtering off and I thought I was safe, but I turned sideways and Waz was there looking in through the window saying, "Off!"

'I got up to get off and just said to myself again, "Don't look at Eddie." I got to the front of the coach where he was sat and looked straight at him. The look he gave me was hell on earth. I got so drunk that night just to block it out.'

Howe's men shook off the remnants of their festive shenanigans to recover from the Morecambe setback with aplomb. Liam Feeney's 57th-minute strike on Boxing Day saw off Cheltenham at Whaddon Road, before Feeney and Pitman were both on target in the final ten minutes against Torquay two days later, sealing a dramatic 2-1 win.

Three straight defeats in January tested the resolve of Howe's threadbare squad once more but again his depleted group answered the questions posed, securing successive victories on the road against Crewe and Rotherham despite benching just four substitutes, including Tindall.

Howe had again gone cap in hand to the League prior to the Tuesday night fixture at the Don Valley Stadium. With just 13 fit professionals travelling to Sheffield, minus the injured Bartley, Howe saw his attempts to sign Doncaster utility man Mustapha Dumbuya on a seven-day emergency loan blocked.

After Pitman and a Hollands double had seen off the Yorkshiremen 3-1, the *Daily Echo*'s back page headline the following day read 'WHAT DO YOU THINK OF THAT THEN, FOOTBALL LEAGUE?' It went down like a lead balloon at HQ in London, perhaps tightening the noose around Howe's neck even further, but the Miracle Man cared little. Just a year into the job, he had developed the rhino skin that served Bond so well.

As January turned into February, a crucial 2-1 win over promotion favourites Notts County, thanks to another Hollands double, kept the Cherries in the hunt for their own elevation against all odds.

'We had a few battles with Notts County that season as we had played them in the FA Cup as well,' says Bartley. 'They'd come into some apparent money and signed people like Kasper Schmeichel and Sol Campbell and brought in Sven-Goran Eriksson as director of football.

'Lee Hughes was there at the time, too,' he adds with a smile. 'I admit I was quite scared of him. I was quite happy to mix it up with most players, but I didn't want any trouble with him – he'd only been out of prison for a couple of years and just had a real aura about him.'

Barnet were dispatched 3-0 under the Dean Court lights on 23 February as the Pitman/Fletcher double act rolled back the years.

But three days later supporters enjoying the relative stability brought by the Murry Group's takeover the previous summer were rocked once more as HMRC issued a winding-up petition for £314,000 in unpaid tax from the Sport-6 regime.

And to make matters worse, Howe's injury crisis was far from over.

Central defender Pearce and winger Feeney were both ruled out of the following game at Shrewsbury with injuries sustained in Friday training so teenager Stockley was called upon again, but this time at the 11th hour.

'We only had three subs again,' reflects Bartley, 'Jeff Goulding, the teenage goalkeeper Dan Thomas and Jason Tindall! So when we got up there, Eddie asked the youth team coach Joe Roach to go back to Bournemouth and get Jayden Stockley and drive him back up to Shrewsbury in time for kick-off. He was only 15 and in the middle of his GCSE mock exams so Jeff Mostyn had to ask the headteacher's permission to take him as he was revising, but even in that game I never thought we'd lose. As long as we had 11 players, I was always confident that season and that was the mentality of all of us.'

Lose, however, they did, 1-0 to a 49th-minute Terry Dunfield strike, but the Miracle Man's men saw other results go their way and remained in second place as the run-in approached at pace.

Having staved off the immediate threat from HMRC, Mitchell watched from his hospitality box as Pitman inspired home wins over Accrington and Bradford City in March before promotion rivals Rochdale were held 0-0 at Dean Court on 5 April.

With Notts County setting the pace at the top of the table, the Cherries and Hill's Rochdale were in position to claim the remaining two automatic promotion spots, with Morecambe and Rotherham close behind.

Their injury woes behind them and with another day of destiny in sight, the Cherries saw off Hereford 2-1 thanks to a Pitman brace and downed Darlington 2-0 four days later to set up a chance to seal promotion at Burton Albion on 24 April.

The East Staffordshire sun was out and thousands flocked to the Pirelli Stadium in hope of the win that would secure the most unlikely return to League One.

'I remember being nervous beforehand,' says Bartley. 'But it felt like a pre-season game, because the sun was out and it was such a lovely place to play football. The pitch was flat and the conditions were perfect. Paul Peschisolido was their manager and I remember making a beeline for him afterwards because I used to use him when playing *Championship Manager* back in the day! He was tiny and I was thinking, "Hang on, I got released by Reading for being too small – look at this guy, how has he gone on to score all these goals and I got released!" I was taller than him at birth!

'It was an amazing day and we played so well. But after an hour it was still 0-0 and I think we were all starting to feel the nerves a bit more then. But we believed in ourselves and kept it together. Brett scored and then Al Connell got the second really late on and it was party time!

'The fans absolutely flooded on to the pitch and I'll never forget how Burton were with us that day – they made it feel like a home game and it was amazing.

'It was as if they had gone up too, the way they were with us. Their fans stayed behind as we celebrated and were amazing.

'We went out again when we got back to Bournemouth that night, but Rochdale were in second and Eddie was desperate to finish above them even though we were already up. The whole thing with Keith Hill had really got to him and we were all desperate to top them so we took it easy on the drink.

'We beat Port Vale 4-0 on the penultimate weekend and Rochdale lost their last four games so we finished second behind Notts County. It was just an amazing achievement considering everything that was against us with the transfer ban and the injuries.

'Eddie was desperate for us to finish as high as we could even though we couldn't win the title and that is something I'll always take from him. He never stops until the final whistle of the last game because he knows that a good finish to the season pays off when you start again the following August. I wasn't thinking that at the time because I was young, but now I am older and wiser I see what he was doing and why he was pushing us.

'We lost the last game at Chesterfield and he was fuming, which just goes to prove what I'm saying!'

A Scottish Cup winner with Hibernian in 2016, Bartley puts his head in his hands when asked to rate the achievements of Howe's tiny class of 2010. He pauses for just long enough.

'Winning the Scottish Cup with Hibs meant so much,' he says, 'but I always look at that team in 2010 as Eddie being a chef. He was given a small and bizarre mix of ingredients that don't go together and told to make a dish. Then he comes out with this Michelin-starred meal and you think, "How have you done that with what you were given?"

'Unless Eddie wins the Premier League, what he did with us those seasons between 2009 and 2010 will surely be his greatest achievement. It's certainly mine.'

But Howe didn't allow himself time to take stock. Back in League One, he knew he needed to add some quality as well as bodies to his wafer-thin squad. Tasked alongside new chairman Mitchell to come up with a Football League charm offensive to end the transfer embargo, there was one name on his target list that he knew better than any other.

CHAPTER SEVEN

THE END OF AN ERA
2010/11

S TEVE Lovell awoke slowly and gently shook the last pieces of tiredness from his eyes. He stretched and glanced out of the bedroom window of his home just outside Glasgow. It was another day, yet only the same uninspiring daily routine beckoned him from his bed. There was nothing, aside perhaps from reflections of glories past.

Oliver Kahn had no chance. What a header.
That atmosphere in 2003 against Rangers at Hampden. Wow.
Left foot, tight angle in front of the away support. Boom!

The Lovell who walks into reception at Dean Court early in 2018 is a very different person to the one who hung up his boots and sunk into despair almost seven years ago. Bright-eyed and keen to talk, he points out the new recruitment office in the stadium's main hub, his place of work since moving back to Dorset from Scotland in order to scout for brother and manager Howe.

He glances out towards the flawless pitch as we slip into an empty hospitality box. 'They used to have a huge image of me scoring the penalty against Huddersfield in 2011 in the corner of the main stand, but then they replaced it with something else. Disgraceful,' he laughs. 'Although to be fair, they'd flipped it in

Photoshop so it looked as if I took it with my left foot. If I'd done that, it wouldn't have gone in!'

Lovell is referring to his stand-out night in a Cherries shirt, during a second stint at the club ravaged by injury. One that, just months later, would signal the end of his career at the age of 30, almost on a par with brother Howe whose own playing time was cut short at 29. The similarities between the pair all but end there, however.

'We lived in a road called The Lea, number 17, in Verwood, a small town in East Dorset, and the house backed on to a green where there was a big row of garages,' recalls Lovell. 'Ed and I would draw a goal on the wall and just stay out there for hours and hours playing football.

'That was all we did to burn energy and with five kids to look after, I think mum was pretty glad of that because it got us out of the house. When we got a little older, I played for Phoenix Youth and Ed was at Rossgarth in Verwood because he was three years older than me. My mum would drive us around everywhere, both of us, playing football. I played Saturdays and Sundays so all my mum did all weekend was watch us play football.

'Now I'm a scout I appreciate how cold it can be just sitting and watching football so our mum was amazing to do that. She used to travel everywhere around Dorset and the New Forest for us.'

Both brothers continued to make waves in the youth game and soon attracted the attention of scouts from professional clubs, but while Howe's work ethic shone through, Lovell was distracted by the temptations of youth.

'There were big differences between myself and Ed,' he admits. 'I probably had more natural ability but Ed worked harder than I did and understood things better, which shows in the way he manages and coaches today. I was probably more naturally gifted at that age I suppose, but when I got older I became more distracted and football was just a laugh. I preferred going out with my friends. We were both starting to get noticed though. I was scoring a lot of goals and had the chance to go to Arsenal but we couldn't afford to get up to London to do training.

'I was only nine so I didn't really appreciate until I got older what that meant. I mean, it was Arsenal in 1990 and they were about to win Division One the following year! I don't think you do appreciate the stature of clubs when you're that age. The scout came to watch me a few times and invited me up there but we just couldn't afford it.

'To me it was just football – I wasn't really aware of the history of clubs at that age so when I was told I couldn't go it didn't really matter to me as I could still play for Phoenix with my friends.

'I went to train at Portsmouth in the end but that was a struggle financially as well so it was cut short – it was just hard to get there to train. It was hard for my mum bringing up five of us and money was tight.

'A couple of years later I started to go down to the AFC Bournemouth centre of excellence at Chapel Gate Sports Club in Bournemouth with Ed on Thursday nights but again I was unaware of what it could lead to at that point. I knew it was a step up, but to me it was still just football and I just wanted to play, wherever it was and with whoever it was.'

By 1994, Howe was making waves in the Cherries youth set-up run by O'Driscoll and would make his first-team debut just a year later, lining up against Hull City in December. Lovell, though, was at a crossroads – combining teenage high jinks around the streets of Verwood and training with the Cherries youth team with games for Dorset village side Cranborne. O'Driscoll became the bearer of bad news. Lovell momentarily looks down.

'Sean was running the youth team and I didn't get offered a deal as a first year YT,' he says with more than a hint of regret. 'It was because my attitude was poor – Sean lived in Verwood the same as me so he knew what I was like around town.

'Ed had just signed as a professional at that stage as he was three years older, but I just shrugged my shoulders and went off and played for Cranborne. I loved it because it was less serious and suited me more at the time.

'I did a plumbing course and I was pretty set that my life would be plumbing and then playing for Cranborne on a Saturday in non-league. My attitude was such that I was pretty happy with that, but Ed asked Sean to give me a second chance as a second-year youth player and he did. I don't know why he did, but he had a great relationship with Ed. Ed has a way of persuading people, too. They respect him and Sean respected him even back then as a youngster.

'From then on I was the only one from that year who was taken on as a professional. If Ed hadn't stepped in then I would never have made it.

'Did it change my approach? Not really. To be honest, it's only in the last couple of years that it's really sunk in how I did everything wrong and how I could have been so much better and achieved so much more. Hindsight is great but it kills you, too.

'I was just a naturally gifted but naughty boy. I might have been given a pro deal but I didn't really progress as a player. I didn't apply myself and didn't do enough. I did only what I needed to.'

A former club legend, though, was to see something in the young Lovell. A goalscoring ability to match his own one day, perhaps. Or the same roguish, lad-about-town demeanour, maybe.

Ted MacDougall, whatever his reasoning, had gleaned enough from just one Lovell reserve team performance against his Portsmouth second string to tip the wink to first-team boss Alan Ball.

'I had literally just signed as a pro and started one first-team game where I was hooked at half-time,' Lovell laughs, 'but I had played well against Portsmouth reserves and Ted, who was managing their reserve team, had liked me. He went back and told Alan Ball that I was worth a look and they put in a bid of £250,000.

'Again I didn't really take it in. The club told me Portsmouth had tabled a bid and I just said, "Okay," and off I went. Looking back now it was silly money for an unproven teenager.

'I phoned my mum and she drove me down there to sign that day. Again, though, I didn't realise the magnitude of the club I was going to.

'They were in Division Two with a World Cup-winning manager but I didn't really know any of that! I just signed. If I was signing for a club now I would do my homework but back then I was just a kid who wanted to play.

'Nothing fazes you at that age,' he smiles. 'You just crack on. I was there for three years and had a load of managers. Alan was there when I signed, then Tony Pulis came in and then Steve Claridge, Graham Rix and Harry Redknapp after him.

'I wasn't really featuring and went out on loan to Exeter, Sheffield United and QPR. It wasn't really until Graham took over in 2001 that I started to play games regularly. There were a good bunch of lads at Pompey and I played with some top players like Robert Prosinečki, Lee Sharpe, Lee Bradbury and Peter Crouch so it was a great learning experience.

'I had another year left on my deal in 2002 but Jim Duffy was the manager at Dundee and had worked at Pompey under Graham, so he knew what I was all about. As soon as I knew they wanted me I didn't hesitate again, despite having to up sticks to Scotland.'

Being pigeon-holed comes with the territory as an Englishman in Scotland. Suggestions Lovell couldn't cut the mustard in the English game, along with claims of a lack of ambition, were commonplace, to such an extent that he agrees with the naysayers. To a point at least.

Lovell, like his brother, was built with an emotional coating, an outer layer of heightened sensitivity perhaps. He does not shy away from criticism or the pains of regret, but his expression changes when we discuss his career north of the border.

'Looking back now I spent too long in Scotland,' he admits. 'But I was never about money when I played – I just wanted to enjoy myself and be happy and I was very happy in Scotland.

'At Dundee I went from being a bench-warmer at Pompey to being a central figure in Jim's team and I enjoyed my time there.

'When I moved to Aberdeen it was another huge step up. I was very fortunate. I had the choice of going to Leicester or Aberdeen and while it's not a regret as such, when I look back at where my career could have gone, it was probably a mistake. I enjoyed my time at Aberdeen but in terms of my career, I probably should have come back to England.

'The standard in Scotland is not as good as England, everyone knows that, but are you better off playing in the SPL in meaningful games against clubs like Rangers and Celtic than playing in League Two in England? Yes, I really believe that.

'Craig Levein was the manager at Leicester and I spoke to him, but I didn't want to leave Scotland as it was my home. I turned down more money to sign for Leicester, but I put myself before my bank balance.

'As soon as you stop enjoying playing, there is no point and that was always my mindset.'

Lovell's Aberdeen career was decorated. Goals against Glasgow's Old Firm won over the Dons' core support before a late consolation against the giants of Bayern Munich in the 2008 UEFA Cup saw Lovell join the likes of Michael Owen, Steven Gerrard, Teddy Sheringham and Emile Heskey as Englishmen to find the net beyond German legend Kahn.

Released at Pittodrie that summer, though, he walked a familiar path. Engaged at the time to Scottish singer Amy

MacDonald, Lovell headed south to Falkirk where a Scottish Cup runners-up medal was secured. After just a year in Stirlingshire, however, he pined for a sibling reunion.

But with the Cherries remaining under the Football League's transfer embargo, the powers-that-be in West Cliff, Preston, weren't interested in family ties. AFC Bournemouth had, according to chairman Mitchell, managed to accrue another £1m of debt during Sport-6's shambolic reign. In the League's mind at least, this was a club that couldn't pay its creditors. New players on the wage bill? No chance.

'In 2009 I felt ready to come back to England and having the chance to play at Bournemouth and for Ed was something I wanted to do,' Lovell recalls. 'But the club was under a transfer embargo.

'Ed wanted to sign Charlie Austin from Poole Town that summer as well but he couldn't bring in either of us. He couldn't even sign a loan player and he only had 13 in his squad at one point in the 2010 promotion season, due to injuries.

'It was very frustrating and so I signed a year with Partick Thistle just to play games really. Eventually I signed for Bournemouth the following summer after the embargo had been lifted and having had an operation on my ankle to remove some floating bone earlier that year.

'Typically on my first day at pre-season in 2010 I felt the ankle pop. Ed jokes about it now because I was his new signing and here I was telling him "Ed, I can't move." He didn't know whether to laugh or cry because he knew I was a bit injury-prone.

'I'd ruptured a tendon in my ankle and we think it was because of the previous operation as it ruptured in a place that it shouldn't have. I still can't move my big toe to this day.'

The embargo had taken its toll on Howe, as the sales of both Brett Pitman to Bristol City in August and Josh McQuoid to Millwall in November had also done, but the manager was able to add summer 2010 resources in winger Marc Pugh from Hereford and Woking midfield prospect Harry Arter.

Mitchell, meanwhile, had been in the chairman's office for just 12 months when the mystery man behind the failed EU UK deal of 2008, Marc Jackson, re-emerged, claiming to be working for Russian firm Convers Group Holdings. The approach? Convers chiefs Roman Dubov and Vladamir Antonov wanted the club and Mitchell's shares, setting a deadline, through Jackson, of 15 July for the chairman to give an answer to their £1.2m takeover proposal. The response? A firm rebuff from Mitchell.

In the League One play-off shake-up by December 2010, for the Cherries to be occupying such a lofty position was a minor miracle. But then this was a club used to acts of a greater being.

Howe, though, remained restless. The endless press conference questions about winding-up petitions and debt were tiresome for a manager who simply wanted to manage. His story of success in the most testing of circumstances was attracting attention and, in January of 2011, both Charlton and Crystal Palace asked Mitchell for permission to speak with his manager.

The press had a field day, camped outside Dean Court for two days waiting for a decision from the Miracle Man. Inside, Howe and Tindall deliberated over remaining in Dorset and seeing through their embryonic project, yet being accused of a lack of ambition, or leaving for a new challenge at a destination where the grass may not be greener.

With training cancelled on 11 January, the players were called in for a meeting with their manager as the media tried to get a steer. Bartley arrived in a Mr Potato Head t-shirt but said nothing, while defender Cummings asked why the circus was in town.

'What are you lot doing here?' probed the Scot. 'The news about my new contract broke last week.' Humour in the face of confusion and change has always been the default Dean Court defence mechanism.

By mid-afternoon, a tired and drawn Howe emerged from the stadium with Mitchell, confirming he was to remain as Bournemouth manager. Five days later, the media having moved on to the next saga, Howe was confirmed as the new manager of Championship side Burnley. Few saw it coming.

In the treatment room, which was fast becoming a second home, Lovell was torn between personal desire to play for his brother and pride at his sibling's appointment in the North West.

'I wasn't around the first team too much as I was doing rehab with the physio Steve Hard, but I obviously knew what was going on with Charlton, Palace and then Burnley,' he reflects. 'As he always does, Ed spoke to his family to discuss what was the right thing to do. He decided Burnley was right for him.

'I was disappointed when he went because I never got a chance to play for him, but I knew he wrestled with the decision for a while. Moving away and out of his comfort zone was a big thing but at that point in his career he felt he needed to do it.'

Mitchell faced his first big decision as chairman. The prodigal son gone, he looked at options in the dressing room. Two senior pros stood out.

'Lee Bradbury and Steve Fletcher took the team and they were two players I knew well from my time at both Bournemouth and Portsmouth,' says Lovell. 'They were likeable characters and important people in the dressing room so there wasn't much of a change after Ed left, really.

'Lee gave his all as a player and when he played right-back for Bournemouth late on in his career, that showed a lot about his character. But management was thrust upon them both without warning and stepping into Ed's shoes wasn't easy for Lee.

'But both of them had played for Ed so they knew how to carry on what he had started and they both had the respect of the players.'

Bradbury's start could not have been better. An opening draw at Rochdale was followed by three wins. Late goals from Fletcher, who had opted to keep playing alongside his assistant manager role, and Danny Hollands completed narrow victories over Plymouth and Swindon.

Hollands was on target again in a 3-0 win at home to Oldham on 5 March, as Bradbury celebrated ten unbeaten games at the helm. His loan signing from Fulham, Finnish striker Lauri Dalla Valle, scored on debut. This management lark was easy.

But a woeful March threatened to derail Bradbury's progress, as five defeats and two draws yielded just two points from seven games at a critical stage of the campaign. A thrilling 3-3 draw at Peterborough, that saw on-loan Tottenham defender Adam Smith bury a 90th-minute chance to deny the Posh all three points, also saw the return of Lovell.

'We'd gone ten games unbeaten after Lee took over,' he recalls, 'but my first game back was against Peterborough coming on as a sub when we were losing and in the middle of a seven-match slump. I came on for Danny Ings only one minute after Fletch had pulled it back to 3-2 with 18 minutes to play. Smithy scored in the last minute to make it 3-3. It was a massive result, but we lost the next two against Bristol Rovers and Tranmere.

'I started against Notts County a week later and we won, which again was crucial, before we drew 2-2 with Yeovil. I'd had a nightmare on the bus down there as one of my fillings fell out, but I remember it more because Shaun MacDonald scored for them in the 90th minute. It was a really horrible moment. We felt like we were only just clinging on to the play-offs.

'We needed something at home against Bristol Rovers, but we went 1-0 down after four minutes and then both sides had a man sent off, Danny Hollands for us and David McCracken for them. It got to the last ten minutes and we scored twice through Mathieu Baudry and Fletch. It was a huge win.'

Bradbury could have been forgiven for thinking luck was suddenly back on his side, but hope was sucked from within when Hartlepool goalkeeper Scott Flinders headed home a 90th-minute equaliser at Victoria Park the following Saturday.

The manager had secured the loan services of Manchester City prospect Donal McDermott in March, a talented, stocky midfielder with a golden touch but a penchant for boozy nights out by the seaside.

McDermott had put the Cherries 2-0 up in the North East, adding to Lovell's 29th-minute strike before Adam Boyd's penalty and Flinders's heroics halted the celebrations.

Lovell laughs, but more out of embarrassment. 'I'm surprised I was good for anything that day in Hartlepool,' he admits. 'The team had flown up such was the length of the journey and the importance of the game, but I went to the wrong airport and missed the flight!

'I ended up driving up with Steve Hard and Neil Moss, the goalkeeping coach, in the back of a van. It was horrendous and a long trip. The lads had been up there for almost a day by the time I got there!

'Luckily for us Leyton Orient lost to Tranmere so we were secure in sixth place by the time we played Rochdale at home on the last day, which was just as well as we lost and Orient beat Plymouth 4-1 away from home.'

For Bradbury and Fletcher it was job done. In the play-off positions when Howe departed for Turf Moor, the rookie duo had maintained the Cherries' equilibrium. The semi-final task ahead, though, was a monumental one.

Huddersfield Town, under the management of Newcastle's home-grown grafter Lee Clark, had spent big on the likes of Irish international Kevin Kilbane, winger Gary Roberts and striker Danny Ward. The likes of Jordan Rhodes, Danny Cadamarteri and young Arsenal loanee Benik Afobe added to their threat.

Lovell chuckles again. 'I remember looking at their team sheet as they were on massive money for that league. We spoke about that and some of them were on £10,000 a week – in League One. They had people like Kilbane and Benik Afobe and were really having a go at promotion. If anything, the play-offs was probably a failure for them.'

On a roasting hot south coast day, Ings saw his penalty saved by Ian Bennett after Kilbane had opened the scoring on 22 minutes. Only McDermott's stunning effort on the hour restored Bradbury's belief. A Wednesday second-leg date with destiny in West Yorkshire awaited.

'Going up there midweek I remember it was perfect conditions for football,' Lovell says, his eyes widening once more. 'The stadium is great and it was an amazing atmosphere. We knew it was our chance to make a big final at Old Trafford and we were up for it.

'We were confident and had a really strong team, the likes of Adam Smith, Jason Pearce, Rhoys Wiggins, Ingsy and Donal. Then there were people like Marc Pugh and Harry Arter on the bench, as well as Fletch, who could always turn a game.

'We knew we had the ability.'

A topsy-turvy battle ensued. Lee Peltier opened the scoring for the home side before Lovell stepped up to the penalty spot after Smith had been felled by Terriers captain Peter Clarke.

The laugh emerges once again. 'I hadn't taken a penalty since I'd missed one for Aberdeen, which probably still hasn't come down from the sky even now. But Ingsy had missed in the first leg so I picked up the ball and said I was taking it. I didn't mess about and just drilled it straight down the middle. As a striker it felt great and relaxed me into the game.

'I'd hardly played for a year and needed something to give me that adrenaline boost. I lasted until extra time which was the longest I'd played in years.'

As the atmosphere in West Yorkshire fizzed, popped and crackled, Ward levelled things up once again. Lovell, though, was rolling back the years, running at Clarke and Antony Kay with pace.

He leans in, arms as wide as his grin. 'The second goal gave me the feeling that was the reason I started playing in the first place. You can't beat that feeling.

'Rhoys crossed from the left wing and I skipped past one player, then went around the keeper but it was a tight angle on my left foot so I needed it to be a great strike and it was. The video of the goal makes my hairs stand up because of the reaction of the supporters at that end. When I'm rating goals in my career, the relevance of the game is the most important factor, so from that point of view the second one that night ranks very highly.'

That adrenaline was needed as the clock ticked into extra time, but the burden of heavy legs was eased when Ings made it 3-2 in the 104th minute. Lovell was spent, though, departing for Michael Symes as Bradbury opted for fresh legs in a bid to cling on. It was in vain.

Kay jumped highest above Pearce and Shaun Cooper, his towering header too much for goalkeeper Shwan Jalal. Pearce then saw red after clattering into Kilbane and Bradbury threw on Baudry for Ings as penalties loomed.

Exhaustion was replaced by agony as Bennett denied Feeney and Anton Robinson's spot-kick cannoned back off the crossbar. For Fletcher, it was too much and the tears flowed, leaving Bradbury to stitch together his broken squad.

Lovell's voice drifts as he gazes out of the window at the Dean Court pitch. 'That game had everything but it just wasn't to be for us,' he says quietly. 'We knew we should have beaten them and it was gutting.

'We knew it was the end of an era with some of the players. I was still living in Scotland so I drove back up there from

Huddersfield and the rest of the lads went back on the coach, so I didn't get the whole emotional experience of how people were feeling on the journey back to Bournemouth.

'I knew the goals had given me a chance of a new contract and I got another year which I was pleased with, but it was sad to see so many players from that team leave that summer.

'Rhoys went to Charlton and so did Danny Hollands, who was out of contract. Anton went to Huddersfield, Feeno went to Millwall, Pearcey went to Portsmouth and Ingsy went to join Ed at Burnley for £1.3m.

'They were all good friends too, as well as my team-mates, and had been around the club a long time in the case of some of them. It was a real shame.

'The core of the squad went and it seemed like every day someone else was leaving. The dressing room felt different and we were obviously weaker for losing those players.'

Lovell's thoughts, though, quickly turned to his own future, injuries of the past catching up with a man who had played only 13 games in 12 months. Inside the dressing room, despair was prevalent, fuelled by departing friends and memories of Galpharm Stadium agony.

The sadness in his eyes is not unexpected as he discusses the end.

'After the game at Huddersfield I had numb feet and didn't have a clue what it was. It was the end of the season so I went away on holiday and forgot about it, but when I came back for pre-season that summer I had it again and was getting numb feet all the time. It was really weird.

'It turned out I had Morton's neuroma in both feet, a condition where your nerves are trapped between your toes. I knew I had to have an operation on it and playing that pre-season was really uncomfortable. But I'd had four operations in a year and I couldn't face another.

'The Huddersfield game was the last game where I really felt okay but it was adrenaline getting me through and I knew I was finished that pre-season in 2011.

'We played Hereford in the Johnstone's Paint Trophy at the end of August and I was replaced on the hour by Jayden Stockley. I had been struggling. Within 20 minutes Jayden had scored twice and we were 3-1 up. I just sat there on the bench, and I hated being subbed anyway, watching Jayden and thinking, "I can't do this anymore."

'It was nothing against Jayden who is a fantastic player. I loved seeing him do well and still do today, but I was subbed because I wasn't good enough and here was a teenager barely past his GCSEs showing me how it was done.

'I was always really self-critical and this was the final straw for me. I was finished, physically and mentally.

'We went into training later that week and I told Lee Bradbury I was retiring. He tried to talk me round but I knew I was finished. People didn't realise how I was feeling and after the game against Hereford they were saying I'd played pretty well, but I hadn't played well in my mind. They weren't aware of how much I was struggling because they couldn't feel it.

'I couldn't let people down and I didn't want to be a burden on the team. I had to stop. I was never the most technical player. I was robust and quick and as soon as I started to lose those traits that was it for me – there wasn't a chance I could change position to stretch my career out, like Bradders had done, because I wasn't technically good enough.'

Lovell decamped back to Scotland in a bid to beat the blues, indulging in some casual scouting but distracted by a yearning for the camaraderie of the dressing room and the buzz of a matchday.

'I really enjoy the scouting and I was doing a bit here and there up in Scotland when I finished playing,' he says, his voice softening once more. 'But I was just doing it at the weekends really. The rest of the time I was doing nothing, just dwelling on the past.

'You don't appreciate how you get paid to stay fit when you're playing. You carry on eating after you've finished but lose that fitness and it affects you. It took me a long time to adjust. I missed the changing room and missed the lads.

'I didn't miss losing or that feeling of disappointment that cripples your brain. A last-minute goal or a missed chance. But I missed being around a club and being around my team-mates.

'I wasted a couple of years literally doing nothing after I finished and I knew I had to do something and stop feeling sorry for myself.'

That sibling bond was to emerge again, only this time it was judgement Howe required rather than goals.

'I spoke to Ed and he said I could scout for him but the only way it would happen was if I moved back to Bournemouth. So I did,' says Lovell, smiling.

'Ed surrounds himself with people he trusts – it's all about that with him. Everyone around him at the club either worked with him in the past or played with him and he trusts them and values their opinion.

'We're a small club despite being in the Premier League, particularly the scouting department, but he gets the best out of us the same as he does his players. I'm loving being back here with him.'

Back in 2011, though, Bradbury was taking stock of the task ahead. And the media were sharpening their pencils.

CHAPTER EIGHT

PAVING THE WAY
2011/12

DARKNESS still dominated, such was the hour. My phone had, as always, been placed on silent mode, yet the flashes of light indicating a call awoke me from my slumber.

Rubbing the remnants of sleep from my eyes, the name on the iPhone screen was 'Lee Bradbury'. It was Monday morning and that day's *Daily Echo* had hit the news-stands hours before. AFC Bournemouth's manager wanted to talk.

Ignoring his persistence with my mind still far from awake, I eventually picked up another call strolling down Bournemouth's Richmond Hill towards the office.

He was not happy.

Fast forward seven years and Bradbury is on the phone to a journalist again, this time a reporter from the *Portsmouth News*, as he walks with confident stride into Fareham's Holiday Inn. We've not seen each other or exchanged a word for almost six years, yet Bradbury's handshake is firm and his smile welcoming.

Now manager of non-league Havant & Waterlooville, Bradbury is bedecked in club tracksuit and pristine trainers. Fuller of figure, in the sense of looking well, than the man who endured a managerial baptism of fire in the dugout of Dean Court, Lee Bradbury is now a man comfortable in his own skin.

'Hello, Neil. Long time no see,' he smiles as we order some coffees. Happy he may be, but he is hungry, too, the pressure of management even at Havant's level denying him any kind of lunch.

'I'll have these, too,' he grins, placing a packet of biscuits on the counter.

With so much to discuss, starting at the beginning seems logical.

It would be harsh and unjust to describe Bradbury as some kind of footballing journeyman, yet the number of clubs on his CV makes that kind of pigeonholing a given.

With so much drama in the twilight of his career in Dorset, it would be easy to forget Bradbury was once a £3m player, albeit 'a £3m player who didn't perform', he laughs.

From the Isle of Wight and Cowes Sports to Manchester City in three years, Bradbury was toiling on the motorways between Hampshire and Essex when Kevin Bond came calling for some much-needed experience in 2007.

'I was at Southend and they spoke to me and said Bournemouth were interested in taking me on loan,' he says, leaning back in his seat, legs crossed. 'I'd travelled to Southend from Fareham for two years and it was taking its toll.

'It was getting to me a bit. We'd been promoted to the Championship and done really well so I was enjoying my football but I'd had enough of the travelling and wanted something closer to home.

'Kevin Bond spoke to Steve Tilson, who was my manager at the time, and I was definitely interested as it was nearer to where I lived.

'I came down and trained with the team at the ground on the Friday and signed on a month's loan. We went to Doncaster for my first game and we won 2-1. Jo Kuffour scored the winner from my flick-on and Bondy asked me after that game if I fancied signing permanently, which I did.

'It was a good move for me and it fitted with me quite well as I was close to the end of my career.'

A model pro with the fitness of players ten years his junior, Bradbury became a big face in Bond's dressing room, able to find a rare balance between commanding authority and respect yet remaining one of the lads.

In the stands, though, supporters being dragged through yet more off-field uncertainty took some convincing.

'Lee Bad-buy I think they called me,' he grins. Bond, though, was looking for more than just goals from his acquisition. The Cherries manager needed someone with a skin as thick as his, who could rally his charges and inspire them as a boardroom time bomb ticked apace.

'As a player you don't take too much notice of the off-field issues – we should probably have taken more notice really,' he reflects, stirring his latte. 'But at the time the biggest thing for me was playing games and the fact it was local to where I lived.

'We knew the club was struggling, of course, as we were reading about it in the newspaper, but you don't take much notice as a player and it certainly wasn't spoken about between me and Bondy.

'There were times when we weren't getting paid and we'd then get paid twice the following week, so it wasn't easy keeping it all together when most of us had families, but as a senior player it was down to me to keep positive and try to keep the younger lads focused. In fairness to the club, they kept to their word most of the time and we would eventually get paid.

'Jeff Mostyn and Steve Sly were doing a lot behind the scenes to help with that. They were good guys, still are, and put their hands in their pockets when it mattered to keep the club going

KASPRZAK TO REPLACE PEDERSEN – SEE PAGE 56

CHERRIES: THE BOND BRAVES

RED ARMY

>>CHERRIES BOW OUT: SEE PAGES 58, 59, 60 AND 61

Darren wants deal extension

NEIL Perrett
neil.perrett@bournemouthecho.co.uk

INFLUENTIAL skipper Darren Anderton has hinted he would consider extending his stay at Dean Court despite Cherries' relegation to the bottom flight.

The 36-year-old former England international is one of a host of players whose contract is due to expire at the end of June.

Anderton, who was sidelined for four months during mid-season, returned to help breathe new life into Cherries' unlikely bid to avoid the drop last month.

He told the Daily Echo: "It's been a real pleasure to play with the lads for the past few weeks. I'm just hopeful we can keep this group together and, if we do, then I think I'd like to be part of it. At the moment, I would have to say I would like to play again next season.

"The past few weeks have been amazing. For me, it's been a privilege to play with the lads. The team I left in November and the team I've been playing with recently is totally different.

"I think they have all grown as players and been outstanding. A lot of that has been down the fact that we haven't been able to bring in loan players so they have had to play and have improved as players.

"The improvement in some has been unbelievable and I'm sure a few of them will go on to have good careers so you can take positives from this season.

"It's all doom and gloom at the moment but you've got to be realistic. The 10-point deduction did for us in the end. I think everyone knew at the time that it made it a mission impossible and it has proved that way. But we gave it a good go."

Anderton again pulled the strings in midfield as Cherries enjoyed the lion's share of the first half at Brunton Park.

He added: "We're very

➤ Continued on page 59

The back page of the Daily Echo after the Cherries were relegated at Carlisle on the last day of the 2007/08 season.

Kevin Bond after the Cherries were relegated at Carlisle United on the last day of the 2007/08 season.

FOOTBALL: CHERRIES

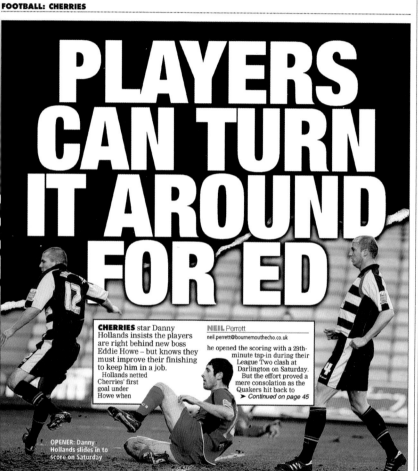

PLAYERS CAN TURN IT AROUND FOR ED

OPENER: Danny Hollands slides in to score on Saturday

CHERRIES star Danny Hollands insists the players are right behind new boss Eddie Howe – but knows they must improve their finishing to keep him in a job.

Hollands netted Cherries' first goal under Howe when

NEIL Perrett
neil.perrett@bournemouthecho.co.uk

he opened the scoring with a 29th-minute tap-in during their League Two clash at Darlington on Saturday.

But the effort proved a mere consolation as the Quakers hit back to

➤ Continued on page 45

SPEEDWAY

Adam: Barker deserved win

PHIL Chard
phil.chard@bournemouthecho.co.uk

ADAM Skornicki admitted the best man won after he had thrown away victory to Ben Barker in the New Year Classic at Poole yesterday.

The Polish champion, who helped Pirates lift the Elite League title last year, scorched to five spectacular qualifying heat wins and was leading the final on the last lap.

But he lifted coming off the back straight for the final time to allow Coventry's Barker to gain valuable ground.

Then the Brit dived up the inside of Skornicki to steal victory and first prize of £1,000 on the line.

Skornicki, who has left Poole Castle Cover to ride for his parent club Wolves this year, said: "I've got no complaints.

"Ben rode well for the whole meeting as well and he deserved his success because he passed me on the last corner.

"It was my mistake. I just lost my racing line coming off the pits bend.

"My arms were a bit tired. I just slowed down a bit and it cost me first place. I'm really happy with five wins. It's just a shame I didn't get that second place in my first race rather than in the last one!"

Skornicki added: "I really enjoyed coming back to Poole and winning five races.

"It was really great racing for Pirates last season and I want to say thank you again to all my friends and sponsors here who made my stay so enjoyable.

"I want to tell the promoters and fans it was a great honour for me to ride for Poole because I'd always wanted to do that since I first rode in England.

"I loved racing here today. The track was nice and slick, but it produced some great racing.

"I just wish Poole the best of luck in 2009 and hope they have a great season like we did last year."

>>FULL NEW YEAR CLASSIC REPORT ON PAGES 42-43

SPORTS DESK – TEL: 01202 411290 FAX: 01202
51246 E-MAIL: SPORT@BOURNEMOUTHECHO.CO.UK

Published by Newsquest (Southern), a Gannett company, from its offices at Richmond Hill, Bournemouth, BH2 6HH (tel: 01202 554601) and printed at 160 Brook Lane, Redbridge, Southampton, SO16 9AX. Registered at the Post Office as a newspaper. (Price: Mon-Fri 40p; Sat 60p). Monday January 5 2009.

ISSN 1368-3837

9 771368 383517

02>

The back page of the Daily Echo after the Cherries lost at Darlington in Eddie Howe's first game as manager in January 2009.

Eddie Howe after tasting defeat in his first game as manager at Darlington in January 2009.

Eddie Howe with Alastair Saverimutto and Adam Murry during the press conference confirming his appointment as manager in January 2009.

SPORT

ditorial: 01202 554601   bournemouthecho.co.uk/sport   **MONDAY APRIL 20, 2009**

FANCY A FLUTTER? RACING IS ON PAGE 46

BACK EDDIE'S BOYS

ALMOST THERE!

NEIL Perrett
neil.perrett@bournemouthecho.co.uk

EDDIE Howe steered Cherries to within touching distance of Football League safety and then questioned the timing of a takeover statement issued by club owner Paul Baker.

Howe and assistant Jason Tindall both expressed their displeasure after Baker had gone public just 48 hours ahead

➤ Continued on Page 53

GOLF

Lee is off the mark on Tour

ANDY Goodall
andy.goodall@bournemouthecho.co.uk

DORSET'S Lee James is up and running after a top-10 finish in the Tusker Kenya Open at the Muthaiga Golf Club in Nairobi yesterday.

The Parkstone-based touring professional is 20th on the European Challenge Tour money list following the first two events.

After a fruitless trip to Colombia last month, James was relieved to make his mark on the order of merit.

"I missed the cut in Colombia and secured a top 10 here, so it's going in the right direction," said James who carded rounds of 70, 68, 71 and 73.

He finished in a share of 10th place on two-under-par to earn 3,456 Euros – 11 shots behind runaway winner Gary Boyd.

Lee James

James struggled with his putter on the final day as he dropped four shots to par while collecting just two birdies.

"It was a weekend of mixed fortunes on the greens," admitted James. "I played a bit scrappy on Saturday but putted brilliantly for a level par round.

"Today I hit more greens in regulation than at any other time this week and took 33 putts.

"Despite missing so many chances on the final day, I'm happy with the way things are going so early in the season."

Next port of call for the Challenge Tour and James is the Moroccan Classic at the El Jadida Royal Golf and Spa on April 30-May 3.

Safety within Cherries' grasp as Howe hits out at Baker's timing

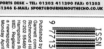
PORTS DESK - TEL: 01202 411290 FAX: 01202
1246 E-MAIL: SPORT@BOURNEMOUTHECHO.CO.UK

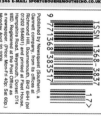
ISSN 1368-3837
9 771368 383517
17>

Published by Newsquest (Southern), a Gannett company, from its offices at Richmond Hill, Bournemouth, BH2 6HH (tel 01202 554601) and printed at Fleet House, Hampshire Road, Poole, Dorset BH17 0HD. Registered at the Post Office as a newspaper. (Price: Mon-Fri 40p: Sat 60p.) Monday April 20, 2009.

The back page of the Daily Echo *after the Cherries won at Chester in April 2009 – a key win on their way to the Greatest Escape.*

Shaun Cooper, Liam Feeney
and Anton Robinson celebrate
Robinson's goal in the 2-0 win at
Chester in April 2009.

Former Cherries owner Paul Baker watches the game
against Grimsby in 2009 that saw the club preserve its
Football League status.

Brett Pitman is mobbed at Dean Court after the 2-1 win over Grimsby in 2009 completed the
Greatest Escape.

Lee Bradbury celebrates the win over Grimsby in 2009 that completed the Greatest Escape.

Steve Fletcher celebrates his goal against Grimsby in 2009 that secured the Cherries' Football League status.

Steve Fletcher turns and fires home his iconic goal against Grimsby in 2009.

Dressing room celebrations after the win over Grimsby in 2009.

Brett Pitman wheels away after his goal against Burton at the Pirelli Stadium in 2010 helped secure promotion from League Two.

Alan Connell celebrates after his goal against Burton at the Pirelli Stadium in 2010 helped secure promotion from League Two.

The players burst from the dugout at Burton Albion after securing promotion to League One in 2010.

Jeff Mostyn after promotion to League One was sealed at Burton Albion in 2010.

Players and fans celebrate as one as promotion to League One was secured at Burton Albion in 2010.

Eddie Howe addresses the media, as Eddie Mitchell looks on, after deciding to reject approaches from Charlton and Crystal Palace in January 2011. Weeks later, he left to join Burnley.

Lee Bradbury with Eddie Mitchell at a press conference to confirm his appointment as manager in January 2011.

Lee Bradbury and Huddersfield boss Lee Clark before the 2011 play-off semi-final second leg penalty shoot-out at the Galpharm Stadium.

Steve Lovell celebrates his penalty during the League One play-off semi-final second leg against Huddersfield in 2011.

Agony for Steve Fletcher as the Cherries lose the 2011 League One play-off semi-final on penalties at Huddersfield.

Eddie Howe talking to the media after he rejoined the Cherries as manager in October 2012.

Eddie Howe and Jason Tindall are introduced to the crowd in October 2012 after their return to Bournemouth from Burnley.

Marc Pugh celebrates his goal in Howe's first game back in charge, against Leyton Orient in October 2012.

Celebrations after promotion to the Championship was sealed at home to Carlisle United in 2013.

The bus tour around Bournemouth after the Cherries secured promotion to the Championship for only the second time in the club's history.

Eddie Howe after the Cherries were promoted to the Premier League at home to Bolton in 2015.

Adam Smith sprays the Champagne after promotion to the Premier League was sealed against Bolton in 2015.

The players celebrate on the pitch after the win over Bolton in 2015 secured Premier League promotion.

Jeff Mostyn savours Premier League promotion following the win over Bolton in 2015.

Matt Ritchie celebrates his goal against Bolton in the Premier League promotion game of 2015.

Harry Arter is held aloft by jubilant supporters following promotion to the Premier League in 2015.

The Cherries squad with the Championship winners' trophy at Charlton Athletic on the final day of the 2014/15 season.

Matt Ritchie and Steve Cook (obscured) with the Championship trophy at the Valley in 2015.

Harry Arter celebrates his goal in the win at Charlton on the final day of the 2014/15 campaign.

Matt Ritchie after scoring against Charlton on the final day of the 2014/15 season.

Ryan Fraser, Yann Kermorgant and Brett Pitman charge from the dugout as the final whistle sounds at the Valley in 2015.

Captain Tommy Elphick holds aloft the Championship trophy at the Valley in 2015.

Eddie Howe with the Championship trophy following the win over Charlton on the final day of the season in 2015.

through the administration in 2008. The club owes those two a huge debt of gratitude.

'Jeff is an upbeat person and very hands on. He wouldn't let things fester and would always come and talk to the players and let them know what was going on. Steve was at every game, too, and their presence allowed us to focus on what we were doing on the pitch. It was a good strategy at that stage.

'We'd worked so hard to stay up that season in 2008/09 and what I remember about that group was the honesty. It was a superb group of players who went out socially and did a lot together and worked hard for each other on the pitch.

'When you are staring into the face of adversity, it pulls people together and that was what happened that season. We had nothing, really. We were training on the park opposite the stadium, which we called Dog Shit Park, and it brought us together. Nothing was too big for us to get over that year, but really we were right up against it. Seventeen points adrift before we'd even started meant nobody gave us a prayer and we had a rough start.

'The rumours went around, of course, so we were aware that Jimmy Quinn was possibly coming in. It was tough because I liked Kevin Bond and had a good relationship with him as a senior player. I learned a lot from that period as someone who had ambitions to go on to coach and manage. When the chips are down, you learn about yourself and the people around you.

'Kevin had his hands tied, there is no doubt about that. When Jimmy came in I was pretty pleased, despite losing Bondy, because Jim was a centre-forward like me, but we didn't start well under him and it unravelled from there.

'It was difficult for him. One good thing he did do was bring in Jason Tindall as his assistant as a lot of the players already knew him. He was a breath of fresh air and very upbeat, which is probably partly why he has done so well with Eddie Howe since.

'He was great around the lads and that gave us a lift when he came in, but at that stage I think some of the lads had accepted that we were going down. Minus 17 points does funny things to you and we knew how tough it was going to be before we'd even kicked a ball that season.

'It was looking bleak under Jimmy, but there was nothing he could do and not many managers would have been able to turn that situation around.'

Howe's New Year's Eve appointment came as no surprise to Bradbury, who had witnessed the young coach's blossoming reputation under the tutelage of Bond. Younger than Bradbury and with only a fraction of the playing experience, the older man welcomed the young pretender into the fold in the most testing of circumstances.

'Eddie was younger than me when he took the job,' he smiles. 'I played with him at Portsmouth so I knew he was unassuming but a deep thinker and someone who doesn't say a lot. What he does say, though, is worth listening to.

'He doesn't spout off and is a strategic thinker. The players respected that straight away as well as how thorough he was. He was very big on timings with regard to coaches, dinners and things like that – a real perfectionist.

'But he was like that as a player, too, and but for the horrendous injuries he had, he would have played consistently in the Championship without a doubt.

'He carried those traits into management and created a strong mentality within the players that season and a togetherness. For a young manager to do that in his first season was experience beyond his years and that's because of the way he thought and planned. He stuck to his strategy and it worked, both when we stayed up with the points deduction in 2009 and when we got promoted to League One with next to no players in the squad a year later.'

Bradbury's roster of illustrious team-mates is almost as long as the list of clubs on his CV: the likes of Paul Dickov, Shaun Goater, Uwe Rosler, Clinton Morrison, Marcus Bent, Attilio Lombardo, Justin Edinburgh, Steve Claridge, Gary O'Neil and Guy Wittingham. Yet Howe's strategy was to bring in young, hungry yet untried youngsters like Liam Feeney and Anton Robinson from clubs like Salisbury and Weymouth to join Marvin Bartley and Mark Molesley who had already made the step up from non-league. They were names that were to serve Bradbury well when, after that intense spell of speculation, the Miracle Man left for Burnley in January 2011.

Bradbury shuffles in his seat, adjusting his position.

'I was 35 so I'd seen it all before, managers coming and going, and it was no surprise that clubs were looking at Eddie as he'd achieved a miracle in keeping us up and then getting us promoted a year later.

'There was a lot of speculation flying around after he went to Burnley about who the board was going to bring in.

'In Eddie's final game at Colchester in January 2011, I played right midfield and got dragged at half-time so I was thinking it might be my last game if someone new came in.

'But in another way I was hoping it was the end of my playing days because I really wanted a shot at being the manager. I wanted the job and I knew that as soon as I knew Eddie was going.

'I had 18 months left on my contract and I was doing okay, but I was clinging on really because I'd lost what pace I had and playing at right-back in League One, you come up against some pretty quick wingers.

'I was already toying with the idea of what I was going to do at the end of that season. I didn't want to cost the team or my team-mates and the job came up at the right time for me.

'Eddie Mitchell's son Tom and his mate Jamie Gleeson from Dorchester Town were training with us at the time and a few conversations I had with Tom made me think his dad was possibly looking to fill the position from within.

'I got the phone call on a Sunday and myself and Steve Fletcher went in to see Eddie Mitchell. He asked if we were interested in taking over and we both were, although Fletch wanted to carry on playing. He felt he still had a lot to offer.

'Eddie asked me about my situation and I just said, "Eddie, I'll hang them up now!"

'I wanted the chance to manage a good club and this was it. You can go your entire career and never have an opportunity to manage a League One club and it was being offered to me.

'I'd played for 18 years but I knew I'd have no regrets finishing. I felt I was coming to the end anyway although I think getting into management quickly helped me avoid the difficulties most players face when they hang up their boots. When you go from being a player to the manager overnight, it has positives and negatives.

'I knew the players, I knew who went out and who didn't, I knew their strengths and weaknesses and what was needed to get the best out of them.

'But the difficulty lies in going from being their mate to their manager. It's a real balance between being approachable but also being a bit standoffish. I think that probably took me six or seven months to truly grasp, but it was all about learning and I don't regret taking it.'

A ten-game unbeaten start would have sparked both delight and fear in the new manager. Gritty and bullish on the pitch, the dugout still felt alien to Bradbury, as did the pre- and post-match media briefings with a press pack fully expecting the rookie to be washed away in the wake of the Miracle Man's achievements.

A poor spring, which saw just one win between 5 March and 9 April, left cracks in the foundations laid by Howe and increased the pressure Bradbury was already putting on himself. A play-off place, where Howe had left his team, was a must. It was secured, but only with minimal time to spare.

'There was pressure because Eddie and Jason had done superbly to get us where we were and I needed to carry that on,' he says, adjusting his position once more.

'I didn't change much at the start because everything was in place. The lads were playing well so it was a case of keeping them at it and keeping the confidence levels high. I slowly put my own ideas into the mix and we managed to do enough to stay in the play-offs with a draw at Hartlepool in the penultimate game of the season, which was a real achievement.'

Job done? Not in the eyes of Bradbury. Before the tape rolled and the biscuits were opened, he was keen to talk about two subjects requiring closure. The first? Huddersfield away, the League One play-off semi-final second leg on 11 May 2011. Bradbury's position shifts again, not through discomfort, but as if to make his point all the more poignant. His elbows rest on his knees and he leans forward.

'The feeling after the first leg in the dressing room was a bit downbeat,' he admits.

'When Danny Ings missed the penalty it was perfectly natural for us to wonder if it was going to be our time, because I'd never seen Ingsy miss a penalty before!

'Things like that have a habit of cropping up when you don't want them to. I had a lad at Havant who scored 20 penalties in a row and then missed one to get us in the play-offs. It's the only one he's ever missed.

'We were going into an away leg on level terms and even though we'd performed well away from home that season and the pressure would be on them in front of 20,000, we felt we should have won the first leg.

'It was an incredible atmosphere at their place for the second leg as they'd given out clappers and rattles to everyone so the noise was deafening. Funnily enough I was on a course with Lee Clark, their manager that day, recently. We didn't get a chance to talk properly but I would have liked to have done as I hadn't seen him since that game.

'When it went to penalties he came over, shook my hand and said "Lee, you and your team have been brilliant. Whatever happens, you've been amazing." And then he said, "I can't watch. Good luck," and went inside to his office! I couldn't believe it, but then started to wonder if I should follow him! But there was no way I could sit inside. I'd drive myself crazy. Every cheer I would have been thinking, "Was that us or them?"

'The disappointing thing for me that night was when we were about to toss the coin for which end the penalties would be taken at, the referee had already decided they were going to be taken at the Huddersfield end. I asked why and he said it was because some Huddersfield fans had got into the Bournemouth end.

'It was completely unfair. There were 8,000 fans behind that goal making a din when my lads were taking their kicks and you could hear a pin drop when they took theirs.

'We missed two penalties and lost. If it had been at the other end, would it have made a difference? I think it would. It just wasn't fair and felt a bit unjust.

'Huddersfield had some wonderful players like Kevin Kilbane and Danny Ward but we more than held our own over the two legs. I'm not blaming Jason Pearce because he was unbelievable for me, but he got sent off in extra time and I really believe if we'd kept 11 players on the pitch we would have won the game. It was late on, but if we had kept him on I think we would have won.

'I've watched the incident back loads of times and I agree with Pearcey that it wasn't a sending-off. Kilbane used all his experience and Pearcey was so committed. He only knows one way and that is 100 per cent. He was amazing for me and the football club – an absolute warrior.

'I'd been through a play-off defeat on penalties for Birmingham against Watford as a player in 1999 but that was 7-6! The goalkeeper even took one that night – it was crazy.

'Shoot-outs are nerve-racking but as a player you just concentrate on your penalty, putting it away and supporting everyone else. As a manager there is nothing you can do beyond picking the right players to take the kicks. Would I have done anything differently that night against Huddersfield? I would, yes. But I won't say what I would have done. You live and learn.

'At the time, I felt I put my performers up – the lads who weren't going to be put off by 8,000 screaming Yorkshiremen behind the goal. We did get affected by that, though, although the two lads who missed, Liam Feeney and Anton Robinson, had been great for me. It just didn't happen for us.'

Like Lovell, Bradbury knew the end of an era was approaching that night at the Galpharm and the first chinks in the armour of his relationship with Mitchell began to show during a summer of sales.

'My hands were tied,' says Bradbury, the pace of his words more abrupt. 'Eddie Mitchell was telling me we had to sell the players just to keep the club afloat. I get that as a bigger picture but from my point of view we'd just reached the play-offs and had a superb bunch of players. I wanted to keep them together to have another go at it, but once two or three left, the others were all thinking, "I don't want to be left here now," and they started looking for moves.

'We ended up losing eight from the starting line-up against Huddersfield. It was unbelievable and very frustrating from my point of view. I was trying my best to keep hold of them but ultimately if the chairman is telling me to sell them then I have to do that if I want to keep my job.

'Ingsy was the one that was the easiest really as in terms of potential he was head and shoulders above anyone else. It was clear he was going to go on to great things. I remember when Eddie Howe brought him into first-team training from the youth set-up and the biggest compliment I can pay him is that he made senior pros stand up and go, "Who's that? He's rapid."

'We were doing one-versus-one in training and me, Jason Pearce and Warren Cummings all said we didn't fancy going up against Ingsy. We were pushing each other to the front of the queue, because he was that good. He runs with the ball so close to him and he'd entice you to have a nibble but by the time you'd got your head back up he was gone. He was incredible.

'You can't stand in a kid's way if he has the chance to go to a Championship club like Burnley as Ingsy did, where he'd earn five or ten times as much as he was on at Bournemouth.

'The tough thing for me to take was with the ones who were offered similar terms at clubs in League One or the Championship. People like Ingsy and Rhoys Wiggins had the chance to earn good money at big clubs like Burnley and Charlton – you can't hold them back.

'The most disappointing one was Marvin Bartley. I didn't want to lose him because he was a real engine in the midfield and broke the play up.

'When you lose that energy from the middle of the park you are losing a massive part of your team and the way the transfer was done, on then off then on again, it all got a bit nasty in the end. I know Marv just wanted to be at the best level he could because we'd had conversations when I was still playing. Of course back then I was telling him to look to get on, so it fell on deaf ears when I was telling him the total opposite as a manager.

'That transfer wasn't very helpful for me and the way it was done wasn't right. Marv was in the car on his way up to Burnley when I tried to talk him into staying, so draw your own conclusions from that.

'But I don't hold it against either Eddie Howe or Marv – they both wanted the best for themselves and Burnley and you can't blame them for that.'

Bradbury moved on quickly. But a poor start to the 2011/12 season, that saw five defeats from the first seven games, including a 3-0 humbling to Danny Hollands's and Wiggins's Charlton on the opening day, gave the supporters little hope in the manager's new recruits.

Goalkeeper Daryl Flahavan and centre-half Adam Barrett brought wily experience to Bradbury's ranks, while Swansea midfielder Shaun MacDonald and loanees Scott Malone (Wolves) and Nathan Byrne (Tottenham) showed Bradbury was already working with an eye on the future.

Results, though, were up and down and uninspiring. Unable to string together more than three successive wins before Christmas, the pressure on Bradbury was mounting in the boardroom despite six-game unbeaten runs coming both before and immediately after the festivities.

Chairman Mitchell, meanwhile, added fuel to the fire by telling fans disgruntled by the club's summer sales spree to "go and support Southampton" if they were unhappy. The chairman then approached supporters on the pitch after the 3-0 home defeat to Chesterfield in September, shouting into a microphone at "the lad in the leather jacket whose eyes seem to be popping out of his head". The newspapers had a field day.

An active January transfer window, though, deflected attention away from Mitchell and on to his rookie manager, who spent big on some names now synonymous with success.

'January was massive and to be fair to Eddie Mitchell, he backed me in the transfer window and I signed players that are still at the club now playing in the Premier League,' reflects Bradbury, his tone restored. 'It makes me really proud to see Simon Francis, Steve Cook and Charlie Daniels playing in that league. I knew Franno from my time at Southend and I spoke to Chris Powell at Charlton to find out why he wasn't playing there.

'Chris said he had fallen out of favour and the Charlton fans were on his back. It got pretty nasty. I asked how much they wanted for him and I can tell you now it wasn't anywhere near the figure that was reported in some papers after I signed him. It was less than £100,000.

'He was quick and great on the ball and cruises through games. All I needed to do was get him confident and I did.

'I played a lot against Charlie Daniels and he came along at a time when the game was really changing for full-backs – they were really attacking and overlapping and Charlie is great at that. His partnership with Marc Pugh was unbelievable and he is a great defender, too. He was a good buy at £175,000. He's worth at least £15m now.

'We were also looking for a centre-half who could play a bit, but who was also good in the air and Des Taylor, who was scouting for us at the time, flagged up this kid at Brighton called Steve Cook.

'I went down to watch him at Lancing and within 20 minutes I knew he was a bit of me. He was cool, calm and aggressive when he needed to be but had a bit of growing up to do. I knew he'd be a great player with a lot of games behind him and that's proven to be the case.

'Cookie had been out on loan a lot and playing games in front of big crowds for us was the making of him. It made him grow up – he was already a good footballer, but he needed to man up and he did.

'I paid £500,000 for Matt Tubbs that January, not the £800,000 you reported in the *Echo* which is still on Wikipedia even now! We needed someone to replace Ingsy and Matt was local and hungry to get back into the professional game. I knew if we could give him chances he would bury them.

'He's with me now at Havant and has scored eight in eight games – he's still doing it now, but it just didn't happen for him and the fans were on my back because of the reported transfer fee.

'If Tubbsy had got off to a better start at Bournemouth I still say he would have been a success. He had a double hernia, though, and being out for a period of time affected him. He needed to play, given the money I spent on him, but he just wasn't available. It happens and you can't put your finger on why it didn't work for him as he has done well everywhere else he's been.

'It's a transfer I look back on a lot and it could have been the best thing I did, but it didn't work out.

'Donal McDermott was a strange one. He'd been in on loan the previous season and I signed him permanently that January. He had all the ability in the world and he could do things at that level that other players couldn't. He was a maverick and a very effective player when he was on it, but he was a very complex character as well. It was a big challenge to contain him and keep him focused. It was a testing time.

'We went away to Oldham, which turned out to be my last game as I was sacked a day later, and he wasn't involved as he was injured. He'd got into some trouble back in Bournemouth and been arrested for drink-driving on the morning of the game.

'Eddie Mitchell phoned me up while I was up there and was bleating on about everything Donal had been up to. But what could I do? I was in Oldham and he was 23 years old – I couldn't babysit him any more than I already was.

'Donal will look back on his career, if he isn't already, and have some regrets. He had real talent on the pitch but couldn't handle himself off it. He was at Manchester City as a kid and you wonder why they let him go? It couldn't have been for football reasons because he had the lot.

'I liked 85 per cent of him as a character but the rest of him was a real challenge.'

Pressure from the stands wasn't the only thing on Bradbury's mind as January and February ticked into March and April. The press, tired of his standoffish soundbites and refusal to provide off-the-record briefings during the January window, began to turn on him and Mitchell.

With the chairman's Chesterfield antics wrapping the fish and chips, Mitchell blotted his copy book once more when he entered the dressing room at half-time with the Cherries 1-0 behind to MK Dons in February.

Bradbury's sacred ground had been soiled – and not just by his chairman, who had seen fit to invite several delegates, including a new investor's wife, inside to address the players.

A demoralising defeat at Sheffield Wednesday on 10 March, where the Cherries were 3-0 behind inside 11 minutes, saw Bradbury let his guard slip post-match when he declared his side had 'been the better team for the opening two minutes'.

The *Daily Echo* had a field day, the word 'IMMATURE' plastered in 200pt across Monday's back page in homage to Bradbury's post-match faux pas. Monday morning's phone call was as expected as it was awkward.

A 1-1 draw at home to Carlisle was followed by a clash against Brentford the following Tuesday evening.

Bradbury had had enough, our phone conversation not appeasing the man who could hear the board sharpening their knives.

Just hours before kick-off against the Bees, the club's media manager Max Fitzgerald dropped a bombshell via email. The paper, its photographers and sports writers were no longer welcome at Dean Court, effective immediately.

With pages to fill and having witnessed press blackouts at the likes of the *Portsmouth News* and *Newcastle Chronicle*, the paper turned the tables and banned the club from the newspaper in retaliation.

Its editorial, on the pages that should have been reporting a 1-0 win against the Londoners, told Mitchell: 'Give our advertising representatives a call, because the days of editorial backing for your football club are over until such time as you come to terms with what "free press" means.'

It is this, issue number two, that Bradbury wishes to clear up.

'The *Echo* ban came from board level and I was told it was happening. It was not my decision,' he says sternly.

'It actually put me on the back foot right away as we weren't doing too well at the time. I thought, "This could be the death of me."

'Now I wonder whether the board did it to achieve exactly that and move me on, sign my death warrant. Who knows? I did feel at the time Eddie Mitchell was behind me. He backed me in the transfer market after all the sales.

'But I asked why the club needed to ban the paper because I knew the only person who would get stick for it would be me. I was the one that the reporters had a relationship with, not the board.

'I told the reporter Neil Perrett at the time that it wasn't my doing and it really wasn't. But the manager can't always get involved in decision-making behind the scenes and that was one of those occasions.

'The Sheffield Wednesday comment was a slip and the paper made a real meal of it. I was young and naive in the job and I wouldn't say things like that now but at the time it caused me a lot of problems. I was angry about it at the time, but I could have managed the situation and relationship with the paper better than I did.

'One of the most important relationships you have as a manager is with the press. If you can keep the press happy, you get an easier ride. If you don't then they can turn on you and then you're out of a job.

'If I was still there now, I'd have a better relationship with the *Echo* boys. I'd have them in for a cup of tea, let them have some off-the-record stuff, tip them off. I'd be more open and trusting, as I am with the guy at the *Portsmouth News* now. You live and learn.'

The paper stuck by its decision to halt all coverage, looking on from watching distance as Bradbury neared the end. The trip to Oldham followed the win over Brentford, but those three points meant little to the beaten and battered manager. He knew what was coming.

'A few weeks before I was sacked, I'd said to Russ Wilcox, my assistant, that I felt like we were in a bit of trouble. He didn't feel like that as we'd only lost a couple but I just had a feeling. People around the club who were normally close to me and wanted to be around me were suddenly taking cover. Eddie Mitchell had a few relatives at the club at that time and it was just a feeling I had.

'By the time we got to the Oldham game, we'd won one in eight and lost five of those. I said to Russ that we needed to win at Oldham. He asked if I knew something he didn't and I didn't – I just felt if we didn't win up there, that was curtains for me.

'We were mid-table, but I thought we needed a result. We lost 1-0 and had a blatant penalty turned down in the 92nd minute and I went up to the referee Robert Madley after the game and said, "You've just cost me my job."

'I'd had the phone call about Donal's antics as well and I just felt like the club was weakening my hand. On the Sunday I took a call from Eddie Mitchell and he said the club was going to make some changes by getting rid of my support staff and bringing in Paul Groves and Shaun Brooks from the youth team as joint managers alongside me.

'I'd brought in my own staff and I felt an allegiance to them. Ryan Garry was one of them and he'd not long retired from playing. I told the chairman that I didn't want to work with Paul and Shaun and he said if I didn't then he would sack me.

'I wasn't prepared to work with them. I'd felt that during the last few months I was in charge, Paul and Shaun hadn't helped my situation. I wanted people around me that I could trust and I didn't know if I could trust them.

'They were running the youth team at the time but I'd taken the team to Notts County in September of 2011 and looked up to see Paul Groves sitting next to Eddie Mitchell in the stand. I phoned him afterwards and asked him what was going on. He just said he had come along to "look at things" but I was the manager and I got a bit defensive about it.

'From there I felt uneasy about them being involved at the club but was told if I didn't comply with what the club wanted then I would lose my job. I got the League Managers' Association involved as I had three years left on my contract, but Eddie came out and said that we had "parted company by mutual consent". Who walks away from a three-year contract? Nobody!

'I'm a fair guy but I'm not a fool and eventually we settled.

'Looking back, things like the dressing room incident against MK Dons were character building I suppose. It was unusual but those things were experiences I wouldn't change.

'One thing I would say about Eddie is that he is a very passionate guy and wanted the best for the football club. He put his hand in his pocket and was passionate, but that passion overflowed at times and he couldn't control it.

'I was doing an interview after a game once and he came down from his box and put his arm around me, saying, "This boy is great, he's going to get us out of trouble," while the cameras were rolling. It was demoralising for me because I felt like a little kid. Support me behind the scenes, not like that.

'Things bubbled over with Eddie at times, like when he went on the pitch at home to Chesterfield. If you're going to do those things, you can't do it like that on the pitch. I'd never seen anything like it and I'm sure Eddie regrets it now.

'I was saddened by the whole situation regarding my sacking because I'd had good times at the club as a player and a manager early on. I always look for Bournemouth's results as the club was a big part of me and I still speak to Simon Francis and Eddie Howe has been great with me. If I have ever rung him, he has always answered. I feel a lot of affinity for the club and Jeff Mostyn has welcomed me in since, too.

'I had great times there and I have no regrets.'

With Groves and Brooks installed as permanent managers and the club and *Echo* still at loggerheads, Mitchell's new managerial duo mustered just one win from six before relations with the local paper eased ahead of the trip to Scunthorpe on 28 April. A season most were pleased to see the back of saw the Cherries finish 11th in League One, with a 1-0 win over Preston closing the door on one of the most tumultuous years in the club's history.

Behind the scenes, though, Mitchell had quietly been wooing his new investor. In October, as Jaffer had done with Mostyn some six years earlier, Russian petrochemicals magnate Maxim Demin was persuaded to purchase Mostyn's 50% stake in the club. It was to be a masterstroke from Mitchell and, prior to stepping down as chairman just 12 months later in 2013, he had one more up his sleeve.

CHAPTER NINE

THE MIRACLE MAN RETURNS
2012/13

S HWAN Jalal sat stock still inside the home dressing room at Dean Court, eyes down, trying to process everything. The silence was deafening. Outside, the press jostled for position as Eddie Howe, alongside chairman Eddie Mitchell and other board members, stood on the stairwell of the stadium's reception deep in conversation.

This was it. Was he staying or was he going? I telephoned one of the board members on the stairs for a last-ditch steer and on the hunt for an 11th-hour exclusive. I watched through the glass as he looked at his phone, deciding whether or not to answer.

He glanced out through the window and picked up, staring at me through the glass.

'Don't say anything,' the voice demanded. 'It's good news. That's all I can say.' He hung up, allowing me time to update the *Daily Echo*'s live blog entitled 'The Eddie Howe Saga – Day Two'.

What a saga it had been, even by the Cherries' standards circa 2008–11.

Sure enough, though, Howe came out alongside Mitchell moments later and confirmed he was, indeed, remaining as manager, rejecting overtures from both Crystal Palace and Charlton Athletic.

The end of a manic 48 hours had reached an unlikely conclusion, both for the gathered media and Howe's players inside the dressing room.

Seven years on, Jalal pulls into Macclesfield Town's pothole-ridden car park and greets me with a familiar handshake.

The Silkmen Cafe outside the National League ground is closed for Easter, but the bar inside is empty so we settle there to talk.

The goalkeeper chuckles when recalling 11 January 2011 although at the time he wasn't sure whether to laugh or cry.

'We were waiting downstairs in the home dressing room,' he recalls. 'We'd been called in to the stadium as all the media were camped outside and they didn't want any of us talking.

'We all thought Eddie was gone but then we heard a kerfuffle outside and he came in and told us he was staying.

'I spoke to Des Taylor, who was scouting for us, and he told me Eddie had changed his mind on the staircase before he went outside to speak to the media. He said he couldn't leave us. I couldn't believe it as I was convinced he was going – we all were.'

Howe's stock had been soaring. The Greatest Escape in 2009 and League Two promotion with a wafer-thin squad a year later had alerted the vultures. Who was this young guy at Bournemouth achieving miracles?

'I first spoke to Eddie about some rumours of him leaving before we'd been promoted to League One in 2010,' says Jalal, his voice rising over the din of the Moss Rose bar's refrigeration unit. 'My contract was up that summer and one of the things I wanted clarity on was Eddie's future.

'Peterborough were said to be keen on taking him at that point and I'd heard that directly as they were my old club.

'But he told me he wasn't going anywhere so I signed the contract and then we hit the ground running in League One in 2010.

'We lost 1-0 on the first day at Charlton but we took enough from that game to know we were going to be able to compete. We went to Peterborough the following week and hammered them 5-1 and played Sheffield Wednesday off the park at Hillsborough in October even though we only managed a draw. People then really started to sit up and ask who this Eddie Howe guy was and we started to hear whispers as players.

'I'd fractured my eye socket at Leyton Orient after Marvin Bartley collided with me at a set piece so I missed a few games in November and December that year and when you are on the sidelines you hear murmurings in the treatment room. We'd heard Crystal Palace were keen and the players started talking. We were convinced he would go so then the talk turned to which of us he would take with him!

'We were doing well in the league but we weren't out of the woods at all off the field and we knew he would probably outgrow the club at some point.

'After he decided he was staying it calmed down for a few days, but then the rumours started up again. We battered Plymouth 3-0 at home on 8 January, but the whispers wouldn't go away and even the *Echo* ran a piece saying, "Eddie, how can you leave after that?" The noises started coming out of Burnley that he was going to go and we had to go to Colchester on the Friday night.

'He called us in after our last training session before that game and we could see he was breaking up. He told us it was his last game. I was devastated and it was no surprise we lost the game 2-1.

'He pulled me aside and thanked me for everything and said if I ever needed anything I knew where he was, but it was a tough one for us all to take.

'Of course, as most managers do, they then take a few players with them and we were convinced Marc Pugh would be the one Eddie wanted and then probably Jason Pearce. But he went for Marv and Danny Ings and that was really the start of all the sales that followed that summer after we lost in the play-off semi-finals to Huddersfield.'

For Jalal, Howe's departure sparked one of the toughest periods of his career. Having signed on the proviso that his manager would remain, the keeper saw Bradbury, his closest ally in the Dean Court dressing room, appointed his new manager. The player-to-manager adjustment dictated that friendship would have to take a back seat.

Having signed a new two-year deal prior to the club's 2010 promotion back to League One, however, Jalal rejected fresh terms in the summer of 2011, looking on as the club's fire sale post play-offs stole the column inches.

The supporters drew their own conclusions.

'I had been assured by my agent at the time that Eddie was looking to move on Brian Jensen and Lee Grant and bring me in at Burnley, but I never had a conversation with Eddie about it,' says Jalal sternly. 'But the news came out that I had rejected a new deal in August 2011 because I was waiting for Eddie to take me to Burnley. That wasn't the case at all.

'There were the likes of myself, Jason Pearce and Liam Feeney who had played pretty much every minute of every game the previous season, but there were other players offered the same terms who had barely played. That was part of the reason so many players left that summer, like Pearcey and Feeno – the terms they were offered just weren't good enough.

'We'd run through brick walls, but we were being offered the same terms as everyone else. At one point the club even tried to reduce my money. I had a year left but they only wanted to give me another year. That, to me, clearly meant they wanted to sell me.

'The contract was never off the table but I told them I didn't want to sign it at that stage. I spoke to Ian Wadley at the *Echo* about it and it obviously went public that I wasn't going to sign.'

On the training pitch, things were little better for Jalal. Bradbury had signed experienced Portsmouth stopper Darryl Flahavan in June 2011, fresh competition for Jalal as his manager battled to bring in reinforcements following the summer sales.

'It was a tough time for me personally as I had lost my place to Darryl Flahavan at the start of the 2011/12 season,' says Jalal.

'Things got a bit out of hand. I think Lee took it personally that I didn't want to play for him when I turned down the new contract, which couldn't be further from the truth. I was just trying to get some security for myself and my family – we'd just lost in a high-profile play-off semi-final so all of our stocks were high at that point and I felt I deserved more.

'I knew the writing was on the wall for me as soon as Flavs came in and Bradders told me at the start of the season he was going to play, even though I'd had a solid pre-season.

'I was angry – in three years I had only missed ten league games and felt like I'd done nothing wrong. It was clear as day to me that the reason I lost my place was because I'd turned down the new contract.

'It got worse because the chairman wasn't prepared to finance two first-choice keepers and Lee pulled me on the training pitch to tell me that Eddie Mitchell had put me on the transfer list.

'In the space of one summer, I'd gone from being the club's number one to being put up for sale.

'We didn't start the season well at all that year and I know that there were calls from Steve Fletcher, who was Lee's assistant at that time, and Neil Moss, the goalkeeping coach, to put me back in.

'I don't think Bradders liked that, but I eventually had a meeting with Eddie Mitchell and we sorted things out so I ended up signing a two-and-a-half-year deal. I've got no idea why he changed his mind but it was done in one afternoon.'

With Demin established as co-owner alongside Mitchell and the ink dry on Jalal's new deal, the keeper set about regaining his starting place from Flahavan. But more trouble was around the corner.

'I'd been playing with a herniated disc since the middle of the previous season and still wasn't right the whole time I was number two to Flavs,' recalls Jalal. 'I had a meeting with Bradders in January 2012 and said I couldn't carry on because I was in so much pain. I had an operation and that kept me out until the last week of the season by which time Lee had been sacked and Paul Groves and Shaun Brooks were in charge.

'I looked at it very much as a fresh start after that. It had been a tough period for me on so many levels.

'It was strange when Lee went as he hadn't long signed a new contract but he was in a tough position. We stuttered into the play-offs in 2011 and if you asked the players from that time, they would say that if Eddie Howe had stayed, we would have had a great chance of automatic promotion.

'Lee was finding his feet and was inexperienced as a manager and it was tough for him.

'He lost so many players in the summer of 2011 and it looked from the players' point of view that the relationship between Lee and Eddie Mitchell had gone south so it wasn't a huge surprise when he went in March of 2012.

'When he told us he had been sacked after the Oldham defeat he kept it together really well but you could see he was angry and he kicked a bin on his way out of the meeting. I didn't see eye to eye with him on a lot of things when he was manager but as a player he had been one of my closest friends in the squad. When he became manager it changed and I found that hard, as I did to see him leave the club the way he did.'

With Bradbury gone after six defeats in eight and the Cherries 13th in League One, Groves and Brooks guided the team to an uneventful finish to the 2011/12 campaign before refocusing their attention on the following season.

With Demin pulling the strings in the Dean Court board-room and resentment from a supporter base still reeling from the summer 2011 sales and demanding a more experienced managerial appointment, pressure was on Groves and Brooks from matchday one in August 2012. Demin was, and is, not your typical oligarch. Certainly not in the big-spending-early-doors manner of the Premier League's most famed Russian, Roman Abramovich.

When he linked up with Mitchell in 2011, paying around £650,000 for a 50 per cent stake in the Cherries, Demin was not a billionaire either, with a modest fortune, by Abramovich standards, of around £165m. More importantly than that, he had an affinity with the area, with Mitchell's company Seven Developments having built him a home near Poole.

While Mitchell had been loyal to Groves and Brooks, promoting them from within as Murry had done with Howe two years earlier, Demin was understood to be unimpressed with the rookie duo. The bad PR generated by their insipid brand of football, meanwhile, also concerned the club's new co-owner.

In the dressing room, for the players who had enjoyed success and glory under Howe, their continued presence was considered a clear step backwards.

'None of us knew Paul or Shaun really, or what they were about, and when they came in the implementation of training and strategy was like we were playing in the youth team,' laughs Jalal. 'They didn't trust the players as far as I could see.

'Tactically they were all about possession and passing and retaining the ball. They tried to change the way we played completely and it took a while to get accustomed to.

'I went away for the summer in 2012 and they released Warren Cummings, Michael Symes, Mathieu Baudry and Lyle Taylor. Shaun Cooper also left that summer. Warren had been at the club for ten years, won a play-off final in 2003 and been promoted with us in 2010, yet Paul told him he was releasing him in a 30-second phone call. It was disgraceful and certainly got Paul off on the wrong foot with some of the more senior players like myself.'

Having parted ways with stalwarts Cooper and Cummings, Groves brought back striker Josh McQuoid from Millwall in May, alongside a £300,000 deal for Rotherham frontman Lewis Grabban. Derby defender Miles Addison signed as Adam Barrett departed for Gillingham, while Bradbury loan signing Simon Francis committed to a permanent deal and playmaker Eunan O'Kane joined from Torquay United alongside Brighton defender Tommy Elphick. Demin was tentatively flexing his financial muscles, while remaining cautious, although Dutch signings Frank Demouge from Utrecht and Lorenzo Davids, cousin of former Juventus star Edgar, from Augsburg raised eyebrows within both the media and the dressing room.

'When we came back for pre-season in 2012/13 it was like a whole new team,' laughs Jalal. 'I walked into reception and met Tommy Elphick for the first time as he was coming in on loan from Brighton, but before the day was out, he'd signed a permanent contract! It was a complete upheaval and I don't think Paul and Shaun grasped how to treat senior players as a management team. We'd come in for training and if you weren't hydrated enough you weren't allowed to train or if you didn't wee before training you'd be fined.

'The medical staff were pulling their hair out as the players all had sore groins because of the repetitions we were being made to do. It just wasn't democratic and it was all about the control they had had with the youth team boys – they tried to bring that into the first team and it just didn't work.

'We went away to Spain for part of pre-season and usually on those trips you get a little bit of time to unwind. Adam Barrett said a few choice words while we were on that trip after we'd gone out for a meal and our food and drink was all monitored. Adam ended up leaving the following month to go to Gillingham, which tells you everything you need to know!'

One positive for Jalal was a starting berth after Flahavan sustained a shoulder injury in pre-season, but four successive draws to start the campaign only heaped the pressure on Groves and Brooks.

'We didn't start well at all that season in 2012/13 and our confidence was down,' says Jalal glumly. 'I started the first league game at Portsmouth and within 20 minutes I'd let Izale McLeod's shot through my legs and wanted the stadium to swallow me up.

'To be fair to Paul Groves, he came out afterwards and supported me and I appreciated it. But it wasn't happening for us. We had all these really good players, people like Miles Addison, Lewis Grabban, Eunan O'Kane and Josh McQuoid, who had signed over the summer, and the likes of Wes Thomas and Tommy Elphick.

'But they had also brought in Frank and Lorenzo and we just didn't see how they fitted in. Frank hadn't even had a medical when he signed and when Steve Hard, the physio, looked at his knees later that summer he said he didn't think he would ever play football again! It was madness and there were players who were injured who didn't want to rush back because they could see the writing was on the wall for Paul and Shaun even then.'

Elphick, Pugh and Southampton loan signing Lee Barnard were all on target in a topsy-turvy 5-3 defeat at Sheffield United on 1 September, before a stunning Richard Hughes free kick secured a 1-0 win at Yeovil a week later. With Mitchell, as under fire as his management duo, having brought in close friend Harry Redknapp in a 'supervisory' role above Groves and Brooks, looking on, the Cherries went a further six games without a win as the disdain from the terraces became deafening.

A 4-0 defeat at Swindon on 22 September looked as if it would be the beginning of the end for Groves and Brooks, yet Mitchell continued to back his appointments in the face of fearsome criticism from both the media and the fanbase.

Jalal, meanwhile, was preparing to once again warm the bench, giving way to an illustrious yet bizarre mid-season signing.

'My last game under Paul was the Swindon game in September,' he recalls. 'They had Matt Ritchie and Gary Roberts on the flanks, who were two of the best wingers in the division, and we played a narrow diamond.

'We just looked at each other in the dressing room and said, "We're going to get absolutely massacred." We just didn't trust Paul and Shaun's selection or tactics.

'Charlie Daniels and Simon Francis were left exposed against Ritchie, Roberts and their two full-backs and we got absolutely shredded to pieces.

'I was culpable for the last goal but by then my head had gone and we were well beaten.

'First thing on the Monday morning, Neil Moss phoned me and said, "Just to let you know, Paul has been on the phone and David James is coming in to train with you." I just started laughing.

'Jamo came in but hadn't trained for five months so when we did a kicking drill, he could barely get the ball off the floor. You could tell he was rusty. He was great to have around and chat to and someone I had the utmost respect for, but it was just strange.

'I was curious though, so I asked him what his plans were. He said he had just come in to get fit and see what happened.

'I had a conversation with Mossy and Paul Groves too and they reiterated what Jamo had said.

'We had Walsall at home on the Saturday after the Swindon game and the day before Shaun Brooks told me to ease up on the training field and get inside because we had the game the next day.

'Later that day it was announced that Jamo had signed and I thought, "fair enough". I wasn't concerned as he hadn't trained or played for five months. I came into the dressing room and got into my warm-up gear on the day of the Walsall game and Mossy came in and said, "Jal, the gaffer wants a word."

'I went in to see Paul and he told me he was going to play Jamo. I didn't know what to say so I just walked out laughing. What could I do?'

Despite Daniels's strike cancelling out Andy Butler's goal for the Midlanders, James conceded a 90th-minute George Bowerman effort to condemn the Cherries to yet another defeat.

Post-match, fans gathered outside the front of Dean Court and called for Mitchell to address them. The chairman emerged but was shouted down by supporters calling for the sacking of Groves and Brooks. Hit on the back of the head by a matchday programme, Mitchell stood firm once again in backing his managers.

The *Echo*'s Monday headline read 'THEY'RE NOT GETTING SACKED IN THE MORNING', but the truth was the end was nigh.

'After losing to Walsall, we went to Crawley on the Tuesday night and got royally turned over again,' says Jalal, shaking his head. 'The fans had completely turned on Paul and Shaun by then and they were dead men walking after that.'

Mitchell could defend the indefensible no longer and Groves and Brooks were sacked just 24 hours after the Cherries' defeat at Broadfield Stadium, with the club 21st in League One and occupying the final relegation place.

Almost immediately, Mitchell was linked with an unlikely return swoop for Howe, who as well as suffering a tough

Championship baptism of fire at Turf Moor, had lost his mother Annie following a short illness in March 2012.

For the young manager, the untimely loss of his greatest supporter brought with it a change of perspective. Family needed to come first and family was in Dorset, not in Hyde, Greater Manchester, where Howe had set up home following his move north.

'The noises about Eddie coming back started quite quickly after Paul and Shaun left,' recalls Jalal, leaning in close once again. 'Every day we'd come in and see the likes of Stephen Purches and big Steve Fletcher and just say, "Is he?"

'There used to be a whiteboard in the changing room and everyone used to write "Is he?" on it every day! It was quite funny and just a laugh really, but then the rumours really started to gather pace and we thought, "hang on, this might actually be happening".'

For the *Echo*, keeping up with the rumour mill was becoming increasingly difficult and big-story paranoia was setting in. At one stage, reporter Perrett was so convinced he saw MK Dons manager Karl Robinson walking into a block of flats close to the newspaper's office that he followed him before shouting "Karl!" The bemused look on the face of the man who was clearly not Karl Robinson was an amusing metaphor for Dean Court's ongoing madness.

'Karl Robinson was in the frame for it without a doubt,' says Jalal, laughing at the story. 'It looked like he might be the one, but then the Eddie stuff really started snowballing.

'We went to Coventry the Saturday after Paul and Shaun went but we were beaten again with Dennis Rofe in caretaker charge.

'For the whole of the next week the new lads were constantly asking me about Eddie. I just said, "If he comes back it will be the best thing that's happened to this club." I was desperate for it to happen because I knew what it would do for us.

'That said, though, even after the club had announced they'd agreed a compensation package with Burnley on the Friday, I didn't believe it until the next day when I turned up for the Leyton Orient game at home and I saw him – just a glimpse as he and Jason Tindall were in a room, but I was speechless. It was happening.'

Those supporters who had drifted away under Groves and Brooks returned en masse as the Miracle Man and Tindall were paraded on the pitch prior to kick-off against the east Londoners.

There was something in the air, a definite change, and those fans who had opted to wipe the slate clean finally saw a performance of genuine quality.

Grabban, whose early displays had promised little, opened the scoring before Pugh doubled the advantage two minutes later. Dean Court was rocking.

'Dennis Rofe took the team and we won the game,' remembers Jalal, 'then Eddie and Jason came to speak to us afterwards and congratulated us. That was it, though, as I don't think they wanted to steal the limelight too much from us and Dennis.

'That night was my other half's birthday and we went out with some of the players and their partners to a place called Koh Thai in Bournemouth and Jason came along, which was great. We talked about a lot and what had been happening while he and Eddie had been at Burnley.

'The following Monday Eddie called us in for a meeting and he explained everything that was going to be expected of us. That was what we needed. We needed that structure after everything had fallen apart under Paul and Shaun.'

The following Saturday, in Howe's first official game back in charge, Harry Arter and Francis were on target alongside a Ben Gibson own goal as Tranmere were safely dispatched 3-1.

A 3-3 draw at Notts County followed and provided some realism to the task ahead for Howe. Two goals behind inside 30 minutes at Meadow Lane, McQuoid's strike and an Arter penalty had restored parity before Jamal Campbell-Ryce's spot kick six minutes from time had seemingly condemned Howe to the first defeat of his second spell in charge. But Matt Tubbs, signed by Bradbury after Howe had opted to send him back to Salisbury following his 2008 loan spell, found the net just 60 seconds later to secure a point on the road.

It was a return of the grit, determination and never-say-die attitude that had served Howe's previous squads so well during more testing times off the field. Demin's financial muscle, meanwhile, had provided greater off-field security initially instilled by Mitchell's arrival. By Dean Court standards, life was rosy.

On 27 October, Howe's men travelled to Carlisle, the scene of their League One relegation on the final day of the 2007/08 campaign. A lot can happen in four years.

Pugh's double, plus strikes from Grabban and Barnard, saw off the Cumbrians 4-2 in a thrilling encounter. Howe's side played with flair and width and were simply proving too strong for all-comers.

'He was different to the manager that left in 2011,' says Jalal. 'He'd learned a lot as he'd gone from an environment where he had a lot of young players who weren't earning a lot to Burnley where there were a lot of senior players, ex-Premier League boys who were on £20,000 or £30,000 a week. He lost his mum as well while he was up there, so you could tell he had changed.

'But he had a set way of how he was going to be with us and it was just what we needed. He told us how our week was going to be and we thought it was brilliant.

'He wanted us to be attacking and flamboyant and wanted his keeper to have good feet. I felt I had the advantage over Jamo there, but Eddie went with the same team for that initial period and the boys went on an 18-game unbeaten run so he couldn't change things.

'I played in the 3-1 FA Cup win over Carlisle in November and the week before Jamo had had a poor game in the 2-2 draw at Bury so I was led to believe that Eddie was going to change things for the game at Scunthorpe on 8 December, but Matt Tubbs had given me a dead leg in training so I missed out. I was gutted because I couldn't even travel and the youth team keeper Benji Buchel was on the bench.

'Jamo ended up saving a penalty in that game, so I had to bide my time until the game at Hartlepool in January. The boys had had a bit of a sticky patch that month with three draws and two defeats but I also think Eddie really wanted the team to be progressive from the back and he knew I could play a part in that. I think he knew Jamo wasn't the answer long-term but I wanted to know what was happening as I knew Neil Moss was looking at other goalkeepers and Flavs was also on his way back from injury.'

Howe was also looking at outfield reinforcements and spent more than £1m of Demin's money in the winter window. The Miracle Man brought back Brett Pitman from Bristol City and punted £400,000 each on young winger Ryan Fraser from Aberdeen and Swindon flyer Ritchie.

Demouge and Davids were moved on, while Bradbury signing Steven Gregory joined Wimbledon and long-serving Mark Molesley moved to Exeter City.

Successive defeats at home to Wigan and away to Walsall during the window, however, reminded Howe that suggestions of an unlikely promotion were perhaps premature. A Grabban penalty, though, secured a tough 2-1 win at Hartlepool, before Pitman notched a hat-trick in a 3-1 home win against Crewe.

In that five-game winning run, Howe's rejuvenated side also secured victories over MK Dons and Portsmouth and completed a quick-fire double over Crewe, but both Jalal and James were about to experience Howe's ruthless streak for the first time.

'In the middle of January, they told me they were going to bring in Ryan Allsop from Leyton Orient but Eddie had told me the shirt was mine and we won five games in a row,' says Jalal. 'But then we had a couple of injuries, including Tommy Elphick, who was on the end of an horrendous tackle from Ryan Lowe at MK Dons, and we went on a ridiculously poor run.

'We lost 2-0 at Preston and I wasn't really at fault but my confidence dropped off from there and we lost at home to Sheffield United and Coventry. Then we went to Leyton Orient and I was at fault for the first goal and after the game Eddie said I didn't seem myself.

'In the heat of the moment I was really disappointed in myself. I had been thinking all week leading up to that game that he was going to drop me and it got the better of me. I worked myself up.

'That week leading up to the next game at Doncaster, I got the dreaded curly finger on the Friday and Eddie told me he was putting Ryan in for the game. I didn't take it well and he didn't take it well that I didn't take it well.

'It's one regret I do have of my time at Bournemouth with the gaffer but it was a confusing time for me because I'd gone from being back on track after Jamo's spell and then back to square one again once Ryan had come in.'

Those five straight defeats in February and at the beginning of March threatened to derail the latest Howe miracle. A Pitman penalty under the lights at Stevenage on 12 March, however, was the catalyst for eight successive victories that would add another promotion to the Miracle Man's CV.

Pitman, Ritchie, Arter and Tubbs were all on target in a swashbuckling 4-1 win at home to Bury on 23 March, before a Pitman-inspired 3-1 win at Shrewsbury meant victory at home to Carlisle the following Saturday would take the Cherries into the Championship – unfamiliar ground for a club that had experienced just three seasons in English football's second tier in its history, between 1987 and 1990.

In front of a full house at Dean Court, Steve Cook's goal handed the Cherries a deserved lead but Lee Miller's equaliser five minutes into the second half added doubt to the cauldron of noise inside the stadium.

Howe's men were not to be denied, though, that steely, gritty ingredient added by the Miracle Man's return in October coming to the fore. Arter made the score 2-1, before a fitting Pitman strike secured promotion in the final minute.

'Tommy Elphick came back from injury and he was imperious during that winning run at the end of the season,' reflects Jalal with a smile. 'Ryan Allsop saved a penalty at Oldham in March, too, which was crucial. At that point there was no doubt we were going to get promoted. We were playing some unbelievable football and Brett and Lewis Grabban were running teams ragged.

'We played Shrewsbury away on 13 April, our third from last game, and on the Friday the only thing we worked on was Marc Pugh receiving the ball on the inside of the full-back because Eddie knew they were vulnerable there.

'Within five minutes we'd won a penalty doing exactly that and I just sat there on the bench and thought, "This manager is unbelievable." Then we scored another goal from the same move before Brett buried an absolute screamer in the second half and we won 3-1. It's things like that that make Eddie the manager he is.

'We'd play games in training that season where we weren't allowed to talk, just so he could emphasise how important communication is during the game, and he brought in a coaching method where the players have to solve a problem themselves.

'He'd set ten players up in a certain shape then tell them they had to work out who was going to play where to achieve the best chance of winning. Then he'd go to the other team and say they were 1-0 behind with ten minutes to go and tell them they had to work out how to win the game.

'Those things show the difference between Eddie and Paul and Shaun. It was like chalk and cheese.

'When it comes to making decisions, he is very much the man in charge but he knew he needed us to be able to figure out problems on the pitch in a live environment. He's obsessive with what he does and he is ruthless – absolutely ruthless.

'Everything has to be right and that's probably why Jason is such a good number two for him because he helps level out that ruthless streak.

'But it was Eddie who got us promoted to the Championship that year as, aside from Brett Pitman, Ryan Allsop and Matt Ritchie, who all signed in January 2013, it was the same bunch of players who couldn't get a result under Paul and Shaun.'

As the celebrations drew to a close in May, Howe turned his attentions to what was looking to be his biggest challenge to date – keeping his boyhood club in a division that included clubs like Middlesbrough, Blackburn Rovers, Queens Park Rangers and Leicester City.

Jalal, meanwhile, spent the summer taking stock after a difficult meeting with his manager.

'I went away that summer and reset myself,' the keeper admits. 'I really wanted to play in the Championship but I'd gone away unsure because a couple of days after the end of the season we had our usual meetings with Eddie pencilled in and I got stuck in traffic in Bournemouth and was late.

'I called him and he was fine with me being late, so straight away the alarm bells were ringing because he was being nice and he hates people being late.

'We sat down and he admitted it had been a difficult season for me. He said it was probably time for me to look for another club where I could be first choice. I was taken aback, but he said

Ryan was going to be his number one with Flavs supporting him as he knew the league.

'He said if I didn't get anything I could come back in pre-season and we'd look at things.

'The first thing he did was recommend me to Sean O'Driscoll at Bristol City and I thought that was going to happen, but it didn't materialise. I started pre-season in 2013/14 at Bournemouth but it became more and more obvious that Ryan and Flavs were going to be the first choices.'

As the last remnants of summer ebbed away, the Miracle Man plotted a strategy to keep the club in the second tier. Mostyn was reinstalled as chairman by Demin in September 2013, but in both the boardroom and dressing room, two key faces were coming to the end of their time and would leave lasting legacies.

CHAPTER 10

SO CLOSE YET SO FAR
2013/14

STEVE Cook and Simon Francis listened intently, hanging on their captain's every word, the hairs on their arms rising through the sweat of 90 minutes' toil.

It had been a long season, and it wasn't quite over, yet Tommy Elphick had looked around Dean Court following the final whistle against Queens Park Rangers and seen, within the swathes of supporters, a vision of what was to come.

Elphick relayed his epiphany in the dressing room as his team-mates sat, drained having held off Redknapp's Premier League elect side for more than 20 minutes with ten men.

It was 5 April 2014, a fourth of five straight wins that would propel Howe's men to within touching distance of the Championship play-offs.

Seven months earlier, staying up was as far as Cook and Francis would allow their minds to travel, the realities of life in England's most backbreaking division dawning on them during the 'hangover' months of August and September.

'That first Championship season was a shock to us,' admits Francis, tracksuited after another intense Howe training session prior to the league visit of Crystal Palace on 7 April 2018. 'We lost some games quite heavily at the start of the season and I think it was the physical side that caught us off guard more than anything. Set plays and long direct balls are a big strength for teams in that league and that took us a while to get to grips with.

'We were still playing some great football and we were never going to change that but it took a couple of months to get used to the physicality of the league.'

The Cherries' current captain is referring to big defeats against both Watford and Huddersfield in the early weeks of the 2013/14 campaign, the club's first in the second tier since 1990.

Howe's men had made the perfect opening day start by dispatching Charlton 2-1 at the Valley, Lewis Grabban's brace sandwiching a Yann Kermorgant (*more on him later*) strike for the hosts, before midfielder Bradley Pritchard had seen red allowing the Cherries to ease to victory.

The following weekend's trip to Watford, though, promised to be something of a bigger test. Howe had added experience to the youthful exuberance of his League One promotion squad over the summer of 2013, defender Elliott Ward joining from Norwich on a free transfer alongside former Irish international and Leeds Champions League hero Ian Harte, who arrived from Reading.

Howe also took something of a punt on South African striker Tokelo Rantie, who arrived from Malmo for a club record £2.5m.

It was a fee that would sit uncomfortably with many of the Dean Court old guard, scarred by a history of over-spending. A Championship club, yes, but this was little AFC Bournemouth, whose club record transfer fee prior to Matt Tubbs's arrival for a lofty £500,000 in 2012 had been Gavin Peacock for £210,000 in 1989.

The eye-watering transfer fee for Rantie, though, was backed up by more genuine tears on the terraces when talisman Fletcher called time on his 21-year stay at Dean Court.

'It's really difficult to put into words my feelings for the big man and what he has done for this football club,' Howe said as the news broke.

With Fletcher positioned in a new scouting role at the club, Howe's men rocked up at Vicarage Road, a venue with a distinct history and under development as the Hornets sought a path back to the riches of the Premier League, on 10 August. Dubbed 'Udinese Reserves' after the club's owners, the Pozzo family, had signed 14 players on loan from the Bianconeri Friuliani and the other club under their ownership, Granada, that summer, the likes of Fernando Forestieri and Diego Fabbrini were something of an unknown quantity.

Within 15 minutes, another Udinese loanee, defender Gabriele Angella, had put the Hornets 1-0 up and despite Grabban's 29th-minute strike levelling matters, the hosts struck five second-half goals without reply, through Angella's second, Lewis McGugan and a Troy Deeney hat-trick, to leave Howe reeling.

Despite a narrow 1-0 home win over Wigan a week later, again thanks to Grabban, the visit to Huddersfield on 24 August had a touch of the Watfords about it. And so it proved.

This time Marc Pugh's goal 22 minutes from time was all Howe had to show for the trip north and by then his side were 4-0 down thanks to Adam Hammill and a hat-trick from evergreen James Vaughan, before Adam Clayton made it 5-1 on 78 minutes. Welcome to the Championship.

Cook winces as we go through the match statistics in the comfort of a small office in the Dean Court pavilion prior to the club's trip to rampant Mo Salah-inspired Liverpool on 14 April.

'The sides that we were coming up against in the Championship were established teams and although we got off to a great start against Charlton, the defeats we suffered early on against Watford and Huddersfield were tough to take,' recalls the defender.

'It brought us back down to earth and it was clear we needed to improve as a team and as individuals quite quickly.

'Eddie hadn't got across everything he wanted to by then as it takes time for a manager to bed in and we were still getting used to everything he wanted from us as a team. It's easy to forget that he'd only been back at the club for less than a year at that point.

'We weren't probably where he would have wanted us to be as a team at that stage and I think that showed in the early defeats we suffered.'

'Those defeats were tough because we'd come from having our own way in League One every week to getting beaten like that,' reflects Francis, crossing his arms. 'The manager was great though. He didn't come in ranting and raving. He could have chosen that option because we were bullied in those games and it wasn't good enough.

'But he chose to take a positive stance and looked at it as a learning curve. When you get promoted, defeats like that are always going to happen and the same thing happened in our first season in the Premier League.

'The way we play, coming up against direct teams and not matching them means we sometimes came out on the losing side, but the manager's approach was right. He knew it would be like that, but he also knew we had to stop it happening again.'

Howe steadied the ship. Three wins from the next seven, a Brett Pitman-inspired 1-0 triumph at Doncaster, single-goal win at home to Barnsley and ding-dong 5-2 victory over Millwall, which included five different goalscorers, two penalties and a sending-off for the Lions, gave his second-tier rookies something to build on.

Off the pitch, though, it was all change again, as chairman Mitchell joined Fletcher in calling time on his Dean Court stay, selling his 50% share in the club to Demin. While both left lasting legacies, Mitchell's time at the helm will forever remain controversial, though few could argue that his involvement between 2009 and 2013 had not been memorable.

Speaking to the *Echo* on behalf of himself and wife Brenda, Mitchell said at the time: 'It goes without saying that we are both immensely proud to have been just a small part of the club's history and I would hope that our short spell at the helm will be viewed as a successful one.' Few could argue with that last sentiment.

Back on the field, while an October/November seven-game winless run threatened to undo Howe's good work, those watching week-in, week-out were very much of the impression the manager's side were settling down in uncharted territory.

Charlie Daniels had replaced Harte at left-back in the 2-1 defeat at Leicester City on 26 October, while Elphick regained his place alongside Cook in central defence after Ward was sent off at the King Power Stadium.

Daniels and Pugh were building a flamboyant rapport on the left, while Francis was relishing having the talent and trickery of Matt Ritchie in front of him on the right. This kind of bombastic, expansive attacking game wasn't the 'Championship Way' but soon sides were sitting up to take notice of Howe's wing men, apart from Redknapp's QPR, who dispatched the Cherries with ruthless ease under the lights at Loftus Road on 3 December.

'We went to QPR and that was a tough day,' says Cook, running his finger down the Hoops line-up that day and shaking his head.

Redknapp's side included former England goalkeeper Rob Green, the pacy Danny Simpson, experienced centre-half Richard Dunne, Joey Barton, Junior Hoilett and strike duo Andy Johnson and Charlie Austin. A 16-minute cameo from winger Matt Phillips left Cook on his backside as the Londoners, a fully formed Premier League team, ran out 3-0 winners.

'They battered us and that was one of my worst games for Bournemouth because Charlie Austin absolutely bullied me,' recalls Cook. 'It was a real learning curve for me that day as they were a Premier League side in the Championship and we were taught a real lesson. Matt Phillips absolutely roasted me for the third goal.'

That result left Howe's men far closer to the Championship relegation zone than they would have liked, but a corner was about to be turned as Howe's offensive philosophy with his full-backs and wingers began to pay dividends.

'We'd worked a lot on mine and Charlie Daniels's roles as full-backs in League One but the first season in the Championship was the most work I have done off the field in improving my game,' says Francis.

'Charlie and I would sit down and watch clips constantly, with the gaffer and without, both of our own games and others. I was watching a lot of Pablo Zabaleta at that time. He was in the form of his life at Manchester City and some of the runs he would make and the decisions he made and the timing was outstanding.

'Charlie was watching a lot of Leighton Baines and his relationship with Steven Pienaar at Everton and how he could implement that with Marc Pugh. They would do the same with Pughie coming inside and Charlie bombing on and it was similar on my side with Matt Ritchie. We all got a great relationship going and I would always know exactly what Matty was going to do when he had the ball.'

Howe, concerned with the form of Ryan Allsop, had drafted in West Ham goalkeeper Stephen Henderson for the victory over Millwall, only to watch his new acquisition go down with a dislocated shoulder a week later in the 1-1 draw at Nottingham Forest. Allsop regained the number one jersey for the game at Leicester, only to be struck down with glandular fever for eight weeks. West Brom keeper Lee Camp was next between the sticks and lined up at Reading's Madejski Stadium four days after the Cherries' Loftus Road shocker.

'I think that game was a real turning point,' says Cook. 'They had some solid Championship players like Billy Sharp and Hal Robson-Kanu but we were fairly comfortable that day and it gave us back some belief.

'Grabbs and Matty Ritchie put us 2-0 up by half-time and although they scored late on, it was a reasonably straightforward day. It was just what we needed at that time.'

There was little belief among the so-called pundits, however, who were critical of Howe's attacking tactics in a league dominated by big men and a reliance of physicality.

'We were brave and played out from the back as much as we could but we knew we needed to compete,' says Francis.

'We weren't a small team that season – we had myself, Tommy Elphick, Cookie, Charlie and Elliott Ward and we are all big guys – but we needed to get our heads around it all early on that season.

'When we went on the bad run in October and November all the critics came out and said, "You can't pass your way through this league like you can in League One. You have to do it the dirty way."

'But we didn't buy into that at all. The manager was never going to change the way we play. Yes, we would change slightly from team to team but our philosophy was always going to stay the same.'

Buoyed by their Berkshire triumph, Cook and Francis led from the front alongside captain Elphick as the Cherries blitzed through Christmas with two wins and two draws from five high-octane games. Ritchie and Grabban were on target in a hard-fought 2-1 win at Sheffield Wednesday, while Eunan O'Kane's strike and a Ritchie double saw off Yeovil at Dean Court on Boxing Day.

As the frantic four weeks of the January transfer window commenced at the turn of the year, Howe, impressed by Camp, signed the goalkeeper on a permanent deal, while also bringing back previous loan defender Adam Smith on a full transfer from Tottenham.

Howe, though, had his eyes firmly locked on one particular target who had been on his mind since the Cherries' opening-day win at the Valley.

'I played a bit with Yann Kermorgant at Charlton and he was a great outlet for us in the second half of that first Championship season,' says Francis fondly.

'He was superb in the air and could hold it up for us. He was one of the biggest signings for us in the Championship because he changed the dynamic and a lot of teams thought we would automatically go long playing Yann.

'But he has great feet and is good with the ball, turning and linking up play, and he worked really well with Brett Pitman that first season.'

Kermorgant hit the ground running. Popular with the supporters from day one, his first goals in red and black came in the form of a hat-trick in a 5-0 win over Doncaster on 1 March, after a barren spell of one win from six in February and March had again threatened to derail the Cherries' progress.

A Grabban penalty saw off Blackpool in the North West a week later, before Grabban was again the match-winner in a midweek fixture at Blackburn, sealing a third consecutive win for the first time that season.

By the time Howe's side visited Barnsley on 22 March, they were knocking on the door of the top half of the table. Cook kept their impressive run of form going with a 90th-minute strike at Oakwell, before braces from Kermorgant and Grabban impressively dispatched Leeds United 4-1 at Dean Court four days later.

Smelling the blood of the sides above them, and having seen off Birmingham City 4-2 at St Andrew's on 29 March thanks to goals from Ritchie, Harte and another Grabban double, the

Cherries had revenge on their minds when Redknapp brought QPR to his old stomping ground at Dean Court.

It was Elphick's day of vision, a 2-1 victory for the hosts against the odds thanks to goals from the captain himself on the stroke of half-time and Grabban on the hour after Armand Traore had got Redknapp's side back in it.

'We were fantastic against QPR and had to dig deep because Harry Arter was sent off midway through the second half,' recalls Cook.

'I remember the game well because I didn't play well and Traore got in behind me for their goal,' says Francis, 'but the lads dug me out of that hole and we got a great result. It was a game where we ground out a result against a team pushing for promotion when we didn't play particularly well and I think it sent a real message to the division ahead of the following season.'

Cook laughs: 'What I remember most from that game was Brett Pitman coming on as a sub in the 96th minute, running straight to the near post and clearing Richard Dunne's header off the line. It was incredible – what a contribution for all of ten seconds!

'After that game, though, we really knew we could do something as we were so committed. Something clicked in that game. I don't know what it was, but beating a side who went on to get promoted while we only had ten men gave us the belief we could do something as a team.'

Elphick was fuelled and gathered his exhausted troops together for the big speech.

'He said some really special things in the dressing room after that game,' says Francis, smiling. 'He was really fired up and said what he thought at just the right time.'

Elphick's Alexander the Great moment was overshadowed by a five-game run-in that yielded a solitary win over Nottingham Forest, with Kermorgant and Grabban both finding the net twice in a 4-1 scoreline at Dean Court. But with Elphick's words ringing in their ears, the Cherries were already looking 12 months ahead.

'The manager prepared us really well for the Championship, but perhaps we were suffering a bit of a hangover early on in that first season,' admits Francis. 'I think we were still enjoying the promotion from League One and it's tough to win back-to-back promotions.

'But as soon as the first Championship season finished, we all said we had a chance the following year, especially after the QPR game, and our focus from the first day in pre-season was on a top-two finish in 2014/15.'

Mighty oaks they now were. Elphick's vision was to become a reality.

CHAPTER 11

THE PROMISED LAND

TOMMY Elphick did what he always did. The traditional pre-match photos taken by AFC Bournemouth's club photographer before every game, home and away, feature only ten players, but Elphick was not about to change his routine for the special occasion.

He ran, as always, to the goalmouth when the players emerged from the tunnel at Charlton's home, the Valley, on 2 May 2015. The words during his bizarre pre-match ritual remain unknown, but the goalpost was headbutted with the usual vigour, the boots cleared of mud and the arms stretched out clinging to the post.

The headbutting, in particular, would have made the visiting fans wince. Sore heads were the order of the day in SE7, celebrations of Premier League promotion following the 3-0 win over Bolton stretching into a fifth day.

For Elphick, though, it was never going to be a case of job done. The Cherries skipper and his team-mates had felt the pain of easing off against Tranmere two seasons before. The history-makers had sealed promotion from League One at home to Carlisle on the penultimate weekend of the 2012/13 campaign but could only muster a 0-0 draw a week later at Prenton Park. The door opened for Doncaster and they walked through with a dramatic, last-gasp win over Brentford. Promotion, yes, but no title.

'There was no way we were going to go to Charlton after the Bolton celebrations and go through the motions,' recalls Elphick. 'Nobody ever remembers the teams that are promoted in second place, do they?

'Who won the league that season? Bournemouth.

'Who went up in second place? No idea.

'The year we went up from League One to the Championship, we did ourselves over at Tranmere and missed out on the title. It was our fault and there was no way we were going to do it again.'

Signed by Paul Groves in the summer of 2012, Elphick was torn between head and heart over leaving his boyhood home in Brighton, not to mention a manager who had instilled flair, a duty of care and real wisdom to the Amex Stadium dressing room.

Gus Poyet had arrived in 2009, as swashbuckling and intense as a manager as he had been in midfield for River Plate, Zaragoza, Tottenham and Chelsea.

'I was part of the furniture at Brighton really,' laughs Elphick, 'but I had been given a really good schooling. When Gus came to the club it really opened my eyes to a different way of playing football. It was just unbelievable and we ended up routing League One in 2010/11 but I ruptured my Achilles on the last day of the season and missed the whole of our first season in the Championship in 2011/12.

'When I came back the following pre-season in August 2012, the plan was to send me out on loan for a few months to get me some game time before coming back to Brighton to stake a claim.

'Bournemouth were one of the clubs interested in taking me and I went to see Paul Groves and Shaun Brooks. Paul had a vision, there was no doubt about that, and they had plans for the training ground and for the stadium. I liked what I saw and it excited me.

'Steve Cook had signed in the previous window from Brighton and I'd kept an eye on what he was doing alongside Charlie

Daniels, who had the same agent as me. Charlie was flying at Leyton Orient and Bournemouth managed to prise him away so I knew they were looking to have a go at promotion from League One.

'Once I had met Paul and seen the town and everything that the club had planned, I wanted to be a part of it and get my teeth into it.

'Gus was reluctant to let me go when the chance came to sign permanently, but he knew it was the best thing for me so I made the move and never looked back.'

But Elphick, like so many before him, was quickly left to wonder if the grass really was greener. Left frustrated and embarrassed following Bradbury's sacking in March and the ongoing off-field uncertainty surrounding chairman Mitchell and silent new investor Demin, the supporters vented their feelings from the off following five defeats from the opening six games.

'We had a rocky start that season,' says Elphick, gazing down. 'I scored in my second game at home, a 1-1 draw against Preston, and then scored again as we lost 5-3 away at Sheffield United in a crazy game. I was happy with what I was doing but something wasn't right and it's hard to put my finger on it, even now.

'We weren't getting the results we needed and for the investment the board had made in the playing squad the previous January in particular, but also the summer I signed with myself, Miles Addison and Lewis Grabban coming in, there was an expectancy. There was a lot of unrest quite quickly that season and the fans had turned on Paul and Shaun and Eddie Mitchell.

'It wasn't a nice place to be and was a tough gig. They'd come in in strange circumstances, Paul and Shaun, and when the fans don't agree with it even before you've started, you know you are going to be kicking uphill.

'I was aware that Eddie Mitchell was passionate, shall we say, and had had a bit of an influence in the dressing room. During one of my first games he rocked up in the dressing room at half-time with an entourage of people. Looking back now, it was just that he wanted the same thing as we did, but I guess the dressing room is really a no-go area for non-playing staff.

'I remember watching the *Football League Show* when I was at Brighton when Eddie went on the pitch with the microphone and called out the supporters so I was aware things were a little tense after Lee Bradbury had gone and Paul and Shaun came in.

'I wondered if I had made a mistake, of course, after the start we had that year. Brighton were flying and having a real go in the Championship and I was thinking I could have been a part of that. It all goes through your head, but all those thoughts were quickly put to bed when Eddie Howe came back.'

The return of Howe was a shot in the arm for Elphick who, alongside his team-mates, had struggled to push through the waves of negativity surrounding Groves's short reign.

Howe had pondered what he had been left with in October 2012, scanning the CVs of the men that were to make history that season. Make no mistake, he made it his business to know the finer details of the players signed by both Bradbury and Groves even before his on-pitch unveiling ahead of the Leyton Orient game that was to turn the season.

Who were the characters? Who would falter when he needed them most? Who was behind him? Who could he do without?

Elphick stood tall, a robust tower of strength. Evolving, he was to become a champion, but first he had to become a leader.

Elphick is not one to put the boot in post failings, nor is his the kind of character who finds someone else to blame. He reflects on the spell of Groves and Brooks intelligently and with balance, yet within his demeanour in the bustle of the Belfry it is clear that, without Howe's arrival, he would have found himself in a football no-man's-land.

'There were two results that essentially did for Paul and Shaun,' he says. 'The 4-0 defeat away at Swindon in September and then away at Crawley where we lost 3-1 at the start of October.

'It wasn't a nice place to be at all and a lot of the lads were in the same situation in that they had stepped away from clubs where they were reasonably settled, so we were all wondering what we'd done. We didn't know why it wasn't happening and things weren't clicking for us.

'Sometimes it takes time for things to gel, but in our case it just took something changing to get us going and that was Eddie's arrival.

'The club announced Eddie was coming back on the morning of the next game at home to Leyton Orient and the lads just clicked that day. Richard Hughes was in the dressing room and it was difficult for him as he was close to Paul but also very close to Eddie.

'But we used to go for a coffee every Wednesday or Thursday and we were sitting there before the Orient game that week just talking about what it would be like if Eddie came back and could get us playing.

'Richard and the likes of Shwan Jalal were telling us the stories of what he had achieved when he was at the club before and we were buzzing. Eddie and Jason came to watch the game against Orient and went on the pitch beforehand and there were probably 1,000 more people in the stadium. It was like a cloud had been lifted from above the pitch and we went on to win the game 2-0.

'It set the tempo and right from that Monday morning when he took his first session with us, we never looked back.'

The aim for the Miracle Man was survival. Taking over a club sitting perilously in 21st place of a division boasting a new-found competitive edge thanks to the likes of Portsmouth, Preston North End and Scunthorpe United, how could his ambitions stretch beyond simply staying up?

'We set all kinds of records that season and it was testament to him as a manager that he was able to turn us from a team 21st in the league to one that won promotion in just a few months,' recalls Elphick, his eyes widening.

'One of the things Eddie was always great at was reminding everyone that while Bournemouth wasn't the biggest club with the biggest stadium or fanbase, it is a really special club that has survived so much. So many people saw it at its lowest ebb and he changed those people's perceptions through what he achieved. He gave them a light and something to celebrate and that can never be underestimated.

'You can't take away the club's achievement in getting to the Premier League but had we not won promotion that year from League One, would the club have strived for the Premier League? Probably not.

'Everyone was happy to take the Championship at that point as the club had only been in that league for one spell before, but the momentum and feel-good factor created from the League One promotion drove everyone on to achieve everything that followed.'

While Howe had added the second-tier experience of Elliott Ward, Andrew Surman and Ian Harte during the summer of 2013, alongside the big money spent on Tokelo Rantie, the following year was to be another defining window for the manager when he acquired Coventry striker Callum Wilson, Junior Stanislas from Burnley and Newcastle United midfielder Dan Gosling.

Big-scoring Grabban was sold to Norwich, meanwhile, while Hughes and loyal Stephen Purches called time on their playing careers to join Howe's backroom team. Tubbs ended his unhappy and ultimately fruitless spell by joining Portsmouth.

Elphick, though, was about to have his post-QPR vision.

'We played them at home in April of that first season in the Championship and I scored as we beat them 2-1,' he recalls. 'I remember sitting in the dressing room after that game, gathering the lads around and thinking the league wasn't actually all it was cracked up to be. QPR went on to win the play-offs that year and we turned them over with ten men.

'We only ended up a few points off the play-offs ourselves in 11th place and there was a feeling that the next season we could potentially do something special. Eddie told us that if we had a good pre-season in 2014 and came back from the summer break really on it, we could do something amazing.'

Three years after the club's penalty shoot-out heartache at the Galpharm Stadium, the Cherries were back in Huddersfield on the opening day of the 2014/15 Championship season. It was to be a defining 90 minutes as Marc Pugh, Yann Kermorgant and a Wilson debut double saw Howe's men thrash their old adversaries 4-0.

'We went to Huddersfield and absolutely wiped the floor with them,' grins Elphick. 'They were an established team and spending big money for the league and we went up there and ripped them apart.

'The next game against Exeter in the League Cup was almost as important as we'd made some big investments in the likes of Junior Stanislas, Callum Wilson and Dan Gosling. Eddie changed the whole 11 pretty much and we won 2-0. We knew we had a squad pulling in the right direction and that's what you need to get out of the Championship.

'The new lads bedded in really well. The best thing about AFC Bournemouth is the dressing room, make no mistake about that. We got those new lads on board really quickly and let them know what the gaffer was about. The way we trained and the way we played that season was pretty unique for the league and it was important to get those lads sorted quickly.

'Moving clubs is a massive step and we were there to help each other. There were a lot of lads around the same age with young families moving down to the south coast and it's not easy, but it's actually a blessing that if you play for Bournemouth, you have to move nearby. You can't really commute so we all lived in town or nearby and it brought us together. We'd often stay after training just to chill out or have a coffee. Eddie was massive on taking us out, doing go-karting or even just a walk down the beach if we'd lost on the Saturday. It kept us together and enabled us to build a spirit.

'But the best way to build team spirit is winning and we certainly did that. Callum and Yann Kermorgant had both hit the ground running that season and really hit it off.'

A 1-0 home win against Brentford courtesy of Stanislas was followed by defeats to Nottingham Forest and Blackburn, while draws at Norwich and Watford and at home to Rotherham completed a lean September that also saw a 2-0 reverse at Derby. Just one win, at home to Wigan, called Elphick's vision into question, surely? He laughs at the suggestion and points to the 14-match unbeaten run from October until the turn of the year that yielded an incredible 11 wins, including an 8-0 annihilation of Birmingham City at St Andrew's.

'We went to Bolton at the start of October and Yann was sent off for a high kick so Eddie made some adjustments,' remembers Elphick. 'We'd gone 1-0 up but they equalised before Callum scored his second to win it. It was that game where I really started to think we could do something because the work rate we showed and the distances we covered that day were immense. I knew our performance that day when up against it would surpass any team in the league.

'Tokelo Rantie had been with us since the previous summer, but it hadn't really worked out for him. He came in for quite a big sum and struggled to settle a bit, but he played a massive part in the season anyway simply by being there and scored a couple in the 8-0 win at Birmingham in October.

'Marc Pugh scored a hat-trick that day and one was a header so we called him "John Toshack" all the way home as we'd never seen him head a ball. To beat any team by that scoreline was a huge feat, but we probably didn't take any more out of it than we did by beating Charlton 1-0 a couple of weeks earlier.

'It was back to work on the Monday for us, but I think people away from Bournemouth started to take note of us after that game. They were thinking, "Hang on, Bournemouth are looking pretty good." We were ruthless that day – after we'd scored the eighth, we were running back to the halfway line saying, "Come on boys, let's get nine or ten." It was brutal.

'A week later we beat West Brom 2-1 in the cup at home after Eddie made ten changes – I was the only one left in from the Birmingham game. They were a good side, doing well in the Premier League, but Junior Stanislas and Eunan O'Kane came in and combined for the first goal. It was superb and showed that your starting 11 is only as good as the underbelly, the lads who were pushing for a starting place.

'Eddie knew he could always turn to the likes of Junior, Dan Gosling, Brett Pitman, Adam Smith and Eunan and get a performance. It's so hard to create that when everyone in your squad thinks they should be playing every week. It was unique and we all knew what we were there for.

'The full-backs and wingers were key for us. We worked on their roles daily and Eddie had noticed straight away when he came back that Simon Francis and Charlie Daniels were absolute flyers.

'He worked with that and developed it. Even now when you watch Marc Pugh and Charlie in the Premier League, you know what you're going to get from them and it was the same with Matt Ritchie and Franno that season in the Championship.

'Me and Steve Cook were a bit worried sometimes as we'd be sitting back while they bombed on, but a lot of it was a joy to watch. The balance and blend in that team was something else and Eddie sculpted it. It was perfect.'

High on confidence, Howe's side pushed on into February but slipped up in successive away games at Brentford and Forest. Surman's third-minute strike at the City Ground was cancelled out by Jamaal Lascelles and Henri Lansbury, but Elphick once again laughs off suggestions of a wobble, pointing once more to a run that would leave Howe's promotion rivals trailing.

'We'd gone to Blackpool in December and they were struggling but the pitch was horrendous that day and we played some amazing football to beat them 6-1, before going to Rotherham and winning 5-1.

'But we had a poor February and won just once so the 2-1 win at home to Wolves in March was massive for our confidence.'

I interject but Elphick beats me to it to bring up a game that had social media purring. Craven Cottage, on the banks of the Thames, was the balmy setting for a Friday night Sky game under the lights – it was to be the moment that ignited Elphick and co into the consciousness of a nation.

Cook's stunning strike on the angle from the edge of the penalty area six minutes from time capped off Ritchie and Pitman's doubles as Fulham were systematically dismantled 5-1. Elphick's eyes light up.

'We got some great press from that game,' he beams. 'It was a devastating performance and Cookie's goal capped it off.

'Cookie is just naturally gifted. Technically he is clean and very athletic and he scored those kind of goals in training all the time. I didn't see much of him when we were both at Brighton as he was a bit younger than me and was with the development squad, but when I came to Bournemouth I knew he was going to be a special player.

'We had a team night out after that game and we were sitting in a restaurant in London on the Saturday afternoon watching the results come in and they all went for us. We went up to second and that was when it dawned on us – after that it was showtime!

'A lot of managers don't like their players talking about promotion but we were talking about it, I promise you! I don't care what anyone says, money is a motivation when you're in the Championship and there were bonuses and financial rewards for all of us potentially. Sky were taking a real interest in us and so were the national papers after the Fulham game. It was all building up.'

Pitman added to his west London brace with a hat-trick as Blackpool were hammered 4-0 at Dean Court the following weekend, while a 1-1 draw at Cardiff and 3-0 win at home to Middlesbrough completed an unbeaten March.

But behind the scenes, the unrelenting pressure and physical demands of the Championship were taking their toll on Howe and his squad. Within touching distance of the ultimate prize, the Miracle Man had one more ace up his sleeve, but not before a disagreement with his captain.

'We lost at Brentford during the poor run in February,' remembers Elphick, 'and me and the gaffer had a bit of a falling out after that game. There had been a bit of talk in the paper about us bringing in a striker on loan and obviously the lads read and hear everything. As we came off the pitch that day I said to Jason Tindall, "JT, we need a lift. A new face. The dressing room has gone flat."

'He looked at me a bit puzzled but I think he felt the same really. We were on the way back from the game and Eddie called me to the front of the bus. He said, "I hear you've made a remark to JT." I told him what I had told Jason, that we needed some kind of lift to get us over the line.

'He didn't take it well and we had a ding-dong on the bus. I wasn't saying it out of spite or for any other reason than what I was seeing in the dressing room. The vibe I was getting as captain was that we needed a kick up the backside and something to boost us.

'A few weeks later he signed Kenwyne Jones.'

Jones's career had taken him from the pure sands of Trinidad and Tobago to the Premier League home of Southampton in 2004 before loan spells at Sheffield Wednesday and Stoke City. A Caribbean Steve Fletcher, Jones's game was not simply about goals but also about unsettling defenders through size and clever thinking, the perfect hulk for a big man, little man combination.

Such was the value in those attributes, he made a £6m switch to Sunderland in 2007 before rejoining Stoke for £8m in 2010. Thirteen goals in 88 top-flight starts, though, told the story of a career that never truly peaked.

At Cardiff City while the Cherries clung on to their dream, Howe couldn't resist when Jones was offered to him on a short-term loan on 26 March. A week later he was named among the substitutes for a tricky Friday night visit to Ipswich.

Refreshed following a warm-weather training camp in Dubai – a reward for the form in early March which erased February's failings and took them back to the top of the Championship, Howe's squad saw Jones make an instant impact at Portman Road.

Trailing to Freddie Sears's sixth-minute strike, Howe's men toiled but to no avail. The Miracle Man removed Cook from the fray and placed an arm around Jones, giving him a gentle push on to the field in the 79th minute.

Three minutes later, bedlam. Jones gave Tommy Smith the slip as Ritchie's cross swung in from the left, his glancing header hitting the net as if some kind of metaphor for pure relief.

'Kenwyne was a massive character and super flamboyant,' recalls Elphick, his smile as wide as Jones's frame. 'A lovely, lovely guy who was very chilled out but who had a huge presence.

'We'd done everything but score when his header went in at Ipswich when we were 1-0 behind. He came on as a sub and headed the goal and set off to do his cartwheel celebration – all of a sudden the feel-good factor was back and we were off and running again.

'That was what I was trying to get across to Eddie and JT at Brentford, although I can see how they may have thought that their captain had lost faith in them. I hadn't – we were good enough, but we had given everything and just needed a lift.

'I think they were going to sign Kenwyne anyway but I was there as captain to bridge the gap between the players and the management team so that was what I did.

'We won three on the spin after the Ipswich draw and were within touching distance when we played Sheffield Wednesday at home on 18 April.'

Jones played just 50 minutes of football in six substitute appearances during his loan spell, including 26 minutes at home to the Owls, but his impact was immeasurable.

With Wednesday at Watford on the last day, the mid-table Yorkshiremen were to play a key part in the final days of the most dramatic and enthralling of campaigns.

'It was 1-1 when Franno got sent off late on against Wednesday,' remembers Elphick, 'but Matt Ritchie scored to make it 2-1 with six minutes to go. But Adam Smith, who had come on as a sub, gave away a penalty in the last minute and they scored. He was absolutely distraught afterwards. He thought he'd ruined the season for us because we stayed second after that result due to Watford beating Birmingham.'

The following Saturday, as Elphick sat engulfed by frustration at the Chewton Glen, his team-mates watched open-mouthed as promotion rivals Middlesbrough were beaten 4-3 by lowly Fulham and fourth-placed Norwich could only muster a 1-1 draw against Rotherham.

'We knew three points against Bolton would take us up barring a ridiculous goal swing on the last day,' says Elphick, 'but Simon Francis was suspended so Smithy had to play.

'Adam was unbelievable that night we were promoted, though, and it just showed how important our squad was. The night we needed him most, he was there.

'The next thing was to win the league and you'd think it would be a big ask to get ourselves right for Charlton on the last day after we'd already been promoted. I assure you it wasn't.

'Eddie told us to enjoy ourselves on Monday night after the Bolton game but he wanted us in at midday on the Tuesday for training. We were then back in on Wednesday preparing to win the title.'

The sun shone over the Valley on the Championship's final Saturday, providing rare warmth for the Charlton supporters who had sat under a dark cloud for much of the campaign thanks to the kind of off-field instability usually reserved for their opponents.

Ritchie and Arter put the Miracle Man's miracle workers 2-0 up inside 12 minutes, before Ritchie doubled his tally five minutes from time. It was par for the course for Howe's side, while the unexpected scenario took place at Vicarage Road.

Needing a win to make sure of the title and eliminate the Cherries' dominance in SE7, Matěj Vydra had set Watford on their way with a goal in the 25th minute. But as the final whistle sounded at the Valley, Atdhe Nuhiu, felled by Smith for the Owls' last-minute penalty two weeks earlier, poked home from close range to deny the Hornets the title by one point.

Elphick scans the host of images on my laptop, Championship title held aloft. He is clearly emotional, perhaps through the feelings evoked by such glorious memories but also through grief that those days are now over.

'There was a lot going on off the field at Charlton,' he recalls, 'and I think their supporters appreciated what we were about and that we had come through dark times to get to the Premier League. Their fans were amazing that day and embraced us.

'They were also great at keeping us up to date with the score at Watford. The Sheffield Wednesday fans were singing, "AFC Bournemouth, they're top of the league" at the Watford supporters after Wednesday scored!

'It was a monumental day, another great performance and an amazing story. Look at Harry Arter – he had been bought for £4,000 from Woking and was sent out on loan to Carlisle by Lee Bradbury. He scored in the game that won us the Championship title. It was another incredible tale and another fitting moment for a player who had committed himself to the club. The likes of Harry, Marc Pugh and Brett Pitman should never be forgotten.

'Post-match at Charlton was a bit of a blur to be honest but I'll never forget the moment I lifted the trophy as long as I live. We were a ramshackle bunch, all from very different backgrounds and all with our own stories to tell. Now I am in an Aston Villa dressing room with internationals boasting 50 or 60 caps and an ex-England captain.

'But do you know what? None of them have won the Championship as we sit here today. Not one of them. I have, with an amazing team at an incredible club and that's special to me and always will be. We made history.'

UP WITH THE BIG BOYS

EDDIE Howe greets me with a smile, but is still clearly simmering inside. It is the first week of March 2018 and Howe's men have, just 48 hours before our scheduled meeting, let slip a crucial 1-0 lead at Leicester City, Riyad Mahrez's 97th-minute free kick coming a full three minutes beyond referee Lee Probert's recommended four minutes of stoppage time.

'It was tough to take,' Howe admits through gritted teeth. 'But that's what football can do to you.'

We leave it there.

Howe is approaching the end of his third season as a Premier League manager, mixing it with the very best just nine years after taking the Dean Court reins for the very first time in that 2009 League Two defeat at Darlington.

It has been a journey of both discovery and self-preservation, the eyes of the country's media focused on a man who many believe will manage England one day.

'I remember the press conferences years ago,' laughs Howe. 'There used to be about four people there and three of them were usually from the *Echo.*'

Howe's engaging weekly briefings now see dozens of journalists jostling for position and they are run with the kind of precision the manager reserves for his own training sessions with the heroes of the past and the stars of the present.

Most of the Premier League press pack learned quickly that attempting to trip up AFC Bournemouth's young manager is an ill-advised pastime. Howe can be as ruthless with the media as he is known to be with his players when required and when away from prying eyes.

He is a decision-maker, one who sticks to his guns often in the face of fierce criticism. A man to whom loyalty means everything. As we settle in to talk in the players' lounge at Dean Court's Pavilion, winger Junior Stanislas says goodbye to his manager, training for another day complete.

Downstairs in the main stadium reception, Jermain Defoe greets a group of charity walkers from the North East, trekking from Bournemouth to Sunderland's Stadium of Light in memory of little Bradley Lowery, the young Black Cats fan who struck up a beautiful friendship with the England striker.

Nathan Ake, the club's £20m record signing, has a laugh with the receptionist as he signs some club memorabilia. Adam Smith joins in, one of many players in whom Howe has showed genuine faith and belief since the days of toil in League One, often in the face of criticism from sections of the supporter base.

As he had done following League One promotion in 2010, Howe had no time to take stock, let alone bask in his achievements, when the 2015/16 Premier League fixtures emerged.

'The moment we won promotion the enormity of the challenge that we were facing began to set in so I didn't have a chance to enjoy it at all,' he laughs.

'Suddenly it wasn't, "Great, we're in the Premier League." It was, "Right, how are we going to stay here?"

'It was a difficult summer in 2015 because there were a lot of unknowns. We didn't know who in the squad was going to step up, we didn't know how good the league was going to be, we didn't know exactly what we were going to need in terms of recruitment. But I knew the bulk of the players who had got us to that point deserved the chance to show they could step up. That was very important to me.

'So, we were going in blind to an extent and we were hoping that a lot of those questions would be answered positively but there were a lot of unknowns to deal with.

'With every promotion we've had, we've had those unknowns because you are never sure how your squad will fare with any step up in standard but it is magnified in the Premier League because of the pressures off the pitch. The pressure and intensity of the media and how the players react to that is a big difference and another thing we all had to adapt to.'

Another adaptation for a manager not traditionally renowned for his big spending during transfer windows was heading upstairs to tell the board to get their cheque books out. A popular misconception around Howe is that he is poor in the transfer market, yet the likes of Callum Wilson, a mere £2m from Coventry, would suggest otherwise.

With the Premier League, though, comes 'more zeros', laughs Howe when asked about the skyrocketing transfer market since the Cherries' promotion was secured.

'Recruitment was top of my list in the sense that all of a sudden we were open to a lot more players potentially wanting to come here,' he continues. 'In the Championship we were fighting against a lot of clubs bigger than us for the same pool of players – of course in the Premier League every club is bigger than us but the difference is players *want* to play in the Premier League. Suddenly we were open to a big pool of players from abroad, but we didn't know anything about them because our scouting network was quite small in the Championship.

'One of the biggest challenges I faced was going to the board to say we needed to expand everything, coaching staff, medical team, scouting team, everything. If we didn't have those things in place, how were we going to recruit players?

'There was a lot of work behind the scenes to make us better as a football club that summer, but it was a shock to the system for everyone because suddenly the numbers we were talking about were huge. The transfer fees were uncomfortable enough in the Championship but even more so in the Premier League. You're sitting there in your seat talking to the board and just looking at all these zeros on the contracts – it's frightening.

'It was a very, very difficult summer in 2015. We were happy with what we'd achieved, of course, but the enormity of what was going to happen was beginning to hit home.

'The recruitment side was very difficult and there were a lot of decisions made with the best intentions but with not a lot of knowledge because we didn't know what we were going to face.

'We tried to be smart and think differently because a lot of the players who were on our original list, we were never going to get. We whittled our way through the list because the established Premier League clubs were taking the names at the top. It was very tricky.'

The Miracle Man, in part at least, stuck with what he knew from successes, and in some cases, failures past. Ivorian Max Gradel, who, despite relegation under Bond, had performed well during a 34-game loan spell at Dean Court from Leicester City in 2007/08, was recruited from Saint-Étienne.

Howe had been impressed with Middlesbrough playmaker Lee Tomlin during his side's time in the Championship so signed him for £3.5m, while Tyrone Mings was recruited from Ipswich for a then club record £8m. Sylvain Distin, the experienced centre-half, joined from Everton on a free, while striker Glenn Murray's £4m switch from Crystal Palace and Josh King's move from Blackburn Rovers completed Howe's summer spending.

But as new men arrived, heroes of the past were coming to the end of their adventure. Brett Pitman had worked with Howe since arriving at the club from the Channel Islands as a raw and untried striker back in 2005 with Sean O'Driscoll still at the helm. Ten years, save for a two-year spell at Bristol City, three promotions and 96 Cherries league goals later, Howe knew it was to be one of his biggest decisions during that summer of realisation.

'Brett was a decision I wasn't relishing at all that summer,' recalls Howe.

'I'd spent so long working with him that it was always going to be tough but I called him into the office and told him that I was more than happy for him to remain at the club and be part of the squad but I couldn't promise him game time.

'He knew we were going to be bringing in other strikers and that he would potentially be more of a squad player so he made the decision to go to Ipswich because he wanted to play regularly.

'I can only speak highly of Brett for everything he achieved here. He was great to have around and a very determined character who wanted to succeed at the club. The goals he scored in League Two, League One and the Championship were key to the club's rise and I can honestly say without Brett, I wouldn't be sitting here today.

'In terms of finishing ability, he's right up there with the very best players I have worked with, but it's very hard to compare him with anyone else because he is such a unique player. He will go down in the history of this club because of everything he achieved here and how he was as a professional.'

Interest had been building throughout the warmer months. How would this little club fare among the giants of the Premier League? The 'fairy tale', words not popular with Howe, of the club's rise from the depths of League Two and administration was garnering international attention from the likes of NBC Sports in America, yet the backing of owner Demin during Howe's recruitment slog was the real story. The Cherries weren't simply there to enjoy a few days out at Manchester United and the like – Howe, and the club's board, meant business.

An opening weekend 1-0 defeat at home to Aston Villa was the kind of drab result the fanfare always delivers, though, and the pyrotechnics of life in the top flight were soon doused by reality of the task ahead.

The following Monday, Howe's men made their debuts on *Monday Night Football* as the Sky cameras clamoured for a piece of the action – another 1-0 defeat did little to excite even the broadcasters, who spent more time elaborating on which members of Howe's starting 11 were Liverpool fans, as if the early season Premier League clash was some kind of FA Cup giant-killing plot.

The heat of an unusual summer refused to abate as the Cherries travelled to Upton Park on 22 August, the swansong season of the famous old ground in London's East End. It was to be a performance that ignited a renewed belief in Howe's players. Wilson put the visitors 2-0 up inside half an hour, before a Mark Noble penalty and Cheikhou Kouyate strike levelled things up before the hour mark.

Substitute Marc Pugh, though, completed a personal milestone of his own when putting the Cherries 3-2 up, his goal capping his scoring exploits in all four divisions, plus the Conference, for the likes of Kidderminster Harriers, Shrewsbury Town and Hereford.

When Wilson slotted home a 79th-minute penalty after Carl Jenkinson had been dismissed for hauling down Gradel, Howe was in dreamland. Or at least he was until the 82nd minute when Modibo Maiga made it 4-3.

'What was I thinking?' laughs Howe. 'Well, my first thoughts were, "Please hold on," because we'd gone 4-2 up and they were starting to pressure us when they scored their third late on.

'But it was an amazing game and certainly gave us the belief we needed at that point in the season. Our wingers were superb that day and Max Gradel gave Carl Jenkinson a torrid time. Marc

Pugh came on in the second half and also ran their full-backs ragged.

'Obviously the game will be remembered for Callum's hat-trick and that's why it was such a blow to lose him just a few weeks later. He was very close to an England call during that spell, there is no doubt about that. He was so unlucky to get the injury he did at that stage.'

Ah, yes. The injuries. As we sit and reflect on the season, it is a stark reminder that almost all of Howe's achievements throughout his time as a manager have been realised by overcoming genuine adversity.

With Hartlepool United dispatched without breaking sweat in the League Cup, Leicester arrived at Dean Court, the latest established Premier League club to try their luck at the little ground on the south coast. Within 27 minutes of the second half, the Cherries in front thanks to Wilson's goal midway through the first period, Howe's masterplan had been torn up and tossed in the trash as both Mings and Gradel succumbed to serious knee injuries.

'We lost them both in that game against Leicester,' reflects Howe, 'and Tyrone was only a few minutes into his debut when he went down. Max's injury affected me more in a way because we'd fought so long to get him, but it was a hammer blow losing both of them like that.

'It was cruel and tough for Tyrone because he had felt all his dreams were fulfilled making a move to the Premier League and suddenly it was taken away from him.

'Max had looked really good for us – in that game against Leicester he was superb in the first half and caused them no end of problems. We lost him and for a player of his age it was difficult for him to come back from an injury like that, especially when he later did it again and we lost him for a second spell.

'I have nothing but good things to say about him because his character is infectious and he's such a positive guy. I just felt for him so much because he was never able to show us his best form.'

A Jamie Vardy penalty just four minutes from time completed a miserable afternoon for Howe – but just four weeks later, and with a solitary victory over Sunderland and stunning Matt Ritchie volley the only high points of a lean September, the manager was to suffer another huge injury blow and the club was to lose one of its most loyal and respected stalwarts.

At Stoke City's Britannia Stadium on 26 September, the Cherries had started brightly, before Wilson suffered a serious knee injury after a clash with Philipp Wollscheid in the 17th minute. And as the Cherries striker lay stricken, Howe was unaware of a tragedy unfolding on the side of the pitch.

Former club photographer Mick Cunningham, working as a freelance for the *Daily Echo*, had collapsed pitchside just moments after photographing Wilson's agony. His first Premier League assignment, Cunningham had spent years covering the club's exploits in the lower leagues. As Howe counted the cost of another defeat, after Jonathan Walters and Mame Biram Diouf had cancelled out Dan Gosling's strike, and the loss of Wilson, news began to filter through that Cunningham had died in hospital.

'I only found out that Mick had been taken ill pitchside very late that night,' says Howe, his eyes softening. 'When I found out he had passed away, it hit me and everyone around the club very hard. It put everything else into perspective.

'Mick was one of those people who was part of the fabric of the football club. He had worked so hard for so long and much of that was in the days when the club was struggling on and off the field. Without people like him, football clubs can't function. We all miss him so much.

'I know he would have been so proud to cover the club in the Premier League, but he is greatly missed by everyone around the club. He was a wonderful guy.'

Grieving, rocked by his injury nightmare and with the transfer window closed, the next five fixtures were to test Howe's resolve beyond anything he had experienced before.

Successive 5-1 defeats at Manchester City and at home to Tottenham were quickly followed by a 2-0 reverse 30 miles down the A31 at Southampton and a 1-0 home defeat to Newcastle United. Howe the pragmatist was left searching for something, anything, to turn his fortunes.

'The thing most people don't consider with injuries like the ones to Callum, Max and Tyrone is what is left behind,' insists Howe. 'We were left with a group of players smaller in number who had witnessed three of their team-mates, who they were banking on, go down with serious long-term injuries.

'The mentality was shaken. They were suddenly thinking, "Are we going to be good enough now?" As a manager, I had to try to build them up to think they would be fine, even without those players. We lost three key players and the window had shut. We felt like we had been hit really heavily before the season had even begun properly.'

Goals from King and Gosling at Swansea were enough to stop the rot and gain a point, but it was the clash at home to Everton a week later that would act as a tonic for the misery inflicted by the heavy defeats to City and Spurs.

In a game that almost reduced Sky Sports' Chris Kamara to tears live on air, four goals came in the final ten minutes as the Toffees went from two goals up to being pegged back to 3-3.

Smith made it 2-1, before Stanislas levelled the match three minutes from time. On the stroke of full time, though, Ross Barkley's strike looked to have won it for Everton before Stanislas popped up in the seventh minute of stoppage time to make it 3-3.

'That spell in October and November was one of the toughest of my managerial career,' Howe admits. 'We'd had the injuries to those key players and I think we lost our identity and what we were about during that period, in part due to the injuries but not solely because of that.

'It was a difficult run of games and when you come up against the likes of Tottenham and Manchester City in the middle of a run like that, in some respects it is only going to go one way. I learned a lot during that period and the players did too and thankfully the games against Swansea and Everton at the end of that run were games that got us back on an even keel.

'The Everton game in particular was a real turning point. We were 2-0 down and I admit I was thinking, "Where do we go from here if we lose this?" We were on such a difficult run of form and the run-in was so hard that we knew we needed results at that stage of the season if we were going to stay up.

'When their goal went in so late, it was just the worst feeling. It was one of the worst I've had as a manager just because it was so late and in such a crucial game.

'But the players were never going to give it up and getting a draw in that game definitely paved the way for the games against Chelsea and Manchester United in December.'

Jose Mourinho's west Londoners were experiencing the kind of slump in form that usually results in Roman Abramovich wielding the axe, yet the Portuguese was remarkably still in situ, despite seven defeats in his past 14 league games, when the Cherries rocked up at Stamford Bridge on 5 December.

Glenn Murray, whose switch to Dean Court from Selhurst Park had yielded a couple of goals during that difficult October, bundled home the winning goal eight minutes from time having been on the pitch for just 99 seconds. It was as unexpected as it was expected, depending on whether you were Howe or Mourinho.

Two weeks later, following a ninth defeat in 16 against front-runners Leicester City, Mourinho was gone. Unintentionally, Howe had done for arguably one of the finest managers in the land.

'It was a huge result,' he says. 'We really needed something from that game to build on what we had done against Everton and it was a typical Glenn Murray goal really. Glenn scored some really important goals for us while he was at the club. He's a very clever player and that showed in his performances for us that season.

'Obviously Jose left Chelsea shortly after that but I never take any pleasure in seeing a manager lose his job. It was a brilliant result for this club, of course, but I would never look at it beyond that and I am always sad when managers lose their jobs, whoever they are and whatever club they are at. Chelsea and Jose was no different.'

Buoyed and with renewed belief, a run of games that would have struck fear into Howe's rookies on fixture release day was fast becoming a sequence of results that would go more than just a little way to securing safety.

Manchester United were next at home, Louis van Gaal's side under a degree of pressure themselves following a tepid stalemate against West Ham. Howe's side, meanwhile, were grieving again – this time for the family of a team-mate.

Unbeknown to the supporters filing into Dean Court for a first look at the Premier League's most successful club, midfielder Harry Arter and his partner had been left devastated by the still-birth of their first child, Renee, just two days earlier.

Howe's man-management was to come to the fore again, giving the grief-stricken Arter the opportunity to play against United with the support of his team-mates.

Stanislas opened the scoring direct from a corner after just two minutes, sparking celebrations that hinted at Arter's inner turmoil. The man himself, though, showed no signs of simmering emotion until an 84th-minute booking. By then, the Cherries were 2-1 to the good and in charge of proceedings, King's 54th-minute strike cancelling out Marouane Fellaini's scruffy equaliser.

In fear of Arter boiling over, Howe substituted his man to a surge of emotion four minutes from time, before embracing him on the final whistle as news of his loss spread through the press box and on to the terraces.

'Arguably the Manchester United result was bigger than Chelsea because of what it meant to the players, who were playing for Harry that day,' recalls Howe.

'I'd spoken to Harry in the days before the game and asked him if he was certain he wanted to play.

'He did and I had to put my trust in his decision. He's a whole-hearted player and of course it was a concern that his emotions could potentially boil over after everything he had been through, but it was arguably his best performance for Bournemouth.

'He was running on pure emotion and you can see how much the players wanted to win for him in the goal celebrations from that game. His performance that day was outstanding.'

In the toughest of circumstances and with Arter at the centre of their thoughts, Howe's men were on a roll. The following weekend at West Brom required a late Charlie Daniels penalty to secure a 2-1 win after the Baggies had seen both Salomon Rondon and James McClean dismissed, before draws against Crystal Palace and Leicester sandwiched a 2-0 home defeat to Arsenal.

The Gunners loss concerned Howe enough to return to the boardroom, some final ingredients required in the Miracle Man's mind. This time the cheque book was opened to the tune of £18m – £10m for Wolves striker Benik Afobe and an £8m return swoop for Lewis Grabban who had gone AWOL from the Norwich team hotel in August after a Howe bid was turned down.

Afobe hit the ground running with a goal in a near perfect 3-0 demolition of Grabban's former employers at Carrow Road, a performance that drew a line through a 3-1 home defeat to West Ham just four days earlier.

Afobe was on target again a week later at Sunderland, although Patrick van Aanholt's goal for the Black Cats spoiled the long trip to the North East. With Portsmouth safely dispatched in the FA Cup, Afobe again found the net in a 2-1 win at Crystal Palace under the lights.

For Howe, though, that was as good as his February got and again the Miracle Man found himself searching for something to ignite his players. Step forward Southampton, a club that had offered him the manager's position after sacking Alan Pardew in 2010.

Under the lights at Dean Court, the Cherries were frenetic. Steve Cook volleyed home after Fraser Forster had parried Matt Ritchie's free kick, before Afobe headed home the second 11 minutes from time. It was another defining result that would pave the way for key victories over relegation rivals Swansea and Newcastle in the following weeks.

'I never want to win against Southampton any more than any other team,' laughs Howe when probed. 'Certainly being offered the position at Southampton had nothing to do with that game and how I felt after the result.

'It was a huge win for the fans, of course, as Southampton are rivals and traditionally have always been a much bigger club playing at a higher level, so it was massive for the supporters.

'In terms of our season it came at a good time and we followed it up with wins at Newcastle and at home to Swansea. It set us up for staying in the division.'

But not before two more heavy defeats to Spurs and City, games that saw the Cherries concede seven goals and score none. A trip to Aston Villa on 9 April, though, was to seal the fate of both clubs.

Cook drilled home from close range on the stroke of half-time before King took advantage of a calamitous defensive mix-up to make it 2-0 on 74 minutes. Despite Jordan Ayew making it 2-1 late on, the defeat all but relegated Villa, while Howe's men passed the magic 40-point mark.

Howe casts a forlorn look as we discuss the run-in, four defeats and a solitary draw that tell the true story of the pressure of the Premier League.

'Looking back now I can reflect on it a little differently,' admits Howe, 'but at the time I was hugely disappointed by the results at the end of the season. But the players were finished – they had nothing left mentally and I see that now. As soon as we were safe that wave of relief swept over them and I can see those results happened largely because of that.'

The drama wasn't finished there, though, with the club's first top-flight visit to Old Trafford curtailed by the now infamous toilet bomb threat in the Sir Alex Ferguson Stand.

'The Manchester United game was huge on the last day and I was really looking forward to it as it was my first visit to Old Trafford,' smiles Howe. 'The players were buzzing too as we approached Old Trafford and the fans were all packed outside.

'I really thought from the way the players were that I was going to get a great performance from them, but then we were told there was a bomb scare in the stadium. Once I got my head around that my first thoughts were for the safety of my family as I had quite a number of people at the game that day.

'It was a bizarre scenario and the rescheduled game the following Tuesday was tough for everyone to get up for after that and that showed in the 3-1 defeat, the performance and the low crowd.'

Howe took time to reflect that summer, a luxury not commonly associated with the Miracle Man, who by keeping the Cherries in the Premier League at the first time of asking had presided over another season of wonder. As well as pondering changes to his playing staff ahead of a second gruelling campaign, the manager took stock on a more personal level.

'Getting into the Premier League hits you like a train,' he smiles briefly, 'and it has been more demanding on my time than any of the seasons before it. It's extremely tough on my family because it does take up so much of my time and it is unrelenting in its nature. You're never any further ahead than the next game and that first season was unquestionably the toughest of my managerial career.

'When I took over in 2009 I didn't have anything to base my knowledge on so tried to instil my own way of working, but I learned more about myself during that first Premier League season than at any other point in my career.

'Being in the Premier League means everything, but largely because of what we have been through as a club to get there. It's unique and very special and being a part of that means everything to me.'

THE MIRACLE MEN FROM LEAGUE TWO TO THE PREMIER LEAGUE*

Players who made at least one league appearance between 2007 and 2016 – information correct June 2018

Miles Addison

Big defender signed on loan from Derby County by Lee Bradbury in February 2012. Signed permanently in July of that year, before falling out of favour following Eddie Howe's return in October. Spent time on loan at Rotherham, Blackpool and Scunthorpe before joining Peterborough United permanently in 2015.

Benik Afobe

Club record £10m signing from Wolverhampton Wanderers when he penned a four-and-a-half-year deal with the Cherries in January 2016.

Started well, finishing the club's maiden Premier League season with four league goals, before bagging six goals in 2016/17. Afobe was loaned back to Wolves in January 2018, scoring six goals as the Molineux side clinched the Championship title, and rejoined the Midlanders permanently in June 2018 before being loaned to Stoke City just 11 days later.

Ryan Allsop

Highly rated goalkeeper who caught Howe's eye while at Leyton Orient. Signed for the Cherries in January 2013 and claimed the number one jersey from David James in March of that year. Struck down with glandular fever in October 2013, though, Allsop was a victim of the Cherries' promotion to the second tier as Lee Camp and then Artur Boruc became Howe's chosen goalkeepers. Allsop was sent out on loan to Coventry, Portsmouth, Wycombe and Blackpool, before signing a temporary deal with Lincoln City in January 2018 and was released by the Cherries in May after five years with the club.

Darren Anderton

Former Portsmouth, Tottenham and England midfielder who won 30 caps for his country between 1994 and 2001. A member of Terry Venables's Euro 96 squad beaten on penalties by Germany in the semi-finals, Anderton spent time at Birmingham City and Wolverhampton Wanderers after leaving White Hart Lane in 2004 after 12 years. Signed for the Cherries on 8 September 2006 on a 'pay as you play' basis – the same day manager Sean O'Driscoll left to take charge at Doncaster Rovers.

Scored a spectacular free kick on his Cherries debut at Scunthorpe and notched a first career hat-trick against Leyton Orient in February 2007, before a stunning strike against Chester in December 2008 ensured he retired from playing on a high.

Harry Arter

Released by Charlton Athletic in 2009 after just one substitute appearance for the Addicks, Arter undertook unsuccessful trials at both Ipswich and Gillingham before signing for non-league Woking.

Spotted by Howe, Arter signed for the Cherries in June 2010 for just £4,000 but was sent on loan to Carlisle by Bradbury in

March 2011 and looked set to leave Dean Court. However, his form was much improved when he returned to Dorset and Arter soon became a mainstay of the Cherries squad during Howe's second spell.

Called up by the Republic of Ireland in 2015, Arter won 11 caps but once again fell out of favour at Dean Court in 2018.

Lee Barnard

Striker who signed on loan at Dean Court from Southampton in August 2012. Scored four goals in 15 appearances under Paul Groves and then Eddie Howe before returning to St Mary's Stadium in December.

After loan spells at Oldham and Southend, Barnard joined the Shrimpers permanently in June 2014 before spells at Crawley and Braintree. Currently playing for Chelmsford City.

Adam Barrett

Imposing centre-half signed from Crystal Palace by Lee Bradbury in July 2011. Barrett went on to make 21 league appearances for the Cherries before joining Gillingham in August 2012. The defender went on to complete spells at AFC Wimbledon and Southend before retiring in 2017 at the age of 37.

Marvin Bartley

A combative central midfielder, Bartley was a mainstay of the 2009 Greatest Escape and 2010 League Two promotion squads under Howe. Signed by Kevin Bond in 2007, Bartley was working as a window fitter in Reading and playing for non-league Hampton & Richmond Borough before moving to Dean Court.

After missing out on the 2011 League One play-off final under Bradbury, Bartley linked up with Howe again at Burnley for £350,000 where he became popular with the Turf Moor supporters.

After Howe departed the North West to return to the Cherries, though, Bartley spent six months on loan at Leyton Orient before signing permanently in January 2014.

After joining Scottish outfit Hibernian in July 2015, Bartley helped the Edinburgh side to their first Scottish Cup in 114 years in 2016 before winning promotion from the Scottish Championship the following season.

Mathieu Baudry

French centre-half signed from Troyes in January 2011 by Bradbury. After finding opportunities hard to come by at Dean Court, Baudry signed on loan for Dagenham & Redbridge in March 2012 before penning a permanent deal with Leyton Orient, for whom he went on to make more than 120 appearances. Signed for League Two Doncaster Rovers in May 2016.

Asmir Begovic

Bosnian goalkeeper who made his Cherries debut under Kevin Bond during an unsuccessful 2007 loan spell from Portsmouth. After further loan deals at Yeovil Town and Ipswich, Begovic joined Stoke City in 2010 where he went on to make more than 150 appearances for the Premier League Potters.

In 2015 he joined Premier League big-guns Chelsea as number two to Thibaut Courtois, but after just 19 appearances for the Blues, Begovic rejoined the Cherries in 2017, taking the number one shirt from Artur Boruc.

Nicholas Bignall

Reading-born striker who spent one month on loan with the Cherries under Howe in 2010, making five appearances. After being released by his home-town club, Bignall spent time at Basingstoke Town and currently plays for Hungerford Town in the National League South.

Artur Boruc

Polish international goalkeeper whose career began with hometown club Pogon Siedice. Boruc moved to Legia Warsaw in 1999 before joining Scottish Premiership big-guns Celtic in 2005.

After five years at Celtic Park, Boruc left to join Southampton and made almost 50 appearances at St Mary's before linking up with Howe in a 2014 Dean Court loan deal.

After signing permanently in 2015, Boruc was relegated to number two after Begovic's arrival in 2017.

Lee Bradbury

Well-travelled striker whose career started with Cowes Sports on the Isle of Wight. Bradbury signed for Portsmouth in 1995 before a string of impressive performances saw Manchester City break their club record to sign the frontman for £3m in 1997.

Bradbury went on to make almost 50 appearances for City before joining Crystal Palace for £1.5m in 1998.

After just a year at Selhurst Park, though, Bradbury rejoined Portsmouth for £300,000 in 1999 where he was loaned out to Sheffield Wednesday and Derby County before joining Walsall in 2004. Spells at Oxford United and Southend followed before Bradbury linked up with Kevin Bond at the Cherries in 2007.

Converted to right-back, Bradbury went on to make more than 100 appearances for the Dean Court side before replacing Howe as manager in 2011.

But having missed out on promotion to the Championship during his first season in charge, Bradbury was sacked in March 2012 and joined non-league Havant & Waterlooville where he piloted the club into the National League in 2018.

David Button

Signed on loan from Tottenham by Howe in January 2009, Button made four appearances during the Greatest Escape season. Loan spells at no fewer than nine other clubs followed before Button joined Charlton in August 2012, making just five appearances.

The keeper signed for Brentford a year later and went on to make more than 100 appearances for the west Londoners before joining rivals Fulham in July 2016.

Nathan Byrne

Stylish full-back who made nine appearances for the Cherries between July 2011 and February 2012, taking in three managers during his short spell at the club on loan from Tottenham.

After further loan spells at Crawley and Swindon, Byrne joined the County Ground side on a permanent basis in July 2013.

He went on to serve Wolverhampton Wanderers before joining Wigan in 2016.

Lee Camp

Experienced goalkeeper signed by Howe on loan from West Brom in 2013. The Northern Irishman went on to make almost 50 appearances for the Cherries after signing permanently in January 2014.

Camp lost his place to Artur Boruc, though, and joined Rotherham in 2015 before signing for Cardiff City two years later. Spent the second half of the 2017/18 campaign on loan at struggling Sunderland.

Josh Carmichael

Poole-born midfielder who came through the ranks at Dean Court and made his league debut under Lee Bradbury in 2011. After loan spells at Gosport Borough, Welling and Torquay United, Carmichael joined Gosport permanently in 2016 before switching to Weymouth in 2017.

Jean-Francois Christophe

French defender signed on loan from Portsmouth by Bond in 2007. Made five appearances as the Cherries were relegated to League Two before joining Yeovil and then Southend on loan.

Released by Portsmouth, Christophe signed permanently at Southend in January 2009 before spells at Oldham Athletic and Lincoln City.

Jack Collison

Cultured Welsh international midfielder signed on loan by Howe from boyhood club West Ham in October 2013. After four appearances for the Cherries, Collison joined Wigan on loan before switching permanently to Ipswich and then Peterborough. Retired in 2016 aged just 27 after failing to overcome a series of knee injuries.

Alan Connell

Enfield-born striker signed from Ipswich by Sean O'Driscoll in 2002, a spell that saw him make more than 50 appearances before being snapped up by Torquay United in 2005.

After spells with Hereford United and Brentford, Connell rejoined the Cherries in 2008 under Bond and made a further 50 appearances before switching to Grimsby Town in 2010.

Further spells at Swindon Town, Bradford City and Northampton Town followed, before Connell finished his playing career in non-league with Havant & Waterlooville and then Poole Town.

Now part of the Cherries' youth set-up, coaching alongside Mark Molesley.

Steve Cook

Centre-half signed by Lee Bradbury, initially on loan, from Brighton in October 2011 as a raw 20-year-old.

After making his league debut against Preston North End, Cook went on to become an established member of Bradbury's starting 11 and signed permanently in January 2012 for £150,000.

The Hastings-born star then flourished under Howe after the manager's return in 2012 and, alongside captain Tommy Elphick, led the Cherries to promotion from League One in 2013 and then the Championship two years later.

Became the first Cherries player to rack up 100 Premier League appearances early in 2018.

Shaun Cooper

Isle of Wight-born utility player signed by O'Driscoll from Portsmouth in 2005.

Cooper went on to spend seven years at Dean Court, making more than 200 appearances.

Rejecting a new deal under Paul Groves in 2012, Cooper joined Crawley Town, before spells back at Fratton Park and with Torquay and Sutton United.

Cooper retired from playing in 2017 after a spell with Poole Town and now coaches in the Cherries academy.

Mohamed Coulibaly

Signed by Howe in 2013 from Grasshoppers in Switzerland, Coulibaly endured an injury-hit spell at Dean Court and managed just a handful of appearances.

After loan spells at Coventry and Port Vale, the Senegalese winger moved to Spain with Racing Santander and then UD Logroñés. Coulibaly currently plays for Swiss side Vaduz.

Warren Cummings

Likeable Scottish international who, following loan spells at Dean Court in 2000 and 2003, signed permanently from Chelsea in time to feature in the 2003 Division Three play-off final triumph over Lincoln. Cummings went on to make almost 250 appearances for the Cherries before he was released by Groves in 2012.

After a loan spell with Crawley Town, Cummings joined AFC Wimbledon before finishing his career with Poole Town and then Havant & Waterlooville.

Charlie Daniels
Full-back who signed for the Cherries on loan from Leyton Orient in 2011. The former Tottenham left-sided defender made the deal permanent in 2012 and has gone on to make more than 200 appearances for the Dean Court club.

A mainstay of the club's promotions in 2013 and 2015, Daniels is a regular in Howe's Premier League starting 11 and has now made more than 100 top-flight appearances.

Lorenzo Davids
A cousin of former Juventus and Holland star Edgar Davids, his was a bizarre signing alongside Frank Demouge in August 2012. Suffering with a knee injury when he put pen to paper, Davids eventually made his debut a month later, but found his first-team opportunities limited when Howe returned in October.

Joined Danish side Randers in January 2013.

Frank Demouge
Like Davids, Demouge had to wait a month for his Cherries debut after sustaining a knee injury shortly after signing from Utrecht. Demouge then sustained a broken nose and concussion in his second start for the Dean Court side, before suffering a calf injury while playing for the reserves.

Howe shipped the Dutchman out on loan to Roda JC in 2013 and he signed permanently for the Eredivisie outfit later that year.

Sylvain Distin

Vastly experienced centre-half who signed from Everton ahead of the Cherries' maiden Premier League campaign in 2015.

A veteran of more than 400 Premier League appearances for the Toffees, Portsmouth and Manchester City, Distin found playing time limited due to the form of Steve Cook and Simon Francis and was released after just one season in 2016.

Ryan Doble

A Welsh under-21 international striker, Doble joined the Cherries on loan from Southampton in August 2011 and made seven appearances before signing for Shrewsbury permanently in June 2012.

Anthony Edgar

Highly rated by parent club West Ham, Edgar joined the Cherries on loan in 2009 and made his professional debut against Port Vale on 3 October. Although the Cherries were keen to extend Edgar's stay, the Football League's transfer embargo saw him return to Upton Park after just three appearances.

After leaving the Hammers in 2011, Edgar went on to play for Yeovil Town, Barnet and Dagenham & Redbridge before moving into non-league with Bishop's Stortford, Braintree, Woking and Hayes & Yeading.

Tommy Elphick

Hugely influential central defender signed from Brighton by Groves in 2012. Brighton-born, Elphick made more than 150 appearances for the Seagulls between 2005 and 2012, before linking up with the Cherries.

Forming a formidable partnership with Steve Cook, Groves handed Elphick the captain's armband later that year and, after Howe had returned from Burnley, Elphick led the Cherries to promotion into the Championship during his first season at the club.

After winning back his place in Howe's starting 11 in 2013/14, following an injury to Elliott Ward, Elphick was once again made captain and played in all 46 games the following season as the Cherries clinched the Championship title and promotion to the Premier League, making Elphick the only Cherries captain to lead his side to two promotions. After making almost 150 appearances for the club, Elphick was sold to Aston Villa in 2016 and joined Reading on loan earlier this year.

Adam Federici

Australian international goalkeeper who joined the Cherries from Reading ahead of the club's first Premier League season in 2015.

A reliable and likeable keeper, Federici made more than 200 appearances during ten years with Reading, but has found playing time difficult to come by at Dean Court as second choice to Artur Boruc and then third choice behind the Pole and Begovic.

Liam Feeney

Flying winger signed by Howe from non-league Salisbury City in 2009. Feeney made more than 100 appearances for the Cherries and was a key figure in the 2009 Greatest Escape before joining Millwall following the club's League One play-off semi-final defeat to Huddersfield in 2011.

After spending time on loan at Bolton and Blackburn, Feeney joined Wanderers in 2014 before relocating to Ewood Park two years later. In 2017, he joined Championship side Cardiff City on loan.

Matt Finlay

Born in nearby Ringwood, Finlay was part of the Cherries youth team when he made his first-team debut as a late substitute against Tranmere in 2008. Took in a spell at non-league club Bashley before joining Ringwood Town in 2014.

Darryl Flahavan

Southampton-born goalkeeper who made almost 400 appearances for Southend United between 2000 and 2008. After a spell with Crystal Palace, Flahavan was signed by Bradbury in 2011 but missed the whole of the 2012/13 season due to a shoulder injury. Flahavan left Dean Court in 2015 to join Crawley.

Steve Fletcher

Legendary, talismanic striker who made a club record 726 appearances between 1992 and 2013. Signed from home-town club Hartlepool United by Tony Pulis, Fletcher suffered relegation in 2002, won promotion in 2003, scored in the club's 5-2 win over Lincoln in the Division Three play-off final, and won promotion again in 2010 under former team-mate Howe.

After being released by Bond in 2007, Fletcher joined Chesterfield for a season and then moved to Crawley Town in 2008. In January 2009, though, rookie boss Howe came calling and the striker was released from his Broadfield Stadium contract to rejoin the Cherries.

After spearheading the Greatest Escape, Fletcher scored the winning goal against Grimsby in April 2009 that preserved the club's Football League status despite a 17-point administration deduction.

After making more than 100 appearances during his second Dean Court spell, Fletcher joined Plymouth Argyle on loan in 2012, linking up with former team-mate and then manager Carl Fletcher.

In 2013, Fletcher called time on his playing career and joined the scouting team at Dean Court. He is now assistant first-team coach under Howe.

Wes Fogden

Brighton-born midfielder who signed on loan at Dean Court from Havant & Waterlooville in October 2011 before penning a permanent deal four months later.

A hard-working and inventive midfielder, Fogden went on to make more than 50 appearances for the Cherries before joining Portsmouth in 2014.

A spell at Yeovil Town followed, before Fogden linked up with Bradbury once again when rejoining Havant in 2016.

Steven Foley

Midfielder signed from Aston Villa by Sean O'Driscoll in 2005. Foley was part of Villa's triumphant 2002 FA Youth Cup side and made more than 50 appearances for the Cherries between 2005 and 2008. He retired in 2008 after failing to overcome a serious back injury and now runs a fitness centre in his home town of Dublin.

David Forde

Capped 24 times by the Republic of Ireland, Forde was a key signing for Bond in 2008.

The keeper made 11 appearances for the Cherries while on loan from Cardiff City between March and May and joined Millwall later that year where he would make almost 300 appearances during a nine-year stay at The Den.

Forde signed for Cambridge United in 2017.

Simon Francis

Swashbuckling full-back signed by Bradbury in November 2011 on loan from Charlton Athletic. Out of favour in south London, Francis made the move permanent in July 2012 and has gone on to make more than 250 appearances for the Cherries, winning two promotions.

A key member of the 2015 Championship title-winning team, Francis was made captain by Howe following Tommy Elphick's move to Aston Villa.

Billy Franks

Defender who rose through the Dean Court youth ranks. Made one appearance in March 2008 in a 2-1 home win over Tranmere Rovers before being released.

Ryan Fraser

Lively Scottish winger signed by Howe from home-town club Aberdeen in January 2013 for £400,000. Recommended by Howe's brother, the former Dons striker Steve Lovell, Fraser has flourished at Dean Court following a season-long loan at Ipswich in 2015/16.

A Scottish international, Fraser made his debut in the 2-2 draw with England in June 2017.

Ryan Garry

Talented but injury-prone centre-half who signed from Arsenal in 2008 after being released by the Gunners. Garry made his Premier League debut in the Gunners' 6-1 win over Southampton in 2003, but missed almost all of the next four seasons due to shin splints.

Signed by Bond after a trial, Garry made more than 50 appearances for the Cherries between 2007 and 2011 but was forced to retire in 2011 at the age of 27 after failing to overcome his injury nightmare.

He is now a coach at the Arsenal academy.

Scott Golbourne

One of four Reading players signed on loan by Bond in 2007, Golbourne made five appearances for the Cherries before leaving the Royals and joining Exeter City in 2009. Spells at Barnsley and Wolverhampton Wanderers followed and Golbourne now plays for Bristol City.

Dan Gosling

Devon-born midfielder signed by Howe from Newcastle United in 2014. Having signed for Plymouth Argyle as a 16-year-old in 2006, Gosling signed for Premier League Everton two years later before moving to St James' Park in 2010.

After a short spell on loan at Blackpool, Howe swooped for the talented midfielder in May 2014 and, although Gosling found Championship appearances hard to come by during the 2014/15 title-winning campaign, he has gone on to be a regular under Howe in the Premier League.

Jeff Goulding

Sutton-born striker who signed from Fisher Athletic in 2008. Goulding scored on his Cherries debut in the Football League Trophy against Bristol Rovers in September and was part of the Cherries squad that miraculously completed the Greatest Escape in 2009. Goulding left Dean Court in 2010 and joined Cheltenham Town, before spells with Aldershot, Chelmsford City and Dover Athletic.

Josh Gowling

Cultured Coventry-born central defender who made more than 80 appearances for the Cherries between 2005 and 2008.

Following relegation to League Two in 2008, Gowling joined Carlisle United, but spent much of his first season at Brunton Park on loan at Hereford United.

After a two-year spell at Gillingham, Gowling moved to Lincoln City before three years at Kidderminster Harriers saw him make more than 100 appearances.

Gowling joined Torquay United in 2017.

Lewis Grabban

Much-travelled striker signed by Paul Groves from Rotherham in 2012. Born in Croydon, Grabban joined Crystal Palace at 13 and made his Eagles debut in 2005.

After three years with Millwall between 2008 and 2011, Grabban spent time at Brentford before joining Rotherham, where he plundered 18 goals in 43 appearances.

Joining the Cherries for £300,000, Grabban netted 13 goals as Howe's return led his new club to promotion into the Championship.

The following season, Grabban scored 22 goals as the Cherries narrowly missed out on the second-tier play-offs, but after attracting the attention of Norwich City, the striker was sold to the Canaries for £3m in the summer of 2014.

However, he rejoined Howe at Dean Court for £7m in January 2016, but failed to make an impact and was loaned to Reading and Sunderland in 2017 before joining Aston Villa on a temporary deal in January 2018.

Max Gradel

Ivorian winger Gradel took in two spells with the Cherries, almost ten years apart.

Signed on loan from Leicester City by Kevin Bond in 2007, Gradel made a big impact despite Bond's men suffering relegation from League One in 2008.

After penning a new deal with the Foxes, the winger joined Leeds United on loan in 2009 before signing permanently at Elland Road the following year.

After scoring 22 goals in 63 appearances for Leeds, Gradel joined St Etienne in 2011 where he went on to make more than 100 appearances.

Gradel rejoined the Cherries for £7m ahead of the club's first Premier League campaign in 2015, but tore his anterior cruciate ligament against Leicester on 29 August and missed six months of the campaign.

Despite returning in February, Gradel found playing time hard to come by and moved to Toulouse on loan in 2017 with a permanent transfer on the cards in June 2018.

Steven Gregory

Midfielder signed from AFC Wimbledon by Lee Bradbury in 2011. Gregory made 28 appearances in his first season at Dean Court, but with limited opportunities the following season, rejoined the Dons on loan in 2012.

After his Dean Court contract was cancelled by mutual consent in 2013, Gregory joined Gillingham and made more than 50 appearances before linking up with non-league Thame United in 2016.

Scott Guyett

Imposing former Gresley Rovers, Southport, Oxford United, Chester City and Yeovil Town defender who joined the Cherries under Bond in 2008.

The Australian centre-half made 34 appearances for the club between 2008 and 2010 before joining non-league Dorchester Town. He is now the fitness coach at Crystal Palace.

Ian Harte

Gifted Irish full-back who made more than 200 appearances during a hugely successful eight years with Leeds United between 1996 and 2004.

After three years in Spain with Levante, Harte represented Sunderland, Blackpool and Carlisle United before joining Reading in 2010 where he made 88 appearances.

Signed by Howe in 2013, Harte made 28 appearances for the Cherries and was part of the squad promoted to the Premier League in 2015.

After retiring the same year, Harte became a football agent.

Stephen Henderson

Dublin-born goalkeeper signed by Howe in 2013 as cover for Ryan Allsop and Darryl Flahavan.

The West Ham stopper made two appearances for the Cherries before injury in his second start at Nottingham Forest ended his time at Dean Court.

Spent 2018 on loan at Portsmouth from Forest.

James Henry

A skilful and inventive winger, Henry was signed on loan from Reading by Kevin Bond in 2007 alongside fellow Royals youngsters Jem Karacan, Alex Pearce and Scott Golbourne.

Henry made 11 appearances as the Cherries were relegated to League Two and after taking in two loan spells at Millwall, was signed by the Lions in 2010. Henry joined Wolverhampton Wanderers in 2014 and is currently with Oxford United.

Zavon Hines

Jamaican winger who joined the Cherries on loan from Burnley in 2012. Hines made eight appearances under Paul Groves and was released by the Clarets in the summer of 2012.

After joining Bradford City, Hines took in spells with Dagenham & Redbridge, Southend United and Maidstone United before signing for Chesterfield in 2018.

Danny Hollands

Combative midfielder who captained the Chelsea youth team and reserves before being loaned to Torquay United in 2006.

Released from Stamford Bridge the same year, Hollands joined the Cherries under O'Driscoll and went on to make just short of 200 appearances between 2006 and 2011.

A member of the side defeated on penalties at Huddersfield in the 2011 League One play-off semi-final, Hollands left Dean Court that summer to join Charlton Athletic.

He made more than 50 appearances for the south London side in between loan spells at Swindon Town, Gillingham and Portsmouth, where he signed permanently in 2014.

However, after two years at Fratton Park, Hollands was on the move again, making 24 appearances for Crewe Alexandra before joining non-league Eastleigh in 2017.

Richard Hughes
Scottish midfielder whose youth career was spent in Italy with Atalanta and at Highbury with Arsenal.

Capped five times by Scotland, Hughes made 131 appearances during his first spell at Dean Court between 1998 and 2002 and joined Portsmouth that year, going on to make more than 100 appearances for the south coast outfit.

Hughes rejoined the Cherries under Groves in 2012, making a further 26 appearances before retiring in 2014.

He is now the head of recruitment at Dean Court.

Steve Hutchings
Striker who came through the Dean Court youth system. Made his debut against Millwall in 2008 but was released a year later.

Went on to play for Dorchester Town and Havant & Waterlooville.

Sammy Igoe
Experienced midfielder who made more than 150 appearances for Portsmouth between 1994 and 2000.

After spending three years with Reading, Igoe served Swindon Town, Millwall and Bristol Rovers before joining Bond at Dean Court in 2008.

After 49 appearances for the Cherries, Igoe joined Havant & Waterlooville in 2010, before a spell at nearby Gosport Borough.

Danny Ings

A pacy and skilful striker, Ings came through the Dean Court youth ranks and made his debut as a 17-year-old against Northampton in the Football League Trophy in October 2009.

After a loan spell at Dorchester Town, Ings made his Cherries league debut in December 2010 at MK Dons and went on a seven-goal scoring spree in early 2011, including a goal in the League One play-off semi-final defeat at Huddersfield.

Ings joined Howe at Burnley that summer and went on to score 38 goals in 122 appearances for the Clarets over four years.

In 2015, Ings joined Premier League Liverpool and won his first England cap, but two serious injuries limited his playing time for the Reds. He returned to action in September 2017 and scored his first goal under Jurgen Klopp in April 2018.

Juan Iturbe

Born in Buenos Aries but of Paraguayan heritage, Iturbe signed on loan at Dean Court from Serie A side Roma in 2016.

Capped eight times by Paraguay, he made just four appearances under Howe before rejoining Roma.

Iturbe, who also spent time at Porto and River Plate earlier in his career, joined Torino on loan in 2017, before penning a temporary deal with Tijuana later that year.

Shwan Jalal

Baghdad-born goalkeeper who joined the Cherries from Peterborough in 2008. Jalal went on to make almost 150 appearances for the Cherries in eight years at Dean Court that took in relegation in 2008 and promotions in 2010 and 2013.

The former Tottenham trainee was released by Howe in 2014 and joined Bury, before spells at Northampton Town, Macclesfield Town and Wrexham.

Jalal rejoined Macclesfield in 2017 and helped the Silkmen to promotion from the National League in 2018, before joining Chesterfield in May.

David James

Former Watford, Liverpool and Portsmouth goalkeeper with more than 800 career appearances to his name.

Capped 53 times by England, James signed for the Cherries in 2012 under Groves and made 19 appearances for the Dean Court side.

James joined Indian Super League side Kerala Blasters as player/manager in 2014 before leaving and then rejoining the side as manager in 2018.

Kenwyne Jones

Trinidadian striker best known for spells with Southampton, Sunderland and Stoke City in the Premier League.

After leaving the Britannia Stadium in January 2014 to join Premier League new boys Cardiff City, Jones was signed on a short loan by Howe in March 2015, with the Cherries leading the race for Premier League promotion.

Despite making just six appearances for the Dorset side, his headed goal on debut at Ipswich on 3 April handed Howe's men a crucial point at Portman Road.

Although a loanee, Jones joined the Cherries squad on a bus tour around Bournemouth after the club's Championship title win that year.

After 17 appearances for Major League Soccer side Atlanta United in 2016/17, Jones retired from the professional game.

Jem Karacan

Turkish midfielder who signed on loan at Dean Court from Reading in 2007 alongside James Henry, Alex Pearce and Scott Golbourne.

Karacan made 155 appearances for the Royals before joining Galatasaray in 2015. However, in two years he made just two appearances and signed for Bolton Wanderers in 2017.

Yann Kermorgant

Hugely popular French striker who joined the Cherries from Charlton Athletic in January 2014.

Scored nine goals as Howe's side narrowly missed out on the Championship play-offs, before forming a formidable partnership alongside Callum Wilson the following season, finding the net 17 times as the Cherries stormed to the Championship title.

Limited to just seven appearances in the Premier League the following season, Kermorgant joined Reading in January 2016.

Joshua King

Powerful Norwegian striker whose youth career began at Manchester United, before a two-year spell with Blackburn Rovers alerted Howe to his abilities.

Loaned to Preston, Hull and Borussia Monchengladbach while at Old Trafford, King signed for Howe's Cherries ahead of the club's first Premier League season in 2015.

After finding the net eight times during that maiden season, King continued to shine the following year, scoring 16 goals as Howe's men finished ninth in just their second top-flight campaign.

Jo Kuffour

Ghanaian Kuffour started his career in the Arsenal youth ranks, before joining Torquay United and then Brentford. Signed by Bond in 2007, the striker made 39 league appearances for the Cherries, scoring 12 goals.

He joined Bristol Rovers in 2008, before spells at Gillingham and Wycombe Wanderers.

Adam Lallana

Hugely talented midfielder who joined Southampton while in the Dean Court youth ranks in 2000.

Although St Albans-born, Lallana's family had moved to Bournemouth when he was five and the star grew up playing five-a-side at the Littledown Centre nearby.

Made his debut for the Saints in August 2006 and joined the Cherries on loan for a month just over a year later.

After making three appearances under Bond, Lallana returned to Southampton and went on to make more than 200 appearances for the St Mary's Stadium side before joining Liverpool for £25m in 2014. Used by Jurgen Klopp as an attacking midfielder, Lallana has won more than 30 caps for England.

Craig Lindfield

Scouser whose youth career was spent at Liverpool. Lindfield signed on loan at Dean Court in 2008 while still at Anfield and made three appearances under Bond.

After leaving his boyhood club in 2009, the striker represented Macclesfield Town, Accrington Stanley and Chester. In 2017, he began a second spell at FC United of Manchester.

Steve Lovell

Popular forward who took in two spells at Dean Court, but spent much of his career north of the border in Scotland.

Brother to Cherries boss Howe, Lovell came through the Dean Court youth system alongside his elder sibling and after just a handful of appearances, Lovell was signed by Portsmouth for £250,000 in 1999.

His playing time was limited at Fratton Park and, in 2002, Lovell signed for Scottish side Dundee, before spells at Aberdeen, Falkirk and Partick Thistle.

After more than 200 appearances in the Scottish leagues, Lovell rejoined the Cherries in 2010.

Scorer of two goals in the club's 2011 League One play-off semi-final defeat at Huddersfield, Lovell retired in September 2011 having failed to overcome an ongoing foot injury.

Shaun MacDonald

A popular player among the Dean Court support, Welshman MacDonald signed at Dean Court from Swansea City in 2011.

After no fewer than five loan spells at Yeovil Town prior to joining the Cherries, MacDonald's game time at Dean Court was limited during his five years at the club, making 84 appearances in all competitions.

Capped four times by Wales, the midfielder signed for Wigan Athletic in 2016.

Scott Malone

Inventive midfielder signed initially on loan from Wolverhampton Wanderers by Bradbury in 2011. After signing permanently in January 2012, Malone went on to make 32 appearances under Bradbury and Groves, before joining Millwall in a swap deal for Josh McQuoid in the summer of 2012.

After three years at The Den, Malone joined Cardiff City and then Fulham. Signed for Premier League new boys Huddersfield in 2017.

Donal McDermott

Talented but roguish midfielder who joined the Cherries on loan from Manchester City in 2011. After signing for Huddersfield following the end of his loan spell at Dean Court and having been released by City, McDermott rejoined the Cherries on a permanent basis under Bradbury in January 2012.

A controversial character, McDermott was reduced to just 20 appearances after falling out of favour following Howe's return and joined Dundalk in 2014.

After a spell at non-league Salford City and Ramsbottom, McDermott joined Rochdale in 2015 before moving to Swindon Town two years later.

Josh McQuoid

Another graduate of the Dean Court youth ranks, McQuoid made 22 appearances during the Greatest Escape season of 2008/09 and was also a regular starter the following season as Howe's side secured promotion to League One.

The following year, after Brett Pitman had joined Bristol City, McQuoid was utilised as a striker by Howe and after five goals in four games at the start of the 2010/11 campaign, began to attract the attention of Championship clubs.

McQuoid went on to bag successive hat-tricks in November 2010 and following his goal against Yeovil Town later that month, joined Millwall on loan on 25 November and signed permanently in January.

Rejoined the Cherries in 2012 in a swap deal for Scott Malone, but was not as prolific second time around and took in loan spells at Peterborough and Coventry City.

Capped five times by Northern Ireland, McQuoid joined Luton Town in 2015, spending three years at Kenilworth Road, before signing for Aldershot Town in 2018.

Tyrone Mings

The Cherries' record signing when he put pen to paper on an £8m move from Ipswich in June 2015.

Mings made his Premier League debut against Leicester that August, but ruptured his anterior cruciate ligament in the game and missed the rest of the season.

After making his comeback in January 2017, Mings received a five-match ban following an incident with Manchester United striker Zlatan Ibrahimovic in March.

The defender returned to training following a back injury in early 2018.

Mark Molesley

Likeable box-to-box midfielder initially signed on loan by Jimmy Quinn from Grays Athletic in 2008. After nine games under Quinn, the midfielder looked set to return to Grays, but was kept on by Howe following advice from assistant boss Jason Tindall.

Went on to make 43 appearances for the Cherries in a spell affected by injury and which included loan time at Aldershot Town and Plymouth Argyle.

After leaving Dean Court in 2013, Molesley played more than 50 games for Aldershot and Exeter City before retiring in 2017.

Now the manager of non-league Weymouth as well as coaching in the Cherries academy.

Neil Moss

Hampshire-born goalkeeper who came through the Cherries' youth ranks and made 22 appearances between 1993 and 1995 before signing for Southampton.

Limited to 24 appearances at The Dell, Moss rejoined the Cherries on loan in 2002 before signing permanently in February 2003.

He went on to make just short of 150 appearances at Dean Court before retiring in 2008 due to a wrist injury. Currently the Cherries goalkeeping coach.

Glenn Murray

An experienced striker with Brighton and Crystal Palace, Cumbrian-born Murray's career began in the North West with Barrow and Carlisle United.

After a prolific spell with Rochdale in 2007/08, Murray joined Brighton and made more than 100 appearances for the Seagulls. A further 112 appearances followed at Selhurst Park before Murray joined the Cherries in 2015 for £4m.

Although restricted to only 19 appearances at Dean Court, Murray scored a crucial goal at Chelsea in 2015 to secure a 1-0 win over the then Premier League champions.

Loaned back to Brighton in 2016, Murray moved back to the Seagulls permanently in 2017 and scored 12 league goals during the Sussex club's first season in the top flight.

Garreth O'Connor

Irish midfielder signed by Sean O'Driscoll from Bohemians in 2000. O'Connor went on to make 168 appearances for the Cherries before joining Burnley in 2005.

A member of the Cherries' 2003 Division Three play-off final-winning team, O'Connor also served Luton Town, St Patrick's Athletic, Drogheda United and Monaghan United.

Eunan O'Kane

Republic of Ireland international midfielder signed by Groves in 2012. Born in Northern Ireland, O'Kane made 106 appearances for Torquay United before joining the Cherries and was part of the victorious 2013 League One and 2015 Championship promotion squads.

After more than 100 appearances, O'Kane joined Leeds United in 2016.

Marcos Painter

Full-back Painter made two appearances for the Cherries in 2013 after joining on loan from Brighton. Released by the Seagulls in 2013, Painter signed a short-term deal with Portsmouth the same year.

Alex Parsons

Worthing-born midfielder who came through the Cherries youth system and made his first-team debut in January 2012. Released the same year, Parsons went on to serve non-league sides Bashley, Whitehawk, Worthing and Bognor Regis Town.

Joe Partington

Luckless midfielder whose Cherries career was blighted by injury. Signed in 2006 after his release from Portsmouth, Partington made just 52 first-team appearances in eight years at Dean Court before joining Eastleigh on loan in 2015. After signing permanently at the Silverlake Stadium, Partington was made captain of the Spitfires and went on to make 64 appearances in two years. Capped at under-17, under-19 and under-21 level with Wales, he is currently with League One side Bristol Rovers.

Jason Pearce

Hard-as-nails central defender who joined the Cherries from Portsmouth in 2007. Part of Howe's promotion squad in 2010, Pearce was made captain the same year.

After missing out on the League One play-off final in 2011, Pearce rejoined Portsmouth for £300,000.

Made captain at Fratton Park in 2012, he left for Leeds United the same year and went on to make almost 100 appearances at

Elland Road. Pearce signed for Wigan Athletic in 2015 and was made captain, but left for Charlton Athletic after just a year at the DW Stadium.

Alex Pearce

One of the 'Reading Four', alongside Jem Karacan, James Henry and Scott Golbourne, signed on loan by Kevin Bond in 2007.

After 11 appearances under Bond, Pearce returned to Reading and made more than 200 appearances for the Royals before leaving for Derby County in 2015. Capped seven times by the Republic of Ireland, the defender spent time on loan at Bristol City in 2016.

Russell Perrett

Former window fitter who signed for AFC Lymington in non-league after being released by Portsmouth. After rejoining the Fratton Park side in 1995, though, Perrett went on to make 72 appearances for the Blues before heading west to Cardiff City in 1999.

After a spell at Luton Town between 2001 and 2007, Perrett was signed by Bond but made just ten appearances as the Cherries were relegated from League One in 2008. Retired the same year after a bout of pleurisy.

Jaime Peters

Canadian full-back who made eight appearances for the Cherries under Bradbury in 2011 after signing on loan from Ipswich Town.

After trials with Yeovil Town and the Vancouver Whitecaps, Peters is currently without a club.

Carl Pettefer

After spells at Portsmouth, Southend and Oxford United, Pettefer was signed by Bond after a successful trial in 2008.

However, the midfielder found opportunities limited at Dean Court and joined Bognor Regis Town the same year.

After signing for AFC Totton later in 2008, Pettefer made more than 200 appearances for the Stags before joining Poole Town in 2013.

Brett Pitman

Highly talented goalscorer who joined the Cherries under Sean O'Driscoll in 2005. Born in Jersey, Pitman made more than 150 appearances under O'Driscoll, Bond, Howe and Quinn until 2010 when his form attracted the attention of Premier League new boys Blackpool. Unable to agree terms with the Seasiders, though, Pitman joined Bristol City in 2010 and went on to make 77 appearances before rejoining the Cherries initially on loan and then permanently in 2013.

During his second spell under Howe, Pitman scored 34 goals in 88 appearances to add to the 59 goals from his first spell.

After helping the Cherries to the Championship title in 2015, Pitman joined Ipswich Town where he made 61 appearances in two years, scoring 24 goals.

After signing for Portsmouth in 2017, the Channel Islander became the first Blues player for 15 years to break through the 20-goal barrier in a single season.

Carl Preston

Pacy winger born in Poole who came through the Cherries' youth ranks to make his first-team debut under Quinn in 2008. However, after the manager's sacking, Preston fell out of favour under Howe and joined non-league Weymouth in 2009.

The 27-year-old went on to make more than 100 appearances for Poole Town.

Ryan Pryce

Cherries youth goalkeeper who graduated to the first-team ranks in 2007. Made just five appearances before joining non-league

Salisbury City in 2010 and then Gosport Borough, The New Saints and Fleet Town.

Marc Pugh

Lancashire-born winger who signed for the Cherries in 2010 from Hereford United. After coming through the youth ranks of home-town club Burnley, Pugh served Kidderminster Harriers on loan before joining Bury in 2006.

After 41 appearances for the Shakers, Pugh joined Shrewsbury Town before moving to Hereford in 2009.

Impressive during his side's League Two clashes against Howe's Cherries, Pugh moved to Dean Court for a tribunal fee of £100,000.

Hugely popular with the Dean Court support, Pugh has gone on to make almost 300 appearances for the Cherries and has scored goals in every league of the English system from the Conference right up to the Premier League.

Stephen Purches

Full-back who joined the Cherries from West Ham United in 2000. A goalscorer in the club's 2003 Division Three play-off final triumph, Purches made almost 240 appearances for the Dean Court side before joining Leyton Orient in 2007.

After a largely successful spell at Brisbane Road, Purches was re-signed by Howe in 2010 and made a further 33 appearances before retiring in 2014. Now one of Howe's first-team coaches at Dean Court.

Michael Rankine

Journeyman striker signed on loan by Quinn in 2008 from Rushden & Diamonds. Rankine made three appearances under Quinn before returning to Rushden and then joining York City in 2009.

Also served Aldershot Town, Grimsby Town, Hereford United, Gateshead, Altrincham and Guiseley.

Tokelo Rantie

A striker capped 40 times by South Africa, Rantie became the Cherries' record signing when arriving at Dean Court from Malmo for £2.5m in 2013. Frustrated by a lack of action, though, making just 44 appearances in three years, scoring five times, Rantie joined Turkish side Gençlerbirliği in 2016.

Matt Ritchie

Tricky winger whose career started at home-town club Portsmouth in 2008. Following successful loan spells with Dagenham & Redbridge, Notts County and Swindon Town, Ritchie signed a permanent deal with the County Ground side in 2011 and went on to make 91 appearances.

Signed by Howe for £400,000 in 2013, Ritchie helped the Cherries to the Championship title 18 months later and scored arguably the finest goal ever seen at Dean Court against Sunderland during the club's maiden Premier League campaign.

Signed by Championship side Newcastle in July 2016, Ritchie helped the Magpies navigate their way back to the top flight the following season and has won 14 caps for Scotland.

Anton Robinson

A combative central midfielder, Harrow-born Robinson's career started at Millwall in 2004 before he joined non-league Eastleigh a year later. After spells with Margate, Eastbourne Borough and Fisher Athletic, Robinson joined Weymouth in 2007 and made 84 appearances for the Dorset side before putting pen to paper at Dean Court in January 2009.

A key member of Howe's Greatest Escape squad, Robinson made more than 100 appearances for the Cherries before joining

Huddersfield following the 2011 League One play-off semi-final defeat.

After just 27 appearances at the John Smith's Stadium, though, Robinson spent time on loan at Gillingham and Coventry before his career was ended through injury.

Now part of Richard Hughes's recruitment team at Dean Court.

Ricky Sappleton

Jamaican striker signed on loan from Leicester in 2008. Sappleton scored on his Cherries debut against Aldershot in August 2008, but made just two more appearances.

After further loan spells at Oxford United, AFC Telford and Macclesfield Town, Sappleton left the King Power Stadium in 2010 to sign for the Silkmen. The Kingston-born player also served Bishop's Stortford, Billericay Town and Kingstonian and is currently with Heybridge Swifts.

Danny Seaborne

Devon-born centre-back whose career began with Exeter City in 2005 where he made 86 appearances.

After a series of loan clubs, Seaborne joined Southampton in 2010 and made 44 appearances as the St Mary's Stadium side piloted their way out of League One.

After a loan spell with Charlton Athletic, Seaborne joined the Cherries on loan in January 2013 and made 13 appearances as Howe led his team to promotion from League One.

Seaborne went on to represent Coventry City, Partick Thistle and Hamilton Academical and is now back with Exeter.

Charlie Sheringham

Son of former Manchester United and England striker Teddy, Sheringham joined the Cherries from Dartford in October 2011.

In his sixth appearance against Brentford on Boxing Day 2011, Sheringham scored his only Cherries goal but suffered a major foot injury following the match.

A year later Sheringham had surgery on the injury and in March 2013, following his rehab, the striker was loaned back to Dartford and released by the Cherries following the end of his loan spell.

Sheringham went on to represent AFC Wimbledon, Ebbsfleet United and Hemel Hempstead Town before joining Saif Sporting Club in Bangladesh in 2017.

Dominic Shimmin

Bermondsey-born central defender who came through the youth ranks at Arsenal before joining Queens Park Rangers in 2005.

Signed on loan by Bond in 2007, Shimmin made two Cherries appearances before moving back to Loftus Road and then representing Crawley Town, Greenock Morton, Dundee and Dover Athletic.

Adam Smith

Born in Leytonstone, Smith came through the youth ranks at Tottenham, making one appearance for the north Londoners between 2008 and 2014. Loaned to Wycombe Wanderers, Torquay United, MK Dons, Leeds United, Millwall and Derby County during his time at White Hart Lane, Smith made a big impact during a 2010/11 loan spell at Dean Court where he made 38 appearances.

After being capped at England under-21 level, Smith signed permanently at Dean Court in 2014 and was part of the 2015 Championship title-winning squad.

A regular in Howe's starting 11, Smith is closing in on 100 Premier League appearances for the Cherries.

Junior Stanislas

London-born winger who made almost 50 appearances for West Ham United after coming through the Upton Park youth system. After a brief loan spell at Southend in 2008/09, Stanislas joined Burnley in 2011 and made a huge impression on Howe.

After 93 appearances for the Clarets, Stanislas linked up with Howe again when signing for the Cherries in 2014 and helped the Dorset side to the Championship title and Premier League promotion in 2015.

Marek Stech

Highly rated by parent club West Ham, Prague-born Stech joined Howe's Cherries on a seven-day emergency loan in 2009. Making his debut the following day at Morecambe, Stech conceded five goals as the Cherries were thumped at Christie Park.

After returning to Upton Park, Stech had brief loan spells at Yeovil and Leyton Orient before joining the Glovers permanently in 2012.

After 72 appearances at Huish Park, Stech moved to Sparta Prague in 2014 before signing for Luton Town three years later.

Jon Stewart

Controversial goalkeeper who came through the youth ranks at Swindon Town before joining non-league Weymouth in 2007.

After two years training with Portsmouth, Stewart signed for the Cherries in 2010 and made his debut at Leyton Orient in November.

However, Stewart made just three more appearances before he was sacked by the club in 2011 for missing training and allegedly damaging hotel rooms.

Stewart joined Howe at Burnley in 2011 but failed to break into the first team and, after a loan spell with Alfreton Town, joined Worksop United in 2013. After a further spell at Alfreton and then Bradford Park Avenue, Stewart joined non-league side Shaw Lane AFC.

Gareth Stewart

Preston-born goalkeeper Stewart started his career at nearby Blackburn Rovers in 1997 but signed for the Cherries in 1999. Despite competition from Neil Moss and then Shwan Jalal, Stewart made more than 150 appearances for the Cherries before leaving for Dorchester Town in 2008.

After spells with Welling United and Yeovil Town, Stewart joined Weymouth in 2017.

Jayden Stockley

Highly rated striker who became the Cherries' second-youngest debutant in the club's history in 2009 when he emerged from the bench aged just 16 years and 21 days against Northampton Town in the Football League Trophy.

After being fast-tracked into the first-team squad by Howe a year later, Stockley made 16 appearances for the Cherries in between loan spells with Dorchester Town, Accrington Stanley, Woking, Leyton Orient, Torquay United, Cambridge United, Luton Town, Portsmouth and Exeter City.

After solid performances for the Grecians, Stockley joined Aberdeen permanently in 2016, before moving back to St James Park in 2017.

Dan Strugnell

A graduate of the Dean Court youth system, Strugnell made one appearance for the Cherries in 2012 against Leyton Orient. After a loan spell with non-league Bashley, Strugnell joined Havant & Waterlooville after being released from Dean Court in 2013.

Blair Sturrock

Son of former Southampton boss Paul, striker Sturrock's career took in spells with Brechin City, Plymouth Argyle, Kidderminster Harriers, Rochdale and Swindon Town before he signed on loan at Dean Court in 2008.

The player made four appearances before rejoining his parent club and also represented Mansfield Town, Southend United, Bishop's Stortford and Basildon United after leaving Swindon in 2009.

Andrew Surman

Born to English parents in South Africa, Surman came through the youth system at Southampton and made his Saints debut in 2006 after a successful loan spell at Dean Court in 2005/06 under O'Driscoll.

After leaving St Mary's Stadium in 2009, Surman joined Wolverhampton Wanderers but signed for Norwich just a year later where he made 52 appearances.

After signing on loan for the Cherries once again in 2013, Surman made the move permanent a year later and helped the Cherries to Premier League promotion in 2015.

A popular midfielder, Surman has gone on to make more than 120 appearances for the Cherries since 2014.

Michael Symes

Striker whose career began at Everton, before he moved to Bradford City in 2004. Symes made just 15 appearances at Valley Parade, while also completing loan spells at Macclesfield Town, Stockport County and Shrewsbury Town.

After joining the Shrews permanently in 2006, Symes went on to make 60 appearances before further loan spells at Moss Rose and then Dean Court, where he made five appearances in 2008 under Quinn.

Following a 41-game spell with Accrington Stanley that yielded 13 goals, Symes joined the Cherries permanently in 2010 after the Football League transfer embargo had been lifted, but after just 37 appearances in two years, he left in 2012 to join Leyton Orient after a brief loan spell at Rochdale.

After signing for Burton Albion in 2013, Symes switched to Southport in 2015.

Lyle Taylor

Greenwich-born striker who started his youth career at Millwall before signing for non-league Concord Rangers in 2009.

After 34 goals in 42 games for Rangers, Taylor signed for the Cherries in the summer of 2010 but found first-team opportunities hard to come by and was loaned out to Lewes, Hereford United and Woking.

After 29 first-team appearances for the Cherries and no goals, Taylor was released in 2012 when he joined Scottish side Falkirk.

Twenty-four goals in 34 games north of the border attracted the attention of Sheffield United and Taylor joined the Yorkshire outfit for an undisclosed fee in 2013.

After struggling at Bramall Lane, though, Taylor was on the move again in 2014, joining Scunthorpe before making the switch to AFC Wimbledon a year later.

In 2017/18, Taylor became the Dons' leading Football League goalscorer with 44 and has made more than 100 appearances for the Londoners.

Paul Telfer

Born in Edinburgh, full-back Telfer's career began with Luton Town in 1988 where he made 144 appearances in seven years at Kenilworth Road before leaving to join Coventry City in 1995.

After almost 200 appearances for the Sky Blues, Telfer joined Southampton in 2001 and helped his side reach the 2003 FA

Cup Final. After four years with the south coast club, Telfer moved north of the border to join Celtic and won two Scottish championships while at Parkhead.

After retiring in 2007 to be with his family in Winchester, Hampshire, Telfer then signed a one-year deal at Dean Court in July under Bond but made just 18 appearances before cancelling his contract helping to assist with the Cherries' financial problems.

After coming out of retirement a second time to join Leeds United, Telfer went on to play for Slough Town and Sutton United, where he was also a coach, before a short spell coaching Indy Eleven in America in 2014.

Jo Tessem

Former Southampton midfielder and Norway international signed by Kevin Bond in 2008. Tessem started his career at Orland, before spells with Lyn and Molde. Signed by the Saints in 1999, he went on to make more than 100 appearances between 1999 and 2005 before returning to Lyn.

After signing for the Cherries, Tessem made 11 appearances before going on to manage non-league side Totton & Eling.

After further brief playing spells at Eastleigh and back at Lyn, Tessem rejoined Totton & Eling as a player in 2010.

Dan Thomas

Cherries youth goalkeeper who graduated to the first-team ranks in 2009 due to a crippling injury crisis.

Thomas made three appearances for the Cherries, while also taking in loan spells at Dorchester Town, Welling United and AFC Totton. After leaving Dean Court in 2012, Thomas joined Havant & Waterlooville, before spells with Poole Town and Aldershot Town. He signed for Gosport Borough in 2017.

Wes Thomas

Essex-born striker whose career began in the Queens Park Rangers youth system. After leaving Loftus Road in 2005, Thomas joined Waltham Forest and made a solid enough impression in non-league to earn a deal with Dagenham & Redbridge in 2008.

After loan spells with Grays and Rushden & Diamonds, Thomas joined Cheltenham Town in 2010 and enjoyed his most prolific spell, scoring 18 times in 41 appearances.

After signing for Crawley Town in 2011, Thomas was signed on loan at Dean Court by Lee Bradbury in September 2011 with the deal made permanent in January 2012.

In total, Thomas played more than 50 games for the Cherries, scoring 11 goals, and also took in loan time at Portsmouth, Blackpool and Birmingham City after Howe's return in October 2012.

Thomas went on to join Birmingham permanently in 2014 and spent two years at St Andrew's before joining Oxford United in 2016.

Jake Thomson

Capped twice by Trinidad & Tobago, Thomson signed for the Cherries on loan in 2009, making six appearances.

A graduate of the Southampton youth system, Thomson returned to St Mary's following his Dean Court spell before joining Exeter City in 2010.

Deals with Forest Green Rovers and Newport County followed, while Thomson also served Salisbury City, AFC Portchester and Bognor Regis Town before joining Havant & Waterlooville in 2016.

Jason Tindall

The Cherries' assistant manager under Howe, Tindall joined the club as a player in 1998 after his release from Charlton.

The Mile End-born utility man made 171 appearances at Dean Court in eight years before leaving in 2006 to join non-league Weymouth where he was made manager in 2007.

Appointed the Cherries' assistant manager under Quinn in 2008, Tindall remained in place when Howe took over on New Year's Day 2009 and alongside the manager, piloted the club to the Greatest Escape in 2009 and promotion from League Two in 2010 before leaving with Howe to join Burnley in 2011.

After returning to Dean Court in 2012, Tindall helped Howe lead the Cherries to promotion from League One in 2013 and then from the Championship in 2015.

Lee Tomlin

Controversial but talented midfielder signed by Howe in 2015 from Middlesbrough for £3.5m. Tomlin began his career at home-town club Leicester City before moving to Rushden & Diamonds in 2005.

After 156 appearances, he left to join Peterborough United in 2010 where he went on to make 135 appearances at London Road.

Following two years in the North East with Middlesbrough, Tomlin moved south to Dean Court but made just six appearances for the Cherries, falling out of favour with manager Howe and attracting criticism for his use of social media platform Twitter.

Loaned to Bristol City in 2016, Tomlin signed permanently at Ashton Gate but left to join Cardiff City in July 2017 and spent the second half of the 2017/18 season on loan at Nottingham Forest.

Matt Tubbs

Prolific striker who left the Cherries youth system in 2001 to join Bolton Wanderers. After two years in the North West, though, Tubbs returned to Dean Court on non-contract terms in 2003.

He signed for Salisbury City later that year and went on to score 108 goals in 248 appearances for the Wiltshire side, including an impressive TV performance against Nottingham Forest in the 2007 FA Cup second round.

After a superb 30-goal season in 2007, Tubbs was called up for the England C team where he scored on debut.

In 2008, Quinn brought Tubbs back to Dean Court on loan where he made eight appearances and scored once, but after Howe had taken over the manager's role in January 2009, Tubbs was sent back to Salisbury.

He joined Crawley Town in 2010 for a club record £55,000 and went on to score an incredible 49 goals in just 65 appearances for the Red Devils before becoming the Cherries' then record signing in January 2012, rejoining the Dorset club for £500,000 under Bradbury.

However, Tubbs struggled to maintain his form and was also sidelined with injury for the latter part of 2012.

After making 38 appearances and scoring seven goals, the striker was loaned to Rotherham United for the first half of the 2013/14 season, before rejoining Crawley on loan for the rest of the season in January 2014.

In June 2014, Tubbs joined AFC Wimbledon on loan but the spell was cut short in January when his Cherries contract was terminated and he joined League Two side Portsmouth permanently.

After a loan spell at Eastleigh, Tubbs went on to join Forest Green Rovers in 2016, before spells with Sutton United, Eastleigh again and Havant & Waterlooville.

Lauri Dalla Valle

Talented Finnish striker who spent time in the Inter Milan youth system in 2005 before returning to his homeland to play for JIPPO.

After a trial with Liverpool, Dalla Valle penned a contract at Anfield in 2008 and spent two years on Merseyside before signing for Fulham as part of the deal that took Paul Konchesky to Anfield.

In 2011, he signed a loan deal with the Cherries and made eight appearances under Lee Bradbury, scoring twice.

After returning to Craven Cottage, Dalla Valle spent time on loan at Dundee United, Exeter City and Crewe Alexandra before signing for Norwegian side Molde in 2013.

Later that year, he joined Belgian side Sint-Truiden, before returning to England in 2014 to rejoin Crewe.

In 2017, he signed for Serbian side FC Zemun.

Sam Vokes

A Welsh international striker capped 58 times by his country, Vokes was born in Lymington and came through the Cherries' youth ranks.

After making his debut under Bond in 2006, Vokes scored 12 goals as the Cherries were relegated to League Two in 2008 and was sold to Wolverhampton Wanderers by administrator Gerald Krasner for £400,000 in May of that year.

Vokes took in loan spells with Leeds United, Bristol City, Sheffield United, Norwich City, Burnley and Brighton while at Molineux and signed for Howe's Clarets in July 2012.

Despite Howe returning to Dean Court in October 2012, Vokes remained at Turf Moor and has gone on to make more than 200 appearances for the Lancashire side, scoring more than 50 goals.

He was part of the Welsh squad that reached the 2016 European Championship semi-finals.

Scott Wagstaff

Midfielder signed on loan from Charlton Athletic by Bond in 2008. He made five appearances while with the Cherries before returning to the Valley and spending further time on loan at

Northwich Victoria and Leyton Orient. Wagstaff left Charlton in 2013 to join Bristol City and make 90 appearances at Ashton Gate before signing for Gillingham in 2016.

Josh Wakefield

Midfielder who came through the youth ranks at Dean Court. Wakefield made three appearances for the Cherries between 2011 and 2016, with the player spending much of his time at Dean Court on loan to the likes of Wimborne Town, Hamworthy United, Dagenham & Redbridge, Dorchester Town, Welling United, Torquay United, Bristol Rovers, Yeovil Town and Walsall. After leaving Dean Court in 2016, Wakefield joined Aldershot Town before a spell at Poole Town. Currently with Weymouth.

Joel Ward

Full-back who signed professional terms with Portsmouth in 2008. Ward was signed on loan by Bond in 2008 and made 21 appearances during his 12 months at Dean Court.

After returning to Fratton Park, Ward made 89 appearances for the Blues before signing for Crystal Palace for £400,000 in 2012 where he has gone on to make almost 200 appearances.

Elliott Ward

Centre-half born in Harrow who came through West Ham's youth system between 2001 and 2003. Ward spent time on loan at Peterborough, Bristol Rovers and Plymouth before signing for Coventry City in 2006.

After 116 appearances for the Midlanders, he joined Norwich City in 2010 and took in two loan spells at Nottingham Forest between 2012 and 2013.

Signed by Howe in 2013 following the Cherries' promotion to the Championship, Ward made 25 appearances in three years at Dean Court before signing for Blackburn in 2016.

George Webb

Midfielder who spent time in the Cherries' youth system between 2000 and 2008. Made his Football League debut against Morecambe on the final day of the 2008/09 campaign and also took in a loan spell with Dorchester Town in 2009.

After leaving Dean Court in 2009, Webb spent time with Gosport Borough, Bournemouth Poppies, Hamworthy United and Wimborne Town. Now an estate agent in Poole.

Rhoys Wiggins

Talented left-back who signed on loan for the Cherries during the Greatest Escape season of 2008/09. After 13 appearances at Dean Court, Wiggins signed for Norwich during the summer of 2009 but failed to make an appearance at Carrow Road and returned to the Cherries for a second loan spell in January 2010, making 19 appearances as Howe piloted the club to promotion from League Two.

After making the deal permanent during the summer of 2010, Wiggins played 35 times as the Cherries narrowly missed out on promotion to the Championship in 2011, but joined Charlton Athletic during that summer.

Following 135 appearances for the south London club, Wiggins moved north to Sheffield Wednesday before joining the Cherries for a fourth time in 2016. The Welsh under-21 international, though, suffered a serious knee injury while on loan at Birmingham City in October of that year and retired in May aged just 30.

Ben Williamson

Striker signed by Bradbury in 2011 from the Glenn Hoddle Academy in Spain. Williamson's youth career had started at Millwall and Croydon, before he joined Worthing in 2009. After spending time at the Hoddle Academy and nearby Jerez

International, Williamson joined the Cherries in January 2011 on a deal until the end of the season but made just four appearances.

After the Cherries' play-off semi-final defeat to Huddersfield, Williamson signed for non-league side Hyde, before joining Port Vale in 2012, where he made more than 100 appearances.

After spells with Gillingham and Cambridge United, Williamson signed for Eastleigh in 2017.

Marc Wilson

Highly rated Irish full-back who signed on loan for the Cherries twice in 2007. After joining Portsmouth from the Manchester United academy in 2006, Wilson spent time on loan at Yeovil Town before linking up with Bond at Dean Court and making 26 appearances during two separate spells in 2007.

After returning to Fratton Park, Wilson made 35 appearances for the Blues until 2010 when he joined Stoke City.

In six years at the Britannia Stadium, Wilson made almost 150 appearances and won 25 Republic of Ireland caps.

He returned to Dean Court in 2016 from the Potteries, but did not make a league appearance that year apart from four games on loan at West Bromwich Albion.

Out of the first-team picture on his return to Dean Court, Wilson signed for Sunderland on a free transfer in 2017.

Callum Wilson

Born in Coventry, Wilson came through the Sky Blues' youth system and made his first-team debut in 2009 and Football League debut 18 months later.

After scoring 22 goals during the 2013/14 League One season, Wilson signed for the Cherries for a fee of around £3m and scored twice on his debut in a 4-0 win over Huddersfield in August 2014.

The striker went on to score 20 league goals as the Cherries sealed the Championship title and promotion to the Premier League in 2015, but after suffering a serious knee injury during the club's maiden top-flight campaign, Wilson missed much of the 2015/16 season.

After returning in April 2016, luckless Wilson ruptured the anterior cruciate ligament in his other knee during training in February 2017, missing a further six months of action.

After returning to action at the start of the 2017/18 season, Wilson notched a hat-trick against Huddersfield Town and went on to finish the campaign with eight Premier League goals.

Neil Young

Harlow-born defender who made more than 500 appearances for the Cherries in 14 years at the club between 1994 and 2008. A graduate of the Tottenham youth system, Young was part of the 1995 Great Escape, before tasting promotion in 2003 in the 5-2 Division Three play-off final triumph over Lincoln.

Relegated to League Two with the Cherries under Bond in 2008, Young moved to Australia and played for South Australian Premier League side Cumberland United until retiring in 2011.

Stephane Zubar

Guadeloupean defender who made just 24 appearances during five years at Dean Court between 2011 and 2016.

Signed by Bradbury from Plymouth Argyle in September 2011, he signed a three-and-a-half-year deal with the club in January 2012 following some solid performances during his debut season.

However, Zubar fell out of favour after Howe's return in 2012 and spent time on loan at Bury, Port Vale and York City before joining Weymouth permanently in 2016. After signing for Yeovil in 2017, Zubar failed to make an appearance at Huish Park due to injury and rejoined Weymouth in 2017.

LEAGUE TABLES 2008–2016

2007/08 League One table

	P	W	D	L	F	A	Pts
P Swansea City	46	27	11	8	82	42	92
P Notts Forest	46	22	16	8	64	32	82
P Doncaster Rovers	46	23	11	12	65	41	80
Carlisle United	46	23	11	12	64	46	80
Leeds United	46	27	10	9	72	38	76
Southend United	46	22	10	14	70	55	76
Brighton	46	19	12	15	58	50	69
Oldham Athletic	46	18	13	15	58	46	67
Northampton Town	46	17	15	14	60	55	66
Huddersfield Town	46	20	6	20	50	62	66
Tranmere Rovers	46	18	11	17	52	47	65
Walsall	46	16	16	14	52	46	64
Swindon Town	46	16	13	17	63	56	61
Leyton Orient	46	16	12	18	49	63	60
Hartlepool United	46	15	9	22	63	66	54
Bristol Rovers	46	12	17	17	45	53	53
Millwall	46	14	10	22	45	60	52
Yeovil Town	46	14	10	22	38	59	52
Cheltenham Town	46	13	12	21	42	64	51
Crewe Alexandra	46	12	14	20	47	65	50
R Bournemouth	**46**	**17**	**7**	**22**	**62**	**72**	**48**
R Gillingham	46	11	13	22	44	73	46
R Port Vale	46	9	11	26	47	81	38
R Luton Town	46	11	10	25	43	63	33

2008/09 League Two table

	P	W	D	L	F	A	Pts
P Brentford	46	23	16	7	65	36	85
P Exeter City	46	22	13	11	65	50	79
P Wycombe Wanderers	46	20	18	8	54	33	78
Bury	46	21	15	10	63	43	78
P Gillingham	46	21	12	13	58	55	75
Rochdale	46	19	13	14	70	59	70
Shrewsbury	46	17	18	11	61	44	69
Dagenham	46	19	11	16	77	53	68
Bradford City	46	18	13	15	66	55	67
Chesterfield	46	16	15	15	62	57	63
Morecambe	46	15	18	13	53	56	63
Darlington	46	20	12	14	61	44	62
Lincoln City	46	14	17	15	53	52	59
Rotherham	46	21	12	13	60	46	58
Aldershot Town	46	14	12	20	59	80	54
Accrington	46	13	11	22	42	59	50
Barnet	46	11	15	20	56	74	48
Port Vale	46	13	9	24	44	66	48
Notts County	46	11	14	21	49	69	47
Macclesfield Town	46	13	8	25	45	77	47
Bournemouth	**46**	**17**	**12**	**17**	**59**	**51**	**46**
Grimsby Town	46	9	14	23	51	69	41
R Chester City	46	8	13	25	43	81	37
R Luton Town	46	13	17	16	58	65	26

2009/10 League Two table

	P	W	D	L	F	A	Pts
P Notts County	46	27	12	7	96	31	93
P Bournemouth	**46**	**25**	**8**	**13**	**61**	**44**	**83**
P Rochdale	46	25	7	14	82	48	82
Morecambe	46	20	13	13	73	64	73
Rotherham	46	21	10	15	55	52	73
Aldershot Town	46	20	12	14	69	56	72
P Dagenham	46	20	12	14	69	58	72
Chesterfield	46	21	7	18	61	62	70
Bury	46	19	12	15	54	59	69
Port Vale	46	17	17	12	61	50	68
Northampton Town	46	18	13	15	62	53	67
Shrewsbury	46	17	12	17	55	54	63
Burton Albion	46	17	11	18	71	71	62
Bradford City	46	16	14	16	59	62	62
Accrington	46	18	7	21	62	74	61
Hereford United	46	17	8	21	54	65	59

	P	W	D	L	F	A	Pts
Torquay	46	14	15	17	64	55	57
Crewe Alexandra	46	15	10	21	68	73	55
Macclesfield Town	46	12	18	16	49	58	54
Lincoln City	46	13	11	22	42	65	50
Barnet	46	12	12	22	47	63	48
Cheltenham	46	10	18	18	54	71	48
R Grimsby Town	46	9	17	20	45	71	44
R Darlington	46	8	6	32	33	87	30

2010/11 League One table

	P	W	D	L	F	A	Pts
P Brighton	46	28	11	7	85	40	95
P Southampton	46	28	8	10	86	38	92
Huddersfield Town	46	25	12	9	77	48	87
P Peterborough	46	23	10	13	106	75	79
MK Dons	46	23	8	15	67	60	77
Bournemouth	**46**	**19**	**14**	**13**	**75**	**54**	**71**
Leyton Orient	46	19	13	14	71	62	70
Exeter City	46	20	10	16	66	73	70
Rochdale	46	18	14	14	63	55	68
Colchester United	46	16	14	16	57	63	62
Brentford	46	17	10	19	55	62	61
Carlisle United	46	16	11	19	60	62	59
Charlton Athletic	46	15	14	17	62	66	59
Yeovil Town	46	16	11	19	56	66	59
Sheffield Weds	46	16	10	20	67	67	58
Hartlepool United	46	15	12	19	47	65	57
Oldham Athletic	46	13	17	16	53	60	56
Tranmere Rovers	46	15	11	20	53	60	56
Notts County	46	14	8	24	46	60	50
Walsall	46	12	12	22	56	75	48
R Dagenham	46	12	11	23	52	70	47
R Bristol Rovers	46	11	12	23	48	82	45
R Plymouth Argyle	46	15	7	24	51	74	42
R Swindon Town	46	9	14	23	50	72	41

2011/12 League One table

	P	W	D	L	F	A	Pts
P Charlton Athletic	46	30	11	5	82	36	101
P Sheffield Weds	46	28	9	9	81	48	93
Sheffield United	46	27	9	10	92	51	90
P Huddersfield Town	46	21	18	7	79	47	81
MK Dons	46	22	14	10	84	47	80
Stevenage	46	18	19	9	69	44	73
Notts County	46	21	10	15	75	63	73

Carlisle United	46	18	15	13	65	66	69
Brentford	46	18	13	15	63	52	67
Colchester United	46	13	20	13	61	66	59
Bournemouth	**46**	**15**	**13**	**18**	**48**	**52**	**58**
Tranmere Rovers	46	14	14	18	49	53	56
Hartlepool United	46	14	14	18	50	55	56
Bury	46	15	11	20	60	79	56
Preston North End	46	13	15	18	54	68	54
Oldham Athletic	46	14	12	20	50	66	54
Yeovil Town	46	14	12	20	59	80	54
Scunthorpe United	46	10	22	14	55	59	52
Walsall	46	10	20	16	51	57	50
Leyton Orient	46	13	11	22	48	75	50
R Wycombe Wanderers	46	11	10	25	65	88	43
R Chesterfield	46	10	12	24	56	81	42
R Exeter City	46	10	12	24	46	75	42
R Rochdale	46	8	14	24	47	81	38

2012/13 League One table

	P	W	D	L	F	A	Pts
P Doncaster Rovers	46	25	9	12	62	44	84
P Bournemouth	**46**	**24**	**11**	**11**	**76**	**53**	**83**
Brentford	46	21	16	9	62	47	79
P Yeovil Town	46	23	8	15	71	56	77
Sheffield United	46	19	18	9	56	42	75
Swindon Town	46	20	14	12	72	39	74
Leyton Orient	46	21	8	17	55	48	71
MK Dons	46	19	13	14	62	45	70
Walsall	46	17	17	12	65	58	68
Crawley Town	46	18	14	14	59	58	68
Tranmere Rovers	46	19	10	17	58	48	67
Notts County	46	16	17	13	61	49	65
Crewe Alexandra	46	18	10	18	54	62	64
Preston North End	46	14	17	15	54	49	59
Coventry City	46	18	11	17	66	59	55
Shrewsbury Town	46	13	16	17	54	60	55
Carlisle United	46	14	13	19	56	77	55
Stevenage	46	15	9	22	47	64	54
Oldham Athletic	46	14	9	23	46	59	51
Colchester United	46	14	9	23	47	68	51
R Scunthorpe United	46	13	9	24	49	73	48
R Bury	46	9	14	23	45	73	41
R Hartlepool United	46	9	14	23	39	67	41
R Portsmouth	46	10	12	24	51	69	32

2013/14 Championship table

	P	W	D	L	F	A	Pts
P Leicester City	46	31	9	6	83	43	102
P Burnley	46	26	15	5	72	37	93
Derby County	46	25	10	11	84	52	85
P Queens Park Rangers	46	23	11	12	60	44	80
Wigan Athletic	46	21	10	15	61	48	73
Brighton	46	19	15	12	55	40	72
Reading	46	19	14	13	70	56	71
Blackburn Rovers	46	18	16	12	70	62	70
Ipswich Town	46	18	14	14	60	54	68
Bournemouth	**46**	**18**	**12**	**16**	**67**	**66**	**66**
Nottingham Forest	46	16	17	13	67	64	65
Middlesbrough	46	16	16	14	62	50	64
Watford	46	15	15	16	74	64	60
Bolton Wanderers	46	14	17	15	59	60	59
Leeds United	46	16	9	21	59	67	57
Sheffield Wednesday	46	13	14	19	63	65	53
Huddersfield Town	46	14	11	21	58	65	53
Charlton Athletic	46	13	12	21	41	61	51
Millwall	46	11	15	20	46	74	48
Blackpool	46	11	13	22	38	66	46
Birmingham City	46	11	11	24	58	74	44
R Doncaster Rovers	46	11	11	24	39	70	44
R Barnsley	46	9	12	25	44	77	39
R Yeovil Town	46	8	13	25	44	75	37

2014/15 Championship table

	P	W	D	L	F	A	Pts
P Bournemouth	**46**	**26**	**12**	**8**	**98**	**45**	**90**
P Watford	46	27	8	11	91	50	89
P Norwich City	46	25	11	10	88	48	86
Middlesbrough	46	25	10	11	68	37	85
Brentford	46	23	9	14	78	59	78
Ipswich Town	46	22	12	12	72	54	78
Wolves	46	22	12	12	70	56	78
Derby County	46	21	14	11	85	56	77
Blackburn Rovers	46	17	16	13	66	59	67
Birmingham City	46	16	15	15	54	64	63
Cardiff City	46	16	14	16	57	61	62
Charlton Athletic	46	14	18	14	54	60	60
Sheffield Wednesday	46	14	18	14	43	49	60
Nottingham Forest	46	15	14	17	71	69	59
Leeds United	46	15	11	20	50	61	56
Huddersfield Town	46	13	16	17	58	75	55

Fulham	46	14	10	22	62	83	52
Bolton Wanderers	46	13	12	21	54	67	51
Reading	46	13	11	22	48	69	50
Brighton & Hove Albion	46	10	17	19	44	54	47
Rotherham United	46	11	16	19	46	67	46
R Millwall	46	9	14	23	42	76	41
R Wigan Athletic	46	9	12	25	39	64	39
R Blackpool	46	4	14	28	36	91	26

2015/16 Premier League table

	P	W	D	L	F	A	Pts
C Leicester City	38	23	12	3	68	36	81
Arsenal	38	20	11	7	65	36	71
Tottenham Hotspur	38	19	13	6	69	35	70
Manchester City	38	19	9	10	71	41	66
Manchester United	38	19	9	10	49	35	66
Southampton	38	18	9	11	59	41	63
West Ham United	38	16	14	8	65	51	62
Liverpool	38	16	12	10	63	50	60
Stoke City	38	14	9	15	41	55	51
Chelsea	38	12	14	12	59	53	50
Everton	38	11	14	13	59	55	47
Swansea City	38	12	11	15	42	52	47
Watford	38	12	9	17	40	50	45
West Bromwich Albion	38	10	13	15	34	48	43
Crystal Palace	38	11	9	18	39	51	42
Bournemouth	**38**	**11**	**9**	**18**	**45**	**67**	**42**
Sunderland	38	9	12	17	48	62	39
R Newcastle United	38	9	10	19	44	65	37
R Norwich City	38	9	7	22	39	67	34
R Aston Villa	38	3	8	27	27	76	17